Autism Spectrum Conditions

FAQs on Autism, Asperger Syndrome, and Atypical Autism
Answered by International Experts

Sven Bölte
Joachim Hallmayer
(Editors)

HOGREFE

Library of Congress Cataloging in Publication

is available via the Library of Congress Marc Database under the
LC Control Number 2010934196

Library and Archives Canada Cataloguing in Publication

     Autism spectrum conditions : FAQs on autism, Asperger syndrome, and atypical autism answered by international experts / Sven Bölte, Joachim Hallmayer, editors.

Includes bibliographical references.
ISBN 978-0-88937-393-8

     1. Autism spectrum disorders--Miscellanea.
I. Hallmayer, Joachim II. Bölte, Sven

RC553.A88A9832 2010   616.85'882   C2010-906738-X

© 2011 by Hogrefe Publishing

PUBLISHING OFFICES
USA: Hogrefe Publishing, 875 Massachusetts Avenue, 7th Floor,
              Cambridge, MA 02139
              Phone (866) 823-4726, Fax (617) 354-6875;
              E-mail customerservice@hogrefe-publishing.com
EUROPE: Hogrefe Publishing, Rohnsweg 25, 37085 Göttingen, Germany
              Phone +49 551 49609-0, Fax +49 551 49609-88,
              E-mail publishing@hogrefe.com

SALES & DISTRIBUTION
USA: Hogrefe Publishing, Customer Services Department,
              30 Amberwood Parkway, Ashland, OH 44805
              Phone (800) 228-3749, Fax (419) 281-6883,
              E-mail customerservice@hogrefe.com
EUROPE: Hogrefe Publishing, Rohnsweg 25, 37085 Göttingen, Germany
              Phone +49 551 49609-0, Fax +49 551 49609-88,
              E-mail publishing@hogrefe.com

OTHER OFFICES
CANADA: Hogrefe Publishing, 660 Eglinton Ave. East, Suite 119-514, Toronto,
              Ontario, M4G 2K2
SWITZERLAND: Hogrefe Publishing, Länggass-Strasse 76, CH-3000 Bern 9

Hogrefe Publishing
Incorporated and registered in the Commonwealth of Massachusetts, USA, and in Göttingen,
Lower Saxony, Germany

Printed and bound in the USA
ISBN: 978-0-88937-393-8

Table of Contents

Section 4: Development and Outcome

Section 5: Causes and Risk

Section 6: Treatment of ASC

Section 9: School, Education, Employment, and Independent Living

Section 10: Legal Issues, Organizations, and Resources

Appendix

Preface

Autism spectrum conditions (ASC) are characterized by limited social reciprocity and thus constitute a substantial public health problem in a world of high social demands. It is now recognized that about 1% of the general population is functionally affected by an ASC. Thus, ASC are not rare conditions and they pose challenges to society, experts, families, and people with ASC themselves. Awareness of and knowledge about ASC has increased tremendously in recent years. Nevertheless, the roots of ASC remain enigmatic, effective intervention options are limited, and outcome as well as quality of life are still low for many people on the spectrum. In addition, many myths and misconceptions about ASC survive.

Countless books have been published on ASC. This volume is novel and unique in bringing together several qualities. It combines 78 contributions from 66 internationally leading clinical and research experts and autism organizations from North America and Europe, thus providing a broad, state-of-the-art view on research and practice in dealing with ASC. The book has a FAQ format that communicates current knowledge on ASC in a well-structured and concise way. It has been written with the clear aim of making it a readable and informative resource for laypersons as a well as experts. Organized in 10 sections, this book includes everything essential you need to know about the symptoms, diagnoses, frequency, possible causes, treatments, education issues, and outcomes in ASC.

Our sincerest thanks to all who made this book possible. And, as always, our best wishes to all people with ASC and their families.

Sven Bölte, Karolinska Institutet, Stockholm, Sweden
Joachim Hallmayer, Stanford University, CA, USA

Section 1

Characteristics, Identification, and Diagnosis

Q1
What Are ASC?

Peter Szatmari

The ASC are a group of neurodevelopmental disorders characterized by impairments across the so-called "autistic triad." These include difficulties with reciprocal social interaction and with verbal and nonverbal communication as well as a preference for repetitive, stereotyped activities, patterns of behaviors, and interests. The age of onset is always prior to 36 months, which is an important characteristic that differentiates ASC from other neuropsychiatric or developmental disorders. The ASC are more common than previously thought and have a prevalence of between 0.5 and 1% (Autism and Developmental Disabilities Monitoring Network, 2009). ASC are treatable using strategies that are intensive, based on behavioral principles, and focus on improving IQ, language, social communication, and play (National Research Council, 2001).

Leo Kanner, a child psychiatrist at Johns Hopkins University, first described 11 children with what he called "infantile autism" in 1944 (Kanner, 1968). These children had difficulties with social communication and presented with patterns of restricted interests and insistence on sameness. However, over the ensuing years, the meaning of the term "autism" became somewhat diluted until more precision was introduced in 1980 with the publication of DSM-III (APA, 1980). In that classification system, the term "pervasive developmental disorders (PDD)" was introduced to describe a group of conditions, all of which are characterized by the autistic triad. PDD included autism, as well as other subtypes. In DSM-IV, there are five subtypes of PDD: autistic disorder, Asperger disorder, PDD not otherwise specified (PDD-NOS), childhood disintegrative disorder, and Rett disorder (APA, 1994).

Asperger disorder is diagnosed in children with ASC who do not present with clinically significant cognitive or language delay. This is usually operationalized as IQ in the typical range and speaking in phrases (spontaneously and functionally) by 3 years of age. In addition, there is a hierarchical relationship between autism and Asperger disorder in that, if a child meets criteria for the former, he cannot meet criteria for the latter (APA, 1994). Children with Asperger disorder, therefore, are usually higher functioning and verbally fluent but with poor conversation skills, and have poor social skills as well as a circumscribed range of interests that are pursued to an unusual degree of intensity and usually alone (rather than as part of a social group) (see Szatmari, 2000; Frith, 2004).

Children with PDD-NOS present with ASC symptoms but do not meet the criteria for either autism or Asperger disorder. It was intended to be used as a leftover category and applied to only a small number of children. This has not turned out to be the case as community studies indicate that a substantial proportion of children with ASC are diagnosed with PDD-NOS, not autism or Asperger disorder (Chakrabarti & Fombonne 2001). Children with PDD-NOS often receive that diagnosis because they are too young to demonstrate many repetitive behaviors, too low functioning to be able to assess communication impairments in excess of developmental level, or too high functioning (or older) and so not demonstrating many impairments in social communication (Walker et al., 2004). Nevertheless, the ability of clinicians to distinguish between PDD-NOS and autism is quite poor (Mahoney et al., 1998) and often results from a lack of information available to the clinician, either from the parent, from direct observation, or from a third source, such as a teacher.

The term PDD has slowly been supplanted by the more commonly used term "autism spectrum disorder" or "autism spectrum condition." This arises from the observation that it is very difficult to differentiate the different subtypes of PDD and it appears, based on current evidence, that the distinctions among these subtypes are not only difficult to make but carry little useful clinical information (for a review see Macintosh & Dissanayake, 2004; Van Lang et al., 2006). The American Psychiatric Association Neurodevelopmental Disorders Work Group developing DSM-V proposes a single term, autism spectrum disorder, to cover all 5 current PDD subtypes (see www.dsm5.org).

It has been clear since the 1970s that autism is caused by biological factors affecting brain development. The first indication of this was the observation that there are approximately 4 boys to every girl with the disorder and that a substantial minority of children with autism also have neurological problems, such as epilepsy, or other medical disorders (Spence & Schneider, 2009). More recently, it has become apparent that genetic factors play an important role in ASC (Weiss, 2009). Approximately 10% of children with ASC have a comorbid single gene disorder, such as fragile X syndrome or tuberous sclerosis. Perhaps as many as another 10% have chromosomal abnormalities (i.e., large duplications, translocations, insertions, and/or deletions) that can be seen under the microscope with routine karyotyping. More subtle genomic or chromosomal abnormalities (known as "copy number variants") are currently being discovered and may apply to a further proportion of individuals with ASC (Merikangas, Corvin, & Gallagher, 2009). Whether more common genetic factors cause ASC is currently not known; however, this is an active area of investigation.

Although there has been quite a bit of research into possible environmental factors that may cause ASC, this has not led to many positive findings (Newschaffer et al., 2002). It is unlikely that environmental factors cause autism in the absence of genetic susceptibility. Perhaps the strongest evidence for environmental etiology comes from maternal use of anticonvulsants (i.e., a mother taking valproic acid during pregnancy), which is associated with an increase in births with ASC (Ornoy, 2009). Extreme prematurity (Limperopoulos, 2009), *in vitro* fertilization (Hvidjtorn et al., 2009), and advanced parental age (King, Fountain, Dakhlallah, & Bearman, 2009), are also factors associated with environmental variables that may be associated with ASC, but these data need to be replicated and more strongly confirmed.

It is also quite clear that a number of biological factors that have been promoted in the media and actively investigated are not involved in the etiology of ASC. These include vaccinations, unusual diet, infections of various sorts, and the so-called "leaky gut."

While it is well known that the majority of individuals with ASC have a poor outcome (Howlin Goode, Hutton, & Rutter, 2004), this picture may shift as the diagnostic criteria broaden to include more higher-functioning individuals, and as universally accessible, early intensive behavioral interventions become available. It is true that recovery can occur in a small number of cases, perhaps as many as 5% (Helt et al., 2008). Most children with ASC show slow but steady improvement in autistic behaviors and in social and communication skills (Bennett et al., 2008). It must be emphasized, though, that outcome is extremely variable, and some individuals with ASC need an extraordinary amount of support, not only in adolescence but also in adulthood (Billstedt, Gillberg, & Gillberg, 2007; Hofvander et al., 2009). The strongest predictors of a positive outcome are early language and average cognitive skills (Szatmari, Bryson, Boyle, Streiner, & Duku, 2003). However, even individuals with these positive prognostic factors may have a poor outcome.

It is true that we have learned a great deal about ASC in the last 20 years. The profession used to think of autism as a psychotic disorder caused by poor maternal-child attachment patterns, with a very poor outcome, and as basically untreatable. This picture has changed dramatically, and it is anticipated that the next 20 years of research will bring even more positive advances. A key challenge will be bringing down the age of diagnosis so that children are able to access intervention earlier than they currently do. At present, the average age at which a child is diagnosed in North America is between 4 and 5 years of age (Mandell, Novak, & Zubritsky, 2005). However, parents first become concerned about the development of their children at around 18 months of age (Zwaigenbaum, 2010). This gap indicates that children are not receiving any services in the meantime and may not benefit from that window of opportunity. Another exciting development is the possibility that, as we gain a greater understanding of the genetic factors that contribute to ASC, more targeted biomedical treatments can be developed that may perhaps reduce some of the cognitive-behavioral changes. Such possibilities are currently being explored in clinical trials and in animal models of fragile X syndrome (Hagerman et al., 2009) and Rett syndrome (Tropea et al., 2009). It is not inconceivable that such advances may be applied to ASC as well.

References

American Psychiatric Association (1980). *Diagnostic and Statistical Manual of Mental Disorders, 3rd edition (DSM-III)*. Washington, DC: American Psychiatric Association.

American Psychiatric Association (1994). *Diagnostic and Statistical Manual of Mental Disorders, 4th edition (DSM-IV)*. Washington, DC: American Psychiatric Association.

Autism and Developmental Disabilities Monitoring Network Surveillance Year 2006 Principal Investigators; Centers for Disease Control and Prevention (CDC). (2009). Prevalence of autism spectrum disorders – Autism and Developmental Disabilities Monitoring Network, United States, 2006. *MMWR* Surveillance *Summaries, 58(10)*, 1–20.

Bennett, T. A., Szatmari, P., Bryson, S. E., Volden, J., Zwaigenbaum, L., Vaccarella, L., ... Boyle, M. H. (2008). Differentiating autism and Asperger syndrome on the basis of language delay or impairment. *Journal of Autism and Developmental Disorders, 38*, 616–625.

Billstedt, E., Gillberg, I. C., & Gillberg, C. (2007). Autism in adults: Symptom patterns and early childhood predictors: Use of the DISCO in a community sample followed from childhood. *Journal of Child Psychology and Psychiatry, 48,* 1102–1110.

Chakrabarti, S., & Fombonne, E. (2001). Pervasive developmental disorders in preschool children. *Journal of the American Medical Association, 285*, 3093–3099.

Frith, U. (2004). Emmanuel Miller lecture: Confusions and controversies about Asperger syndrome. *Journal of Child Psychology and Psychiatry, 45*, 672–686.

Hagerman, R. J., Berry-Kravis, E., Kaufmann, W. E., Ono, M. Y., Tartaglia, N., Lachiewics, A., ... Tranfaglia, M. (2009). Advances in the treatment of fragile X syndrome. *Pediatrics, 123*, 378–390.

Helt, M., Kelley, E., Kinsbourne, M., Pandey, J., Boorstein, H., Herbert, M., & Fein, D. (2008). Can children with autism recover? If so, how? *Neuropsychological Reviews, 18*, 339–366.

Hofvander, B., Delorme, R., Chaste, P., Nydén, A., Wentz, E., Ståhlberg, O., ... Leboyer, M. (2009). Psychiatric and psychosocial problems in adults with normal intelligence autism spectrum disorders. *BMC Psychiatry, 9*, 35.

Howlin, P., Goode, S., Hutton, J., & Rutter, M. (2004). Adult outcome for children with autism. *Journal of Child Psychology and Psychiatry, 45*, 212–229.

Hvidjtorn, D., Schieve, L., Schendel, D., Jacobsson, B., Svaerke, C., & Thorsen P. (2009). Cerebral palsy, autism spectrum disorders and developmental delay in children born after assisted conception: A systematic review and meta-analysis. *Archives of Pediatrics & Adolescent Medicine, 163*, 72–83.

Kanner, L. (1968). Autistic disturbances of affective contact. *Acta Paedopsychiatrica, 35*, 100–136.

King, M. D., Fountain, C., Dakhlallah, D., & Bearman, P. S. (2009). Estimated autism risk and older reproductive age. *American Journal of Public Health, 99*, 1673–1679.

Limperopoulos, C. (2009). Autism spectrum disorders in survivors of extreme prematurity. *Clinical Perinatology, 36*, 791–805.

Macintosh, K. E., & Dissanayake, C. (2004). Annotation: The similarities and differences between autistic disorder and Asperger's disorder: A review of the empirical evidence. *Journal of Child Psychology and Psychiatry, 45*, 421–434.

Mahoney, W. J., Szatmari, P., MacLean, J. E., Bryson, S. E., Jones, M. B., & Zwaigenbaum, L. (1998). Reliability and accuracy of differentiating pervasive developmental disorder subtypes. *Journal of the American Academy of Child and Adolescent Psychiatry, 37*, 278–285.

Mandell, D. S., Novak, M. M., & Zubritsky, C. D. (2005). Factors associated with age of diagnosis among children with autism spectrum disorders. *Pediatrics, 116*, 1480–1486.

Merikangas, A. K., Corvin, A. P., & Gallagher, L. (2009). Copy-number variants in neurodevelopmental disorders: Promises and challenges. *Trends in Genetics, 25*, 536–544.

National Research Council. (2001). *Educating Children with Autism. Committee on Educational Interventions for Children with Autism*. Washington, DC: National Academy Press.

Newschaffer, C. J., Fallin, D., & Lee, N. L. (2002). Heritable and nonheritable risk factors for autism spectrum disorders. *Epidemiologic Review, 24,* 137–153.

Ornoy, A. (2009). Valproic acid in pregnancy: How much are we endangering the embryo and fetus? *Reproductive Toxicology, 28,* 1–10.

Spence, S. J., & Schneider, M. T. (2009). The role of epilepsy and epileptiform EEGs in autism spectrum disorders. *Pediatric Research, 65,* 599–606.

Szatmari, P. (2000). The classification of autism, Asperger's syndrome, and pervasive developmental disorder. *Canadian Journal of Psychiatry, 45,* 731–738.

Szatmari, P., Bryson, S. E., Boyle, M. H., Streiner, D. L., & Duku, E. (2003). Predictors of outcome among high functioning children with autism and Asperger syndrome. *Journal of Child Psychology and Psychiatry, 44,* 520–528.

Tropea, D., Giacometti, E., Wilson, N. R., Beard, C., McCurry, C., Fu, D. D., … Sur M. (2009). Partial reversal of Rett syndrome-like symptoms in MeCP2 mutant mice. *Proceedings of the National Academy of Sciences of the United States of America, 106,* 2029–2034.

Van Lang, N., Boomsma, A., Sytema, S., Bildt, A., Kraijer, D., Ketelaars, C., & Minderaa, R. (2006). Structural equation analysis of a hypothesised symptom model in the autism spectrum. *Journal of Child Psychology and Psychiatry, 47,* 37–44.

Walker, D. R., Thompson, A., Zwaigenbaum, L., Goldberg, J., Bryson, S. E., Mahoney, W. J.,… Szatmari, P. (2004). Specifying PDD-NOS: A comparison of PDD-NOS, Asperger syndrome, and autism. *Journal of the American Academy of Child and Adolescent Psychiatry, 43,* 172–180.

Weiss, L. A. (2009). Autism genetics: Emerging data from genome-wide copy-number and single nucleotide polymorphism scans. *Expert Reviews of Molecular Diagnostics, 9,* 795–803.

Zwaigenbaum, L. (2010). Advances in the early detection of autism. *Current Opinion in Neurology, 23,* 97–102.

Q2
What Are the Most Common Characteristics of ASC?

Peter Szatmari

Clinical experience has characterized ASC as a set of signs and symptoms that fall under three main categories: Impairments in reciprocal social interaction, impairments in verbal and nonverbal communication, and a pattern of repetitive, stereotyped behaviors, interests, and activities. While this has served as a very useful guidepost, more detailed measurement studies have somewhat changed this clinical picture (Snow, Lecavalier, & Houts, 2008; Lecavalier, Gadow, DeVincent, Houts, & Edwards, M., 2009). It is now generally thought that there are two main dimensions along which ASC children are placed (Georgiades et al., 2007). One is impairments in social communication, and the other is repetitive, stereotyped, behaviors. It has been shown, through measurement studies, that such children also have independent difficulties either with general cognitive skills or with more specific skills in one or two areas (Szatmari et al., 2002; Matson & Shoemaker, 2009; Fernell et al., 2010). Therefore, intellectual disability (ID) is seen in roughly 50% of individuals with autism and in 25% of those with ASC (Fombonne, 2005). Among those who do not have ID, some form of specific learning disability, either in reading, spelling, or mathematics or a nonverbal learning disability, is almost universally present (Jones et al., 2009).

Another universal characteristic of the disorder is that onset is prior to 36 months of age (American Psychiatric Association, 2000). Until recently, there has been much debate as to when children with ASC first begin to present with their difficulties. Retrospective reports, early videotapes, and parental reports have all suggested that, between 12 and18 months of age, if not earlier, signs of difficulties in social communication, visual attention, and motor difficulties begin to present themselves (Rogers, 2009). Infant sibling studies (i.e., where the infant sibling of a child with autism is followed longitudinally from birth to 36 months of age) have provided much richer data on this topic (Zwaigenbaum et al., 2009). It now appears as though most children with ASC develop normally until 6 months of age, and there is then a slowing down in their social communication, as well as in cognitive and language skills over the following 12–18 months (Zwaigenbaum, 2010). Therefore, the most obvious time at which difficulties begin to appear is between 12 and 18 months of age, whereas the full syndrome is not present until 24–36 months of age.

Difficulties in social communication are then an essential part of ASC. Such problems can be broken down into different subdomains, including social reciprocity, eye contact, smiling in response to another, directing attention, greeting, empathy, and offering and asking for comfort. Imitation, peer relationships, and social initiative with peers and adults are other key aspects of social interaction (Anderson, Oti, Lord, & Welch, 2009). Communication problems are seen in virtually all children with ASC (Fodstad, Matson, Hess, & Neal, 2009). These might include reduced babbling, speech delay (either of phrases or single words), and unusual speech patterns, such as echolalia, pronoun reversal, and making up words. There are significant difficulties in the pragmatics of communication, such as poor conversation skills, unusual inflection, and little expression of emotion in speech. In addition to these verbal communication difficulties, almost all children with ASD have nonverbal communication difficulties: They do not use gestures, will not point at objects close by or far away, and won't nod or shake their head.

There are, finally, many examples of repetitive stereotyped behaviors (Szatmari et al., 2006; Lam, Bodfish, & Piven, 2008; Richler, Huerta, Bishop, & Lord, 2010). These include preoccupations with parts of objects (e.g., playing with a toy but not in the way in which it was meant to be played). Fascinations with concrete sensory experiences, such as smell, sight, touch, and taste, are also common. Older children with ASC often have extremely intense, circumscribed interests, such as specific cartoons and shows on TV such as the Weather Channel, and unusual hobbies and interests, such as listening to thunderstorms or reading science fiction. Repetitive motor movements, such as flicking one's fingers in front of the eyes, flapping one's hands, or running back and forth in a certain pattern, are also common, particularly among younger children with ASC. Rituals, such as an insistence on doing things in a particular way, are also not uncommon and should be differentiated from resistance to change, which signifies children not wanting to go from one activity to another, particularly if they are interested in that activity. This is a common problem in young children in general and is often confused with ASC.

A lot of research has gone into trying to understand how to characterize cognitive delays so often seen in children with ASC. Delays in expressive and receptive language are common, but children with Asperger syndrome do not show such language problems (Williams, Botting, & Boucher, 2008). Indeed, Asperger syndrome is characterized by an absence of clinically significant cognitive and language delay (Woodbury-Smith, Klin, & Volkmar, 2005). Perhaps a more parsimonious explanation of cognitive difficulty that virtually all ASC children share is a difficulty with abstract, metaphorical thinking, as opposed to more rote thinking or concrete understanding, which they are able to do well (Williams, Goldstein, Minshew, 2006). The more complex the cognitive operation, the more abstract, the more metaphorical, the more difficulty the ASC child will have with learning that concept, with understanding it, and with being able to perform certain roles.

Another active area of research has focused on trying to understand the fundamental deficit associated with ASC. Various theories have been proposed and studies undertaken to test the extent to which difficulties in joint attention, theory of mind (ToM), executive dysfunction, weak central coherence, and shifting and disengaging attention might be a unifying paradigm to understand children with ASC (Happé & Frith, 2006; Martin & McDonald, 2003; Miller, 2006; Landry & Bryson, 2004)). It now seems apparent that there will not be a single explanation or a single cognitive model for the disorder, but rather that different components of the condition might be associated with different cognitive models (Happé & Ronald, 2008). For example, a lack of ToM may be a good explanation for some of the social difficulties that children with ASC experience but some other model would need to be proposed for the preference of repetitive, stereotyped behaviors, such as weak central coherence (Mandy & Skuse, 2008).

References

Anderson, D. K., Oti, R. S., Lord, C., & Welch K. (2009). Patterns of growth in adaptive social abilities among children with autism spectrum disorders. *Journal of Abnormal Child Psychology,* 37, 1019–1034.

American Psychiatric Association (2000). *Diagnostic and Statistical Manual of Mental Disorders (4th ed.).* Washington DC: American Psychiatric Association.

Fernell, E., Hedvall, A., Norrelgen, F., Eriksson, M., Höglund-Carlsson, L., Barnevik-Olsson, M., … Gillberg, C. (2010). Developmental profiles in preschool children with autism spectrum disorders referred for intervention. *Research in Developmental Disabilities, 31,* 790–799.

Fodstad, J. C., Matson, J. L., Hess, J., & Neal, D. (2009). Social and communication behaviours in infants and toddlers with autism and pervasive developmental disorder-not otherwise specified. *Developmental Neurorehabilitation, 12,* 152–157.

Fombonne, E. (2005). Epidemiology of autistic disorder and other pervasive developmental disoders. *Journal of Clinical Psychiatry,* 66, *Suppl. 10,* 3–8.

Georgiades, S., Szatmari, P., Zwaigenbaum, L., Duku, E., Bryson, S., Roberts, W., … Mahoney, W. (2007). Structure of the autism symptom phenotype: A proposed multidimensional model. *Journal of the American Academy of Child and Adolescent Psychiatry, 46,* 188–196.

Happé, F., & Frith, U. (2006). The weak coherence account: Detail-focused cognitive style in autism spectrum disorders. *Journal of Autism and Developmental Disorders, 36,* 5–25.

Happé, F., & Ronald, A. (2008). The "Fractionable Autism Triad:" A review of evidence from behavioural, genetic, cognitive and neural research. *Neuropsychological Reviews, 18,* 287–304.

Jones, C. R., Happé, F., Golden, H., Marsden, A. J., Tregay, J., Simonoff, E., … Charman, T. (2009). Reading and arithmetic in adolescents with autism spectrum disorders: Peaks and dips in attainment. *Neuropsychology, 23,* 718–728.

Lam, K. S., Bodfish, J. W., & Piven, J. (2008). Evidence for three subtypes of repetitive behavior in autism that differ in familiality and association with other symptoms. *Journal of Child Psychology and Psychiatry, 49,* 1193–1200.

Landry, R., & Bryson, S. E. (2004). Impaired disengagement of attention in young children with autism. *Journal of Child Psychology and Psychiatry, 45,* 1115–1122.

Lecavalier, L., Gadow, K. D., DeVincent, C. J., Houts, C., & Edwards, M. C. (2009). Deconstructing the PDD clinical phenotype: Internal validity of the DSM-IV. *Journal of Child Psychology and Psychiatry, 50,* 1246–1254.

Mandy, W. P., & Skuse, D. H. (2008). Research Review: What is the association between the social communication element of autism and repetitive interests, behaviours and activities? *Journal of Child Psychology and Psychiatry, 49,* 795–808.

Martin, L., & McDonald, S. (2003). Weak coherence, no theory of mind or executive dysfunction? Solving the puzzle of pragmatic language disorders. *Brain and Language, 85,* 451–466.

Matson, J. L., & Shoemaker, M. (2009). Intellectual disability and its relationship to autism spectrum disorders. *Research in Developmental Disabilities, 30,* 1107–1114.

Miller, C. A. (2006). Developmental relationships between language and theory of mind. *American Journal of Speech and Language Pathology, 15,* 142–154.

Richler, J., Huerta, M., Bishop, S. L., & Lord C. (2010). Developmental trajectories of restricted and repetitive behaviors and interest in children with autism spectrum disorders. *Development and Psychopathology, 22,* 55–69.

Rogers, S.J. (2009). What are infant siblings teaching us about autism in infancy? *Autism Research, 2,* 125–137.

Snow, A. V., Lecavalier, L., & Houts, C. (2008). The structure of the Autism Diagnostic Interview-Revised: Diagnostic and phenotypic implications. *Journal of Child Psychology and Psychiatry, 50,* 734–742.

Szatmari, P., Georgiades, S., Bryson, S., Zwaigenbaum, L., Roberts, W., Mahoney. ... Tuff, L. (2006). Investigating the structure of the restricted, repetitive behaviours and interests domain of autism. *Journal of Child Psychology and Psychiatry, 47,* 582–590.

Szatmari, P., Merette, C., Bryson, S. E., Thivierge, J., Roy, M. A., Cayer, M., & Maziade, M. (2002). Quantifying dimensions in autism: A factor-analytic study. *Journal of the American Academy of Child and Adolescent Psychiatry, 41,* 467–476.

Williams, D, L,, Goldstein, G., & Minshew, N. J. (2006). Neuropsychologic functioning in children with autism: Further evidence for disordered complex information-processing. *Child Neuropsychology, 12,* 279–298.

Williams, D., Botting, N., & Boucher, J. (2008). Language in autism and specific language impairment: Where are the links? *Psychological Bulletin, 208,* 944–963.

Woodbury-Smith,M., Klin, A., & Volkmar F. (2005). Asperger's syndrome: A comparison of clinical diagnoses and those made according to the ICD-10 and DSM-IV. *Journal of Autism and Developmental Disorders, 35,* 235–240.

Zwaigenbaum, L. (2010). Advances in the early detection of autism. *Current Opinion in Neurology, 23,* 97–102.

Zwaigenbaum, L., Bryson, S., Lord, C., Rogers, S., Carter, A., Carver, L., ... Yirmiya, N. (2009). Clinical assessment and management of toddlers with suspected autism spectrum disorder: Insights from studies of high-risk infants. *Pediatrics, 123,* 1383–1391.

Q3

What Are the Differences (and Similarities) Between Autism, Asperger Syndrome, and PDD-NOS?

Fred R. Volkmar

This is an excellent question with a short and then a longer answer. The short answer is that, as currently defined in DSM-IV-TR (American Psychiatric Association, 2000), autism is defined on the basis of characteristic difficulties in the areas of social interaction, communication and play and restricted/unusual interests and behaviors. Asperger disorder differs from autism in that early language ability is relatively preserved, while pervasive developmental disorder not otherwise specified (PDD-NOS) is a category used for individuals with problems suggestive of autism but not meeting full criteria for that condition. All these conditions are currently recognized as members of the pervasive developmental disorder (PDD) class – a term that was coined in 1980 when autism was first included as an officially recognized diagnosis. In practical terms, PDD means the same thing as autism spectrum disorder (Volkmar & Klin, 2005).

Of these disorders, autism has been far and away the most frequently studied and, somewhat paradoxically, the least studied disorder, PDD-NOS, is the most frequent. This disparity in research reflects an understandable focus on the more "prototypic" disorder. However, interest in the broader spectrum of autistic-like conditions has increased dramatically in recent years, and it likely includes a number of subtypes, though none of these are, as yet, officially recognized (Towbin, 2005).

The condition termed "Asperger syndrome" was first described in 1944, the year after Kanner's first description of autism. In the initial cases described by Hans Asperger, the children (all boys) had remarkable trouble in social interaction and weak motor skills, but good verbal abilities. They also exhibited circumscribed interest in various topics (e.g., trains, rocks, the weather, American gangsters), and this interest interfered with their abilities to learn other skills (McPartland & Klin, 2006). The issue of whether or not Asperger syndrome is truly different from autism or represents, essentially, more cognitively able children with autism has been controversial. As a practical matter, the reasons for according it a separate diagnostic status have included the important implications of preserved verbal abilities for intervention, associations with specific learning profiles, comorbid conditions (like depression), and what may be an even stronger genetic component (Baron-Cohen & Klin, 2006). Research on all these conditions has strongly implicated genetic factors, and there is some suggestion that all three conditions are transmitted within families (Abrahams & Geschwind, 2008; O'Roak & State, 2008).

References

Abrahams, B. S., & Geschwind, D. H. (2008). Advances in autism genetics: On the threshold of a new neurobiology. *Nature Reviews Genetics, 9,* 341–355. [erratum Nat Rev Genet 2008 Jun;9(6):493].

American Psychiatric Association (APA) (2000). Diagnostic and Statistical Manual. Text Revision (4th ed.), Washington, D.C.: APA Press.

Baron-Cohen, S., & Klin, A. (2006). What's so special about Asperger syndrome? *Brain and Cognition, 61,* 1–4.

McPartland, J., & Klin, A. (2006). Asperger's syndrome. *Adolescent Medicine Clinics, 17,* 771–788.

O'Roak, B. J, & State, M. W. (2008). Autism genetics: Strategies, challenges, and opportunities. *Autism Research, 1,* 4–17.

Towbin, K. E. (2005). Pervasive Developmental Disorder Not Otherwise Specified. In: F.R. Volkmar, A. Klin, R. Paul and D. J. Cohen, *Handbook of Autism and Pervasive Developmental Disorders* (pp. 165–200). Hoboken, NJ: Wiley.

Volkmar, F. R., & A. Klin (2005). Issues in the classification of autism and related conditions. In F. R. Volkmar, A., Klin, R. Paul, and D. J. Cohen, *Handbook of Autism and Pervasive Developmental Disorders* (pp. 5–41). Hoboken, NJ: Wiley.

Q4
Why Is It Important to Differentiate Between High- and Low-Functioning ASC?

Sven Bölte

ASC can appear on all levels of cognitive function, from profound mental retardation to intellectual giftedness. Therefore, the intelligence level is not part of the definition of any ASC. However, there is an excess of mental retardation in ASC. It is assumed that about 55% of all affected individuals also show a mental handicap (Baird et al., 2006), whereas the expected rate in the general population is approximately 3%. Thus, it is the most frequent coexisting psychiatric problem in ASC. Females with an ASC are even more likely to show a low intelligence quotient (IQ). On the other hand, most people with Asperger syndrome have an IQ in the average or high range.

It is common in clinical settings today to also label people with ASC according to their general mental capacity in order to enhance communication between experts. One often hears the terms "high-functioning" (HF) or "low-functioning" (LF) in association with ASC individuals. These are still unofficial and not clearly defined subcategories. HF refers to the absence of mental retardation (i.e., IQ > 70) or sometimes even to the absence of learning disability (i.e., IQ > 85), whereas LF generally indicates mental retardation (i.e., IQ < 70). This differentiation is a little misleading and may be misunderstood by laypersons, as HF ASC does not necessarily indicate that the respective individual does particularly well in everyday life (Bölte & Poustka, 2002).

Nevertheless, there are several good reasons to make the HF versus LF differentiation. First, IQ has been demonstrated to be the most robust predictor of outcome in ASC (Gillberg & Steffenburg, 1987). To be HF is a prerequisite for school attainment, social integration, and independence. LF ASC, in the vast majority of cases, is accompanied by continuously low adaptive skills, challenging behavior, and the need for support (Howlin, Goode, Hutton, & Rutter, 2004). Second, people with HF ASC are less easily recognized as deviant. While LF individuals are increasingly being diagnosed within the first years of life, HF people are often overlooked because their intellectual capacities, and perhaps verbal skills, camouflage their behavior difficulties. In these cases, it is also more likely that the environment will expect the individual to "grow out of" existing problems or denies the existence of a developmental problem in the face of the intellectual strength exhibited. To the untrained eye, it may appear a contradiction that a serious behavior problem can be present in an individual of normal or high intelligence. Third, HF and LF people with ASC differ considerably in how much they are aware of their behavior. In adolescent and adult HF ASC, a certain insight into distinctiveness can be encountered, and self-report is a possibility of collecting information. This is hardly ever the case, however, in LF ASC. Finally, HF and LF individuals with ASC require quite different amounts and kinds of intervention. For an prototypic LF individual with ASC, intensive autism-specific behavior therapy, separate education, and supportive medication may be an option, whereas individuals with HF ASC will often benefit most from social skills training and integrative education.

References

Baird, G., Simonoff, E., Pickles, A., Chandler, S., Loucas, T., Meldrum, D., & Charman, T. (2006). Prevalence of disorders of the autism spectrum in a population cohort of children in South Thames: The Special Needs and Autism Project (SNAP). *Lancet, 368*, 210–215.

Bölte, S., & Poustka, F. (2002). The relation between general cognitive level and adaptive behavior domains in individuals with autism with and without co-morbid mental retardation. Child Psychiatry and Human Development, *33*, 165–172.

Gillberg, C., & Steffenburg, S. (1987). Outcome and prognostic factors in infantile autism and similar conditions: A population-based study of 46 cases followed through puberty. *Journal of Autism and Developmental Disorders, 17*, 273–287.

Howlin, P., Goode, S., Hutton, J., & Rutter, M. (2004). Adult outcome for children with autism. *Journal of Child Psychology and Psychiatry, 45*, 212–229.

Further Reading

Prior, M., & Ozonoff, S. (2007). Psychological factors in autism. In F. R. Volkmar, Autism and Pervasive Developmental Disorders (pp. 69–128). 2nd ed., Cambridge University Press.

Q5
What Are the First Signs of ASC?

Tony Charman

Much of the historical literature in both the clinical and research fields starts with descriptions of children with ASC at the age of 4 or 5 years, because, until the last decade, we knew little about the early emergence of ASC in infants and toddlers. Several factors have driven this change, including efforts to improve earlier identification with the recognition that earlier-delivered intervention may improve outcome (Dawson, 2008). Aside from retrospective reports from parents about how their children were in the first few years of life, which might suffer from a number of reporting and reliability biases, several strands of recent research have broadened our understanding of the early signs of autism. More objective retrospective information has been analyzed from home videos of the children taken prior to the child receiving the diagnosis. Prospective studies involve samples of young children from a general (or referred) population, who have some initial risk marker, such as failing a screening questionnaire or being a younger sibling of a child diagnosed with ASC. Children in the latter group are genetically at a higher risk compared to other children (see Yirmiya & Charman, 2009; Zwaigenbaum et al., 2009, for reviews).

Palomo, Belinchon, and Ozonoff (2006) reviewed 8 studies of retrospective analyses of home videos from the first 2 years of life of infants who later developed ASC. The early signs of autism during the first year of life that consistently emerged were reduced response to name calling and reduced frequency of looking at faces; in the second year of life, pointing as a means of request and sharing behaviors, such as pointing to show and showing/giving objects, differentiated the ASC groups from the comparison groups. Seeking physical contact, participating in social games, and the frequency of negative affective responses did not differentiate the ASC groups at 12 months. Other studies have suggested that sensory abnormalities might be present as early as 9 months of age in some children. An advantage of such home movie studies is that naturally occurring behavior prior to diagnosis is evaluated; however, a disadvantage may be that parents may chose to videotape their children when the children are at their best and not necessarily while manifesting some of the behaviors that may be early signs of the emergence of an ASC.

Prospective screening studies (see Webb & Jones, 2009, for a review) have shown that it is possible to prospectively identify ASC, including in children about whom parents and professionals did not have preexisting concerns, from the age of 18 or even 14 months of age. The most common early signs captured by these screens are impairments or delays in early emerging social communication, such as response to name calling, joint attention, and play; although, at least in one study, there was a suggestion that sensory abnormalities and a restricted repertoire of play activities might also be early indicators of later ASC. In none of the studies that have included systematic follow-up of the screened populations to identify all cases of ASC at outcome, however, have the signs been universal (i.e., these screens do not identify all cases). This suggests that caution is required when recommending universal population screening, although the American Academy of Pediatrics has made such a recommendation (Johnson & Myers, & the Academy of Pediatrics Council on Children with Disabilities, 2007). Clinically, such screens work better in referred populations or when the screening result is used alongside parental or professional concern about development.

Many investigators are currently conducting prospective longitudinal studies of younger siblings of children with ASC, who, as a group, are at a genetically higher risk to develop an ASC compared to the general population. A considerable amount of literature regarding the developmental trajectories of these younger siblings is now available (for summaries, see Rogers, 2009; Yirmiya & Charman, 2009; Zwaigenbaum et al., 2009). However, to date, only a few studies have followed the at-risk siblings up to the age of 36 months to determine outcome, lessening the certainty that the early signs detected are necessarily predictive or indicative of a later ASC. From those that have conducted such follow-ups, a number of early manifestations have been found, including some towards the end of the first year of life.

Zwaigenbaum et al. (2009) examined the development of high-risk and low-risk infants from 6 to 12 months and identified several behavioral markers at 12 months (but not at 6 months) that predicted later diagnoses of ASC at 24 months, including atypical eye contact, visual tracking, disengagement of visual attention, orienting to name, imitation, social smiling, reactivity, social interest, and sensory-oriented behaviors. Landa and Garrett-Mayer (2006) found that at 14 months (but, again, not at 6 months) the children who went on to receive a diagnosis of an ASC scored lower than controls on the motor and language subscales of the Mullen assessment. In a separate publication, the same group (Landa, Holman, & Garrett-Mayer, 2007) also reported differences in social communication and play behavior, especially for those children who received an early diagnosis (a tentative ASC diagnosis made at the 14-month visit). Studies of young at-risk siblings have found that both early signs of social communication (not responding when one's name is called) and nonsocial signs (more spinning and rotating of objects, prolonged and unusual visual inspection) at age 12 months distinguished between the at-risk siblings who went on to receive a diagnosis and those who did not (see Yirmiya & Charman, 2009, for a review).

Another early sign of an ASC is developmental regression or "setback." Pickles et al. (2009) found that regression or loss of skills (most commonly language, but also social and play behaviors) was highly specific to children with an ASC, particularly those with core autism, and was rarely seen in those with other neurodevelopmental disorders, including language delay.

Indeed, regression is one of the red flags, alongside failure to meet social and communication developmental milestones, that make referral of a child to a pediatrician imperative, as recommended by the American Academy of Pediatrics (see www.aap.org/publiced/autismtoolkit.cfm) and other professional groups (Johnson & Myers, & the Academy of Pediatrics Council on Children with Disabilities, 2007). There has been significant international interest in training and educating community practitioners and parents in the early signs of ASC, and useful and accessible websites that show the best-validated early signs are now available (see www.firstsigns.org; www.autismspeaks.org/whatisit/learnsigns. php). To finish on a note of caution, no signal sign (or indeed a score on an ASC screening checklist) equates to a diagnosis, and consideration of the meaning of any individual behavior, usually in consultation with parents and other professionals, is required before any decision, for example to refer for an ASC assessment, is made.

References

Dawson, G. (2008). Early behavioral intervention, brain plasticity, and the prevention of autism spectrum disorder. *Development and Psychopathology, 20,* 775–803.

Johnson, C. P., & Myers, S. M., & The American Academy of Pediatrics Council on Children With Disabilities (2007). Identifiaction and evaluation of children with autism spectrum disorders. *Pediatrics, 120,* 1183–1215.

Landa, R., & Garrett-Mayer, E. (2006). Development in infants with autism spectrum disorders: A prospective study. *Journal of Child Psychology and Psychiatry, 47,* 629–638.

Landa, R. J., Holman, K. C., & Garrett-Mayer, E. (2007). Social and communication development in toddlers with early and later diagnosis of autism spectrum disorders. *Archives of General Psychiatry, 64,* 853–864.

Palomo, R., Belinchón, M., & Ozonoff, S. (2006). Autism and family home movies: A comprehensive review. *Journal of Developmental and Behavioral Pediatrics, 27,* S59–68.

Pickles, A., Simonoff, E., Conti-Ramsden, G., Falcaro, M., Simkin, Z., Charman, T., … Baird, G. (2009). Loss of language in early development of autism and specific language impairment. *Journal of Child Psychology and Psychiatry, 50,* 843–852.

Rogers, S. J. (2009). What are infant siblings teaching us about autism in infancy? *Autism Research, 2,* 125–137.

Webb, S. J., & Jones, E. J. H. (2009). Early identification of autism: Early characteristics, onset of symptoms, and diagnostic stability. *Infants & Young Children, 22,* 100–118.

Yirmiya, N., & Charman, T. (2010). The prodrome of autism: Early behavioral and biological signs, regression, peri- and post-natal development and genetics. *Journal of Child Psychology and Psychiatry, 51,* 432–458.

Zwaigenbaum, L., Bryson, S., Lord, C., Rogers, S., Carter, A., Carver, L., … Yirmiya, N. (2009). Clinical assessment and management of toddlers with suspected autism spectrum disorder: Insights from studies of high-risk infants. *Pediatrics, 123,* 1383–1391.

Further Reading

Volkmar, F. R., State, M., & Klin, A. (2009). Autism and autism spectrum disorders: Diagnostic issues for the coming decade. *Journal of Child Psychology and Psychiatry, 50*, 108–115.

Q6
At What Age Can ASC Be Detected?

Tony Charman

Until the 1990s, it was rare for children to receive a diagnosis of autism until the age of 3 or 4 years, and in some cases much later. This was despite the fact that both the DSM and ICD diagnostic systems are clear that, in order to meet the criteria for core autism, symptoms have to be present in the first 3 years of life, as evidenced by abnormalities in language development, social attachment and interest, and early play skills. Motivation to achieve early diagnosis comes from the recognition that earlier-delivered intervention may improve outcome (Dawson, 2008), and the clinical desire to help parents understand their child's development and behavior, which can be both difficult to understand and hard to manage, as well as to inform family planning given the increased risk for children born subsequently.

However, an increasing number of children in many countries are currently diagnosed with an ASC by 2 or 3 years of age. Alongside the positive message that these developments bring, there are also challenges and concerns regarding our ability to diagnose ASC in children so young. One critical question has been whether the diagnosis was possible, accurate, and stable when applied to toddlers at the age of 2 or 3 years. Over the past decade, a number of research teams have followed up on children first diagnosed at the age of 2 years into early and, more recently, middle childhood to allow us to answer this important question to some extent.

A first series of studies conducted 10 years ago (see Landa, 2008, for a review) followed children from initial early assessments at 2 years of age to later assessments at 3–4 years of age, and all showed high stability of diagnosis, in particular for core autism with somewhat lower stability for milder ASC (i.e., pervasive developmental disorder not otherwise specified (PDD-NOS)). The movement across the ASC/PDD-NOS diagnostic category boundary was somewhat different in the studies; in some, individual children who met broader ASC criteria at the initial assessment did not meet criteria for an ASC at follow-up, whereas in others, children who did not receive an ASC diagnosis at the initial assessment met criteria for milder ASC at follow-up. The samples in these early studies differ in a number of characteristics, including how and for what purposes they were ascertained (e.g., prospective screening studies vs. clinically referred samples, IQ, language ability, and the different use and implementation both of standard diagnostic instruments but also of DSM-IV and ICD-10 diagnostic criteria), and these might account for the differences found.

In the last few years, a number of second wave follow-up studies of children initially diagnosed around the age of 2 have been published. The more recent studies differ from those described above in a number of features, most notably in that some have considerably larger sample sizes (Chawarska, Klin, Paul, Macari, & Volkmar, 2009; Lord et al., 2006) and that the follow-up periods extend to age 7 in the Charman et al. (2005) study and to age 9 in the Lord et al. (2006) studies. Broadly, the lessons are the same: Diagnosis of core autism is highly stable in these samples but that of milder ASC is less so. Compared to the first wave of studies, there was greater movement from having an ASC diagnosis at 2 years to a non-spectrum diagnosis at 4 years in several of these recent studies. Whilst the authors report the factors associated with these good outcomes, principally higher IQ and better language competency, it is important to remain cautious regarding prognosis and outcome at such a young age. Usually both the diagnostic picture and the child's prognosis become clearer over time. However, the general pattern is of reasonably high stability of diagnosis, extending downwards in age the earlier pioneering longitudinal work of Sigman and colleagues, who, over a decade ago, demonstrated high stability for a diagnosis of childhood autism from 4 years of age through to mid-childhood and even young adulthood.

It is generally accepted that, for the diagnosis of ASC in toddlers, as for that in older children, expert clinical judgment is more reliable than the standard diagnostic instruments, the Autism Diagnostic Interview-Revised (ADI-R; Rutter, LeCouteur, & Lord, 2003) and the Autism Diagnostic Observation Schedule (ADOS; Lord, Rutter, DiLavore, & Risi, 2001). Many, but not all, studies also found that behaviors from the third symptom cluster that defines autism (restricted and repetitive behaviors and activities) were less evident at 2 years of age than at 4–5 years of age. However, where these features are seen in combination with social and communication impairments in a toddler, they are highly indicative of autism. What has emerged from these programs of work are some clear messages (core autism *can* be accurately diagnosed in 2-year-olds) but also some areas of uncertainty that will take continued study to resolve (in some studies, diagnosis, particularly of the milder ASC, appears less stable).

For clinicians, the lesson is to accept that autism is a developmental disorder, and at a very young age there may be less certainty regarding the pattern of behavior that a child is showing and the likelihood of them continuing to meet diagnostic criteria into the future. Charman and Baird (2002) discuss the importance of understanding the diagnostic process as an iterative process to be worked out between clinical teams and parents over time, and that concepts such as a "working diagnosis" or "working hypothesis" (that a toddler is showing sufficient features that they likely have an autism spectrum condition, even if it cannot be confirmed at such a young age) can be helpful. An important aspect of early diagnostic consultation is an open and straightforward approach to the negotiation of the diagnostic view with parents over time. The diagnosis needs to be explained to parents in such a way that they recognize their child and the difficulties they are experiencing in the description that is given. At the same time, clinical teams should be aware of the need to provide sufficient certainty regarding the child's condition that they are not refused services following assessment.

Another important clinical reminder is that, whilst for some children with an ASC their presentation may make diagnosis possible by an experienced clinical team by 2 or 3 years of age, there is a subgroup of verbally and intellectually able children who go on to receive a diagnosis of autism (sometimes called high-functioning autism) or Asperger syndrome, who may not receive a diagnosis in the preschool years. There is also another group who may meet diagnostic criteria for an ASC who do not receive an explicit diagnosis at a young age – those individuals with moderate to severe intellectual disability (ID) or those with an already identified preexisting associated medical condition. In a recent epidemiological study (Baird et al, 2006), we found that, for cases meeting research diagnostic criteria for an ASC following in-depth assessment, low IQ was associated with not having received a clinical diagnosis by local clinical services by the age of 9, though all had a diagnosis of some form of developmental disorder, mostly ID or language delay (a process referred to as "diagnostic overshadowing").

One final caveat is that the studies summarized above have largely come from expert clinical research centers specifically studying young cohorts of children. In community settings in many countries, there is evidence that for many children and their families a diagnosis is not confirmed until children are well into school age, and this has implications for the training of community practitioners (Wiggins, Baio, & Rice, 2006).

References

Baird, G., Simonoff, E., Pickles, A., Chandler, S., Loucas, T., Meldrum, D., & Charman, T. (2006). Prevalence of pervasive developmental disorders in a population cohort of children in South East Thames: The Special Needs and Autism Project (SNAP). *The Lancet, 368,* 210–215.

Charman, T., & Baird, G. (2002). Practitioner review: diagnosis of autism spectrum disorder in 2- and 3-year-old children. *Journal of Child Psychology and Psychiatry, 43,* 289–305.

Charman, T., Taylor, E., Drew, A., Cockerill, H., Brown, J. A., & Baird, G. (2005). Outcome at 7 years of children diagnosed with autism at age 2: Predictive validity of assessments conducted at 2 and 3 years of age and pattern of symptom change over time. *Journal of Child Psychology and Psychiatry, 46,* 500–513.

Chawarska, K., Klin, A., Paul, R., Macari, S., & Volkmar, F. (2009). A prospective study of toddlers with ASD: Short-term diagnostic and cognitive outcomes. *Journal of Child Psychology and Psychiatry, 50,* 1235–1245.

Dawson, G. (2008). Early behavioral intervention, brain plasticity, and the prevention of autism spectrum disorder. *Development and Psychopathology, 20,* 775–803.

Lord, C., Rutter, M., DiLavore, P. C., & Risi, S. (2001). *Autism Diagnostic Observation Schedule (ADOS).* Los Angeles, CA: Western Psychological Services.

Landa, R. J. (2008). Diagnosis of autism spectrum disorders in the first 3 years of life. *Nature Clinical Practice Neurology, 4,* 138–147.

Lord, C., Risi, S., DiLavore, P. S., Shulman, C., Thurm, A., & Pickles, A. (2006). Autism from 2 to 9 years of age. *Archives of General Psychiatry, 63,* 694–701.

Rutter, M., LeCouteur, A., & Lord, C. (2003). *Autism Diagnostic Interview, Revised (ADI-R).* Los Angeles, CA: Western Psychological Services.

Wiggins, L. D., Baio, J., & Rice, C. (2006). Examination of the time between first evaluation and first autism spectrum diagnosis in a population-based sample. *Journal of Developmental and Behavioral Pediatrics, 27,* S79–87.

Q7
Is Autism a Common Personality Trait?

John N. Constantino

Although the term "autism" has historically been reserved for children with severe and disabling deficits in the capacity for reciprocal social behavior, the observation that such deficits are quantitative in nature (continuously distributed rather than all-or-nothing) and that they also occur in much milder forms in the general population raises the question of whether ASC represent the pathological extreme of a common personality trait or traits. Several large population-based studies (e.g., Contantino & Todd, 2003; Ronald, Happe, Price, Baron-Cohen, & Plomin, 2006; Skuse et al., 2009), each using different methodologies to ascertain autistic traits, have all demonstrated unimodal (skewed normal) distributions for these traits in nature (as depicted below in Figure 1 from the study by Constantino and Todd, 2003), and have demonstrated that the magnitude of

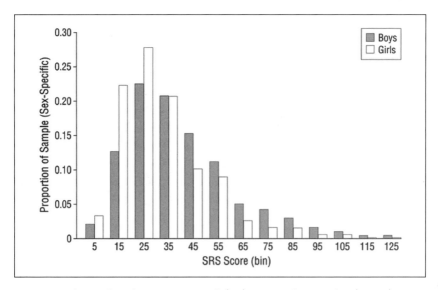

Figure 1. Distribution of Social Responsiveness Scale (SRS) scores as a function of sex (*n* = 1576). Reprinted from Constantino and Todd (2003).

inherited influence on these traits is as pronounced as for ASC themselves (in the order of 80%).

Personality traits are generally conceptualized as enduring styles of interpersonal behavior that are largely (though not completely) inherited and that predict the quality of an individual's relationships with other people. In this sense, it is difficult to imagine a more potent inherited personality trait than autistic impairment, because its most profound impact is on social (interpersonal) behavior. In a recent study of adolescents with high-functioning ASC, about half met criteria for schizoid personality disorder (Constantino et al., 2009). Given the prevalence of ASC in childhood (affecting close to 1% of the male population) and the relative rarity of an ASC diagnosis in adulthood, it is quite likely that many adolescents with higher-functioning ASC get diagnosed with personality disorders (rather than ASC) when they become adults, even though it is extremely unlikely that their ASC have completely resolved. Thus, there appears to be substantial continuity between the respective states of being mildly affected (at the level of personality variation) versus severely affected (at the level of classification of an ASC).

Remaining questions are whether the autistic-like traits that are seen in the general population exist on the same continuum as those of clinical ASC, and whether their causes overlap. In support of the concept of ASC as an extreme personality trait, the prevalence of children with extreme (clinical-level) scores for autistic traits in general population distributions is essentially identical to that which has been estimated for ASC (Constantino & Todd, 2003). Children with milder levels of autistic symptomatology are known to be more common than those with severe symptomatology, and this is true in the general population as well. Finally, the common observation of children with intermediate phenotypes (exhibiting, for example, "odd," "nerdy" preservative, or socially aloof behavior) bolsters the notion of continuity between clinical-level syndromes and "normality."

The issue of overlap in causality is still being explored. Although it is true that a minority (10–15%) of ASC are explainable on the basis of specific genetic mutations, some of the causal mutations that have been discovered have resulted not only in autism, but in very mild phenotypes that fall within the range of phenotypic expression observed in the general population. In some complex diseases, rare mutations that contribute risk for disease have also explained normal variation within the population. In autism, particularly among families with multiple affected individuals, the *unaffected* males exhibit a pronounced pathological shift in their distribution of autistic traits (Virkud, Todd, Abbacchi, Zhang, & Constantino, 2009). The aggregation of subclinical autistic traits in this population suggests that the genetic causes of those traits overlap with those of ASC themselves.

Therefore, there are many reasons to consider the possibility that some clinical ASC represent the severe end of variation in personality, particularly traits affecting capacity and motivation for reciprocal social behavior.

References

Constantino, J. N., Abbacchi, A. M., Lavesser. P. D., Reed. H., Givens. L., Chiang, L., … Todd, R. D. (2009). Developmental course of autistic social impairment in males. *Developmental and Psychopathology, 21*, 127–138.

Constantino, J. N., & Todd, R. D. (2003). Autistic traits in the general population: A twin study. *Archives of General Psychiatry, 60*, 524–530.

Ronald, A., Happe, F., Price, T.S., Baron-Cohen, S., & Plomin, R. (2006). Phenotypic and genetic overlap between autistic traits at the extremes of the general population. *Journal of American Academy of Child and Adolescent Psychiatry, 45*, 1206–1214.

Skuse, D., Mandy, W., Steer, C., Miller, L., Goodman, R., Lawrence, K., ... Golding, J. (2009). Social Communication Competence and Functional Adaptation in a General Population of Children: Preliminary Evidence for Sex-by-Verbal IQ Differential Risk. *Journal of American Academy of Child and Adolescent Psychiatry, 48*, 128–137.

Virkud, Y. V., Todd, R. D., Abbacchi, A. M., Zhang, Y., & Constantino, J. N. (2009). Familial aggregation of quantitative autistic traits in multiplex versus simplex autism. *American Journal of Medicine Genetics B Neuropsychiatry Genetics, 150B*, 328–334.

Further Reading

Constantino, J. N. (2009). How continua converge in nature: Cognition, social competence, and autistic syndromes. *Journal of the American Academy of Child and Adolescent Psychiatry, 48*, 97–98

Q8
What Are Idiopathic and Syndromal Variants of ASC?

Brett Abrahams

Available research suggests that ASC are not one or even several conditions with easily defined causes but rather dozens or even hundreds of entities that share common behavioral features. Under the umbrella of ASC, a distinction has traditionally been made between cases largely attributable to single genetic or environmental risk factors (syndromal) and those in which the causes are unclear but thought to be more complex (idiopathic). Current science, however, is beginning to blur the boundaries between these two categories and argues against such a distinction. More detailed information written for geneticists (Abrahams & Geschwind, 2010) and nongeneticists (Abrahams, 2010) is also available elsewhere.

The early identification, in a small fraction of ASC cases, of single gene disorders in which autism is observed at higher than expected frequency (e.g., fragile X syndrome), led to the notion that the vast unexplained majority of cases were more complex. This small fraction of syndromal cases was held to be something distinct, superficially similar to the ASC, but neither representative nor informative with regard to individuals with an idiopathic (i.e., poorly understood) form.

Surprisingly, and really counter to predictions made as little as 5 years ago, there are now more than 25 rare syndromes in which autism occurs at much higher than expected frequency. Although none *individually* accounts for more than 1–2% of cases, these syndromes *collectively* account for upwards of 20% of cases. Importantly, insights from genetics can be useful for medical management for this subset of individuals. As additional risk factors are identified – and this is happening more rapidly than ever before – this new knowledge will result in improved outcomes for patients and families.

References

Abrahams, B. S. (2010). Many roads to the autism spectrum disorders. In Deborah A. Fein (Ed.), *Neuropsychology of Autism*. Oxford, UK: Oxford University Press.

Abrahams, B. S., & Geschwind, D. H. (2010). Genetics of Autism. In M. R. Speicher, S. E. Antonarakis, & A. G. Motulsky (Eds.), *Human Genetics: Problems & Approaches* (4th ed.). Berlin: Springer-Verlag.

Q9
What Is Neurodiversity?

Sven Bölte

Neurodiversity is a notion which postulates that neurodivergent or atypical neurological development should be considered normal human variation. It should, therefore, not be considered a disorder or disease, but rather respected as an aspect of human diversity, such as being gay or left handed. The concept of neurodiversity is particularly applied to some mental disorders, among them attention-deficit/hyperactivity disorder (ADHD), dyslexia, tics, schizophrenia, and bipolar disorders. It is argued that most people diagnosed with these disorders are not truly ill, with no need for cure, only definite social acceptance. Neurodiversity embodies a rejection of medical labels or diagnoses for many psychiatric conditions.

The idea of neurodiversity is put forward by people with ASC, especially the online community, as well as some parents, clinicians, and researchers. They advocate tolerance and acceptance instead of pathologization of autistic individuals. It is argued that autism cannot be separated from a person and autistic people should be allowed to develop naturally, without interference by attempts to heal. To the contrary: Neurodiversity indicates that society, not people with ASC, needs to change. Neurodiversity is therefore often the maxim of the autism rights, autism culture, or autism pride movement. In order to stress neurodiversity, healthy, typically developing people are often labeled "neurotypicals" (NT), as opposed to autistics.

Further Reading

Gernsbacher, M. A. (2004). *Autistics need acceptance, not cure*. Retrieved from http://www.autistics.org/library/acceptance.html

Woodford, G. (2006). "We don't need to be cured," autistics say. *National Review of Medicine, 3*. Retrieved from http://www.nationalreviewofmedicine.com/issue/2006/04_30/3_patients_practice05_8.html

Q10
What Is a Savant?

Sven Bölte

The word "savant" is French and means knowledgeable individual. In medicine and psychology, it is often used to describe the coexistence of cognitive, mental, or sensory disability, on the one hand, and outstanding capacity in a circumscribed domain of intellectual or artistic function, on the other. The appearance or development of a savant skill is obviously unexplainable, and a comparable discrepancy between global and specific function is hardly ever found in typically developing people. Exceptional abilities can emerge in the area of memory, drawing, music, calculating, reading, technical and geographical ability, fine motor coordination, and sensory discrimination. The terms idiot savant, savant syndrome, mono savant, or islets of ability are also sometimes used to label the savant phenomenon. Truly exceptional (prodigious) savants are rare: Only some 100 cases are known. However, so-called "splinter abilities" and "talented savants" are quite frequent. Here, the exhibited skill is primarily outstanding in comparison to the general level of functioning of the respective individual, but not necessarily outstanding when compared to the average level of abilities in the general population. For instance, a profoundly mentally retarded person showing average mathematical skills may be viewed as a talented savant.

Savants can be found in a range of disorders, but they are obviously most frequent among people with ASC (Howlin, Goode, Hutton, & Rutter, 2009). Rimland (1978) reported a savant talent rate of 9.8% for autism, with markedly more males than females showing savant skills. While there are many theories to explain the emergence of savant skills in general (Heaton & Wallace, 2004), two try to explain why there is an excess of savants in ASC. One theory proposes that the development of special skills is strongly connected to repetitive, obsessive, and restricted behaviors or interests, which are core symptoms of autism. According to this assumption, preoccupations favor the emergence of extraordinary skills because they lead to a very intense and rehearsed activity within a circumscribed field from an early age (O'Connor & Hermelin, 1991). The other hypothesis assumes that savant skills in autism are supported by a cognitive style coined by local processing of information or attention to detail (Pring, Hermelin, & Heavey, 1995).

References

Heaton, P., & Wallace, G. L. (2004). Annotation : The savant syndrome. *Journal of Child Psychology and Psychiatry, 45*, 899–911.

Howlin, P., Goode, S., Hutton, J., & Rutter, M. (2009). Savant skills in autism: Psychometric approaches and parental reports. *Philosophical transactions of the Royal Society of London. Series B, Biological sciences, 364*, 1359–1367.

O'Connor, N., & Hermelin, B. (1991). Talents and preoccupations in idiot-savants. *Psychological Medicine, 21*, 959–964.

Pring, L., Hermelin, B., & Heavey, L. (1995). Savants, segments, art and autism. *Journal of Child Psychology and Psychiatry*, 36, 1065–1076.

Rimland, B. (1978). Savant capabilities of autistic children and their cognitive implications. In G. Serban (Ed.). *Cognitive defects in the development of mental illness* (pp. 44–63). New York, NY: Bruner & Mazel.

Further Reading

Hermelin, B. (2001). *Bright splinters of the mind*. London, UK: Jessica Kingsley.

Treffert, D. (2006). *Extraordinary people*. New York, NY: Harper & Row.

Q11

Do Autistics Have Cognitive Strengths? Should ASC Be Defined as Disorders?

Michelle Dawson & Laurent Mottron

In their original accounts of autism, both Leo Kanner and Hans Asperger noted areas in which autistics had obvious strengths in acquiring and processing certain kinds of information. However, in the ensuing decades, there has been very little systematic investigation into what autistics do well. In spite of this neglect, evidence for numerous autistic cognitive strengths has emerged from several different sources.

One source is descriptive work, of which Kanner's accounts (collected in Kanner, 1973) are excellent examples. Kanner reported evident strengths, impressive achievements, and good later outcomes in many autistics, including in extremely atypical individuals. Similarly, Asperger (1944/1991) reported unusual cognitive strengths in an individual judged to be "grossly autistic" with "impossible behavior," whose eventual achievements and success were outstanding. While the autism literature as a whole provides numerous descriptive reports of autistics performing well, these reports are mostly haphazard, if not entirely accidental. Clear autistic strengths (e.g., strong focused interests) have, in recent decades, often been described as pathological and, therefore, as targets for remediation through treatment.

Another source of evidence for autistic strengths comes from the study of savant syndrome. Individuals displaying the exceptional skills regarded as savant abilities – in areas such as musical performance, calculation, drawing, and memory – are often found to be autistic. It is now agreed that savant syndrome is strongly associated with autism and with autistic traits (Heaton & Wallace, 2004). Using conservative methods, a recent study has shown that about 1/3 of autistics have exceptional or savant abilities (Howlin, Goode, Hutton, & Rutter, 2009). In addition, areas of strength that are obvious in savant autistics have consistently been found when investigated in non-savant autistics whose abilities are far less obvious. This raises the possibility that many more autistics could develop exceptional or savant abilities were they given the opportunity. However, little is known about how autistics learn well and, therefore, about the best ways to enhance, and not to suppress, autistics' inherent cognitive advantages (Mottron, Dawson, & Soulieres, 2009). To the contrary, savant-level abilities have been listed among autistics' presumed-to-be dysfunctional behavioral excesses and deficits, with more emphasis on eliminating these obvious atypicalities than on encouraging them (Dawson, Mottron, & Gernsbacher, 2008).

A final source of evidence for autistic strengths arises from experimental work comparing the performance of autistics to the performance of nonautistics on various tasks. Most often, the goal of the research has been to locate presumed core autistic deficits. Regardless, autistics have performed better than nonautistic controls in numerous existing studies involving social, nonsocial, and language-based information. Tasks on which superior autistic performance has empirically been found range from embedded figures, visual search, and block design tasks; to logical consistency, fluid reasoning, and resistance to false memory tasks; to sentence comprehension, picture labeling, and phonological processing tasks; to auditory pitch discrimination and chord disembedding tasks; to familiar-face image recognition and intention-understanding tasks. In this incomplete list, some findings are highly replicated and others are not. It is also clear that several strengths in unexpected areas have inadvertently been found, raising the question of how much would currently be known about the full range and importance of autistic strengths had this question been studied in a systematic manner.

Contrary to many current assumptions, autistic cognitive strengths empirically reported in the literature are not confined to any small or exclusive category of autistics. Strengths have been found in autistic toddlers, children, adolescents, and adults; in males and females; and in autistics judged to be (and not to be) intellectually disabled via commonly used instruments. Strengths have been more frequently found among autistic individuals than Asperger individuals, although less research has been conducted, in general, among Asperger individuals.

Because autism has most often been regarded as a disorder, numerous autistic cognitive strengths have been interpreted not as possible autistic advantages to be studied and encouraged, but as evidence for autistic cognitive deficits. For example, autistics' superior performance on a series of visual and auditory tasks has been interpreted not as evidence of enhanced autistic abilities, but instead as evidence of an ability that autistics lacked ("weak central coherence"). Indeed, it is routine for data showing autistics performing better than nonautistic controls to be interpreted solely as evidence for speculated deficits that were not actually found (Gernsbacher, Dawson, & Mottron, 2006).

Similarly, popular autism screening and diagnostic instruments judge exceptional autistic abilities as "symptoms," contributing to greater autism "severity." From early in development, autistic strengths lead to the appearance of atypicality (e.g., Klin, Lin, Gorrindo, Ramsay, & Jones, 2009), and atypicality in itself, regardless of any other consideration, is judged negatively through the metric of "severity." The current standard in the autism literature defines "optimal outcomes," not as successful autistics whose atypical strengths have been given every opportunity to flourish, but as individuals who are no longer autistic and therefore have lost their strong but atypical abilities (Helt et al., 2008).

In a world where autism is defined as a disorder, strenuous efforts, to the point of irrationality, have routinely been made to define all traits and abilities associated with autism as suboptimal and pathological (Baron-Cohen, 2005; Gernsbacher et al., 2006). Classifying autistics as disordered has clearly interfered with the progress of autism research and has, in other ways, been harmful to autistics, including by constructing a daunting obstacle to good outcomes (Mottron, Dawson, & Soulieres, 2008). Autistics, like nonautistics, have genuine difficulties in many areas, and, like nonautistics, require assistance in areas where their performance is weak. However, autistics uniquely are seen as pathological when displaying significant or dramatic strengths, creating for autistics a nearly insurmountable disadvantage or disability not faced by nonautistics. The "only a disorder" view of autism should be rejected in favor of a more scientific and ethical recognition of the genuine strengths and weaknesses of all human beings, regardless of their cognitive phenotype.

References

Asperger, H. (1944/1991). "Autistic psychopathology" in childhood. In U. Frith, U. (Ed.), Autism and Asperger Syndrome (pp. 37–92). Cambridge, UK: Cambridge University Press.

Baron-Cohen, S. (2005). Enhanced attention to detail and hyper-systemizing in autism. Commentary on Milne, E., Swettenham, J., & Campbell, R. Motion perception in autism: A review. Current Psychology of Cognition, 23, 59–64.

Dawson, M., Mottron, L., & Gernsbacher, M. A. (2008). Learning in autism. In J. H. Byrne (Series Ed.) & H. Roediger (Vol. Ed.), Learning and memory: A comprehensive reference: Cognitive Psychology (pp. 759–772). New York, NY: Elsevier.

Gernsbacher, M. A., Dawson, M., & Mottron, L. (2006). Autism: Common, heritable, but not harmful. Behavioral and Brain Sciences, 29, 413–414.

Heaton, P., & Wallace, G. L. (2004). Annotation: The savant syndrome. Journal of Child Psychology and Psychiatry, 45, 899–911.

Helt, M., Kelley, E., Kinsbourne, M., Pandey, J., Boorstein, H., Herbert, M., & Fein, D. (2008). Can children with autism recover? If so, how? Neuropsychology Review, 18, 339–366.

Howlin, P., Goode, S., Hutton, J., & Rutter, M. (2009). Savant skills in autism: Psychometric approaches and parental reports. Philosophical Transactions of the Royal Society B: Biological Sciences, 364, 1359–1367.

Kanner, L. (1973). Childhood Psychosis: Initial Studies and New Insights. Washington D.C.: Winston

Klin, A., Lin, D. J., Gorrindo, P., Ramsay, G., & Jones, W. (2009). Two-year-olds with autism orient to non-social contingencies rather than biological motion. Nature, 459, 257–261.

Mottron, L., Dawson, M., & Soulieres, I. (2008). A different memory: Are distinctions drawn from the study of non-autistic memory appropriate to describe memory in autism? In J. Boucher and D. Bowler (Eds.) Memory in Autism (pp. 311–329). Cambridge, UK: Cambridge University Press.

Mottron, L., Dawson, M., & Soulières, I. (2009). Enhanced perception in savant syndrome: Patterns, structure and creativity. Philosophical Transactions of the Royal Society B: Biological Sciences, 364, 1385–1391.

Further Reading

Miller, L. K. (1999). The savant syndrome: Intellectual impairment and exceptional skill. *Psychological Bulletin, 125,* 31–46.

1

Section 2
Diagnosing Autism

2

Q12
How Are ASC Diagnosed?

Carl Feinstein

ASC occupy a special place among medical disorders due to the uniquely social and communicative nature of their symptoms. Because of this, there are inherent obstacles that make diagnosis more challenging, as well as difficult to explain to patients and to the parents of children with these conditions. Although neurodevelopmental in origin, the symptoms of ASC reflect deficits in uniquely human attributes that most people don't commonly regard as "biological," unlike other expressions of our neuronal activity, such as physical movement or sensory experience. The uniquely human attributes that are impaired include the sensitive social attunement in realtime interpersonal situations that characterizes our interactions with others, the capacity to infer the cognitive and emotional perspective of other people, and the capacity to exchange information by verbal and nonverbal communication.

Furthermore, it is not widely recognized that very young children possess these social and communicative capacities, despite abundant research proving that babies embark on their social development and nonverbal communication in highly meaningful ways during the first year of life. Yet this is precisely the stage of development at which ASC arise and when prompt diagnosis is so urgent, if remediation is to begin in a timely fashion. It can, therefore, be quite challenging for parents to recognize and describe to doctors the profound but subtle differences observed when comparing their child to other unimpaired children or to their own expectations of how young children should behave.

It is equally difficult for parents to connect the diagnosis of autism, fraught with dire implications, to the subtle and elusive deficits of their toddlers in what may appear to them to be minor issues, such as failure to make eye contact or inability to point or to share attention. More overt behaviors, such as not responding to the voice of parents, leading to suspicion of a hearing impairment, or speech delays are more likely to start parents off on the chain of evaluations that lead to a diagnosis of an ASC. However, modern parents are certainly familiar with autism as a very serious condition, implying that their child is categorically impaired and different from other children. How are they to come to terms with a diagnosis that appears to be based on such elusive phenomena that are so difficult to conceptualize, especially when there is no simple explanation of what led to their child's difficulties and no laboratory test that can confirm it?

Last, but not least of the inherent obstacles to diagnosis, is the great variability in type and severity of symptoms that are all subsumed under the label of ASC. The fact is that each person with an ASC is a unique human being, embodying a distinctive profile of aptitudes, mood, and temperamental features, distinctive family circumstances, and cultural influences. No person is defined solely by whether or not they have an ASC. Furthermore, parents often have their own perception of what is important about their child's development that may not map neatly on the medical formulation of ASC.

For example, parents may be more concerned that their child is hyperactive or won't obey instructions, or cannot tolerate deviations from a standard routine than whether he or she understands the feelings of others. A parent may be more impressed that their child can read precociously than concerned that the child never plays with other children. In addition, some of the behavior issues commonly experienced by children with ASC and of obviously great concern to parents are not caused by autism, but rather stem either from other aspects of the children's biological makeup or from their life experiences. These might include concurrent disabilities not infrequently found in children with ASC (e.g., intellectual disability or seizure disorder). These are highly significant problems that demand medical and educational attention, may well reflect a common underlying cause for the autism symptoms, and offer clues to a specific biological cause for the autism symptoms. However, they are not core features of an ASC.

A proper diagnostic evaluation for ASC must, therefore, consist of obtaining a detailed history and description of the person's (usually the child's) problems and how they developed over time. It should include an extended opportunity for the parents to describe their child's behavior as they formulate it, in addition to a detailed elicitation by the diagnostic clinician of all the known cognitive and behavioral features of ASC. Ideally, multiple adult informants, such as pre-school teachers, speech therapists, and others should provide information about the child, in addition to the information given by parents.

Even though much important information suggesting or ruling out the diagnosis of an ASC can be elicited by interview of the parents, all diagnostic evaluations of autism should include an extended period of direct observation of the child. This observation must include a sustained, direct interview, using both language and play materials to elicit the child's ability to communicate, to play, and to share attention with the examiner. Given the young age of most children being evaluated, the child's social and communicative engagement should be assayed between the child and parent, as well as between the child and the examiner. It is often necessary, and always desirable, to have the parent present for at least part of the interview between examiner and child. The interview should include blocks and other nonspecific play objects, as well as age-appropriate imaginative play materials, including both familiar objects, such as toy cars and toy furniture, and dolls, puppets, or actions figures to determine if the child can use these to engage in reciprocal or thematic imaginative play. Often age-appropriate art materials or children's books are helpful in eliciting the optimal social interactiveness of which the child is capable.

Separate from these direct interviews, a thorough diagnostic evaluation for an ASC should include appropriate medical and cognitive testing. Hearing and

2

vision must be evaluated. Oral motor handicaps that may impede communicative speech must be ruled out. A pediatric history should explore the possibility of traumatic brain injury, as well as familial, infectious, or other major illnesses that might explain developmental delay or regression. A pediatric examination and basic genetic and chromosomal testing should be done to determine if one of numerous known medical causes for ASC is present. Cognitive testing, as well as systematic speech and language testing, should be done if there is clinical evidence of intellectual deficit or delayed language.

In carrying out the diagnostic assessment described above, it is invariably more helpful and supportive to the parents and patient if there is a single expert clinician who follows the family through all the interviews and testing required and who takes responsibility for both the conduct of the evaluation and the presentation of the diagnostic findings to the parents and patient. Unfortunately, some clinics are structured so as to provide multiple parallel subspecialty assessments by numerous clinical subspecialists, following which only one of these (often a junior member or the "team") meets with the parents to provide feedback when all testing is done. Such a method diffuses responsibility and often provides derivative and poorly integrated information to the parents, at a time when they most need committed and compassionate involvement by a responsible and familiar doctor.

When all the diagnostic evaluations are done, it is absolutely critical to allow for a full interpretive interview (often more than one is necessary) between parents and doctor (or between patient and doctor for adults being evaluated). This should include a full and comprehensive discussion of the findings of the diagnostic evaluation, as well as treatment and education recommendations. Parents must be encouraged to ask questions and express their own views in such an interview. The presentation of a diagnosis of an ASC is usually a highly emotional experience, and it is often difficult to cover all the issues and concerns of the parents in a single meeting. Therefore, at least one follow-up interview should proactively be offered to the parents. The optimum treatment and educational placement of their child depends on the healthy empowerment of the parents to be effective advocates for their child's educational and treatment needs, as well as to be direct and loving agents for positive change in their child's clinical condition. The conduct of the interpretative diagnostic interview(s) should be aimed at achieving such parental empowerment, as well as providing the compassionate support most parents can well use to help them weather the turmoil or sadness associated with having received an ASC diagnosis for their child.

Q13
What Are the Essential Aspects of ASC Assessment?

Carl Feinstein

ASC are brain-based disorders of development arising in very early childhood that result in specific categories of impairment in social, communicative, cognitive, and behavioral functioning, ranging widely in degree of severity. Medical science has identified numerous genetic and medical condition factors of both large and small effect that, in combination with environmental factors that are still poorly understood, underlie these specific impairments. These impairments, in turn, lead to delays in the normal progression of adaptive functioning normative for the age of the child or adult who has ASD. Adaptive functioning refers to the wide array of skills and behaviors that are required for an individual to participate fully in human society at a level appropriate for their age.

A thorough diagnostic assessment of ASC requires specific tests of the patient's impairments in socialization, communication, and specific characteristic behaviors, the categories of symptoms, and delays in adaptive functioning that define the disorder. These tests are mostly not the conventional medical examination and laboratory tests doctors use to diagnose medical illnesses, but are evaluation procedures that describe and measure the behavioral traits characteristic of ASC. They utilize tests and structured or standardized observations that have been developmentally normed, so that the behaviors of the patient being evaluated are compared to what would be expected of a person (usually a child) of the same age and cognitive capacity.

Developmental Assessment

An essential component of every diagnostic assessment for ASC is the careful and systematic developmental history, with special attention to each age period of the child's social and communicative functioning, including questions about common behavioral features of autism. The ASC are not static or developmentally frozen conditions. Children with ASC, while lagging or deviant in socialization and communication, do make progress in these skills, particularly if they receive effective behavioral, communication, or educational interventions. Thus, during the developmental history examination, each of these core functions must be accurately described for the ASD child and compared by the interviewer to normative skills at the comparable age. For example, the manifestations of the core symptoms of autism are quite different, in most cases, in a 10-year-old child from what they were when that child was 3 years old. The diagnostician must be highly trained to recognize what the main manifestations of autism are at every stage of child development.

Currently, the universal developmental cutoff for the diagnosis of autism, the age before which one of the core deficits in autism must have been present, is 36 months. It is possible for the future, since there have been advances in the reliable diagnosis at an even younger age and there are some older children with ASC symptoms whose parents or caretakers did not notice early childhood issues, that the age criteria for diagnosis may shift. Nevertheless, it seems clear that, under ideal circumstances, positive screening and confirmatory diagnosis can be achieved by age 3. It must be stressed, however, that what is most useful to the patient and family in diagnosis is the identification of the social, communicative, and behavioral characteristics present in the child at the age of evaluation, since these symptoms become the starting point for formulating an effective treatment plan.

There are several scientifically developed developmental history interviews for ASC that require special training to administer consistently and to rate reliably. Of these, the best known are the several variants of the Autism Diagnostic Interview (ADI; Rutter, LeCouteur, & Lord, 2003). Because these interviews are systematic surveys of the child's entire development, they may be fairly lengthy. Not surprisingly, the older the child at the time of the evaluation, the longer the interview may be. For example, a 2-year-old toddler being evaluated might be tested for the ability to name and understand specific objects or to make simple requests, while the teenager would have to be evaluated for the skills of the younger child, but also the ability to carry on extended conversation about topics such as school activities, family relations, or current events. Also, for an older child, it is likely that information must be obtained from schools and other social agencies, whereas for the toddler, information from the parents might be sufficient.

In order to be sure that the symptoms or delays in development observed in the child aren't simply attributable to a more generalized intellectual disability (ID) (i.e., a delay in general cognitive development) rather than the specific impairments of autism, it is most often necessary to perform psychometric testing of intelligence. While many children with ASC have some measure of intellectual delay, in order for a diagnosis of ASC to be made, the core deficits that characterize ASC must be disproportionate to whatever the intellectual decrement might be.

Assessment of Social Functioning

Central to the diagnostic assessment for ASC in the office setting are specialized interviews of the child to assess reciprocal social engagement and imaginative play. Of these interviews, the Autism Diagnostic Observation Scale (ADOS;

Lord, Rutter, DiLavore, & Risi, 2001) is the current standard. This type of interview should be performed by clinical experts in ASC, who are trained to score the child's responses in a reliable and standard fashion. In addition, the diagnostician must administer behavior and communication rating scales, as well autism symptom questionnaires, to supplement and complete the information obtained by direct interviewing. It is important for the diagnostician to obtain descriptions of the child's typical behavior in naturalistic settings such as the home or school. These descriptions are provided by parents, teachers, and other adult caretakers. Ideally, the diagnostic expert should also observe the child in a naturalistic setting, outside of the stressful and unfamiliar environment of the doctor's office.

Evaluation of Language and Communication

Tests of communication similarly involve expert interviews and office testing of the child's ability to understand and effectively express written and spoken language, as well as to communicate effectively, taking into account the needs and perspectives of the person with whom the child is communicating. While the use of spoken language is the centerpiece of the evaluation, some children may have poor verbal use in this modality but use sign language, gestures, picture exchange systems, or even written exchange systems to communicate. All means of communication should be assessed. The three components of language and communication assessment are: basic linguistic skills and usage, pragmatic communication, and oddities of speech commonly found in individuals with ASC.

Basic linguistic skills often require the administration of psychometric tests of specific language skills that are scored to indicate how the child being tested performs relative to normal skill levels of unimpaired children. Assessment of pragmatic communication focuses on all the nonverbal elements, such as intonation, hand, facial, and bodily gestures, looking in the direction of the person being spoken to, knowing how to gauge if the communicative partner is interested in or understands what the child is saying, and providing sufficient contextual background information so that the listener can fully understand the meaning of what the child is saying. Assessment of oddities of speech measures the presence and severity of verbal behaviors, such as repetition of phrases that are out of context (echolalia), inability to use pronouns correctly, or perseverative questioning or verbal rituals.

Evaluation of Characteristic ASD Behaviors

This part of the diagnostic process is based on both direct observation in the interview and the reports provided by knowledgeable adults. It describes and, if present, rates the severity of numerous odd or deviant behaviors, such as repetitive nonfunctional movements and physical mannerisms, unusual sensory responses to sounds, lighting, or texture, restricted and perseverative range of interests or behaviors, and failure to develop age-appropriate imaginative play, the normal functional use of various object, tools, utensils, play materials, etc. In addition to these groups of behaviors, the diagnostician directly observes for other maladaptive behaviors, such as poor attention and impulse control, destruction of objects, aggression, self-injurious behavior, incontinence, and refusal to cooperate, as well as collecting written checklists and descriptions from knowledgeable adults. While these maladaptive behaviors are not diagnostic of ASC, they create many problems for the child's participation in school and other community environments, as well as inconvenience and disruption of family life in the home. Therefore, describing them systematically in the diagnostic process is absolutely essential to formulating a treatment plan to improve the quality of life of the ASC child who has such problems.

2

Assessment of Adaptive Functioning

While much of the focus in the diagnostic assessment of ASC is on checking for the core diagnostic criteria (social, communicative, and characteristic behaviors), it is not sufficient to simply list all the child's problems, in order for the diagnostic process to be truly useful. The ultimate purpose of the diagnostic process is to plan for optimal treatment and remediation. Each symptom should be appraised not only in terms of how it defines what is wrong with the child but also how it impacts the child's optimal ability to function at an age-appropriate level in their self care, as well as in home and peer, school, and community life. This type of practical functioning, which has everything to do with the overall quality of life of the person with ASC, is referred to as adaptive functioning or adaptive behavior. Adaptive behavior is measured by specific interviews and checklists that are usually referred to as adaptive behavior scales. Competent and increasing autonomous adaptive behavior is the ultimate goal of treatment, and, therefore, adaptive functioning must be part of the diagnostic findings, if there is to be optimal treatment.

Expertness in Assessment

The reader will notice that the term "expert" is frequently used in this chapter to characterize the diagnostician(s) who should be responsible for the evaluation of children for ASC. There are two general considerations related to expertise for the diagnosis of autism: one is related to professional discipline and the second is related to the degree of specialized training in the assessment and treatment of ASC.

The professional disciplines (subspecialties of medicine) include, most commonly, pediatrics (in some geographic areas this includes developmental-behavioral pediatricians), child psychiatry, and pediatric neurology. At least equally critical to the diagnostic evaluation are the skills of the child clinical psychologist and the speech and language pathologist. The audiologist may also play

2

an important role since adequacy of hearing is a prerequisite for the normal development of language and communication. There are also roles for the social worker, the occupational therapist, and, at times, the physical therapist. If the child is suspected of having a specific genetic abnormality, the role of the medical geneticist may be critical.

In the field of ASC, where much remains unknown about environmental and medical causes, specialists outside of the disciplines mentioned, such as allergists, immunologists, gastroenterologists, etc., may play a role in treating specific medical problems in ASC. However, the diagnosis of an ASC requires, first and foremost, specialized training in child development and neurodevelopment, child psychiatry, cognitive and behavioral functioning (clinical psychology), and communicative and language functioning. The symptoms that define ASC fall in the psychological, behavioral, cognitive, and communication realms, and, whatever other specialized medical assessments that might be helpful or point the way to some form of relief of pain and suffering for the child, it is the professionals trained in the core realms of ASC who are most likely to recognize and measure the severity of ASC symptoms.

Having said this, however, another important, albeit unfortunate, consideration for parents is that, at present, many doctors, even in the most relevant disciplines listed above, have no specialized training in recognizing the social, communicative, and behavioral deficits that define ASC. Within each of these disciplines, only a minority of practitioners have obtained this special training. Many of the information-gathering interviews, structured play interviews, "behavioral interview probes" for the child, observational rating strategies for ASC, and tests for adaptive behavior require specialized training to use validly and reliably.

Furthermore, while there are many screening questionnaires potentially available that are designed for use in general medical practice to detect clinical warning signs of ASC in young children, many doctors are not familiar with these questionnaires or simply maintain that they "know it (ASC) when they see it." There remain far too many rueful testimonials of worried parents who were told, "your child will outgrow it" or "I just don't see it," and who thereby got a late start on prompt diagnosis and critically important preschool intervention programs because the ultimate ASC diagnosis was delayed. Until the knowledge of how to assess ASC is fully disseminated throughout the entire medical and psychologist community, parents somehow must be sufficiently confident, assertive, and empowered to know when to keep pursuing answers for their child and to search until they find an expert clinician or clinical center that can help them address the concerns they have about their child.

References

Lord, C., Rutter, M., DiLavore, P. C., & Risi, S. (2001). *Autism Diagnostic Observation Schedule (ADOS)*. Los Angeles, CA: Western Psychological Services.

Rutter, M., LeCouteur, A., & Lord, C. (2003). *Autism Diagnostic Interview, Revised (ADI-R)*. Los Angeles, CA: Western Psychological Services.

Q14
Who Diagnoses ASC?
Who Are the ASC experts?

Sven Bölte

Getting a proper DSM-IV-TR/ICD-10 diagnosis is a prerequisite for receiving care in most countries. Professions qualified and certificated to diagnose ASC may vary somewhat across cultures, and the numbers of professionals in the health care systems qualified to diagnose ASC are still rather limited. This is especially true for diagnosing ASC in toddlers or adults. Many primary care physicians, general practitioners, and other health care experts whom people with ASC and their relatives encounter when they first search for help are still unable to identify ASC or do not have the time for comprehensive diagnostics. As a consequence, those looking for support may face no diagnosis, a false diagnosis, or "doctor shopping" over an extended period of time until a correct diagnosis of an ASC is established. Even if referred to an autism specialist, waiting lists may be so long that clients have to wait weeks or months for an appointment.

Child psychiatrists, along with clinical child psychologists, pediatricians, and child neurologists with several years of experience within the field of ASC, are the most qualified to make appropriate diagnoses during childhood and adolescence and are formally legitimated. To diagnose an ASC in adulthood, a general psychiatrist familiar with the presentation of neurodevelopmental disorders beyond childhood should also be consulted. Although ASC are among the most reliable diagnoses in psychiatry (Klin, Lang, Cicchetti, & Volkmar, 2000), this is not necessarily true for lesser variants like PDD-NOS (Volkmar et al., 1994). Therefore, additional training on standardized diagnostic instruments (e.g., Autism Diagnostic Observation Schedule (*ADOS;* Lord, Rutter, DiLavore, & Risi, 2001) and Autism Diagnostic Interview, Revised (*ADI-R;* Rutter, LeCouteur, & Lord, 2003) is desirable, even for experienced experts diagnosing ASC.

Different professions are involved in a comprehensive diagnostic assessment and subsequent intervention strategy development in ASC. Aside from those previously mentioned, these include behavior analysts, speech therapists, occupational therapists, social workers, special needs teachers, geneticists, specialized physicians (e.g., neuroradiologists, optometrists, otologists) and others. One professional alone can hardly account for all necessary procedures or provide the complete range of information that is of interest. Clinical professionals

2

involved in assessment of ASC often have special expertise in a certain area of diagnostics (e.g., psychiatric diagnosis, intelligence and neuropsychological testing, language, somatic/neurological examination) and intervention (e.g., applied behavior analysis (ABA), Picture Exchange Communication System (PECS), Treatment and Education of Autistic and related Communication-handicapped Children (TEACCH), cognitive behavior therapy, medication, education, employment), or they are qualified to provide help in a circumscribed age range (i.e., infancy, childhood, adolescence, adulthood).

Respected ASC research groups are an effective resource to inquire about new scientific evidence, developments, and ongoing trials. National and regional parent organizations are often able to give information on local ASC experts. In general, qualified clinicians and researchers are those who are familiar with, and acting in accordance with, current best practice parameters published by relevant expert committees and organizations (e.g., Filipek et al., 2000).

References

Filipek, P. A., Accardo, P. J., Ashwal, S., Baranek, G. T., Cook, E. H. Jr., Dawson, G., ... Volkmar, F. R. (2000). Practice parameter: Screening and diagnosis of autism: Report of the Quality Standards Subcommittee of the American Academy of Neurology and the Child Neurology Society. *Neurology, 55*, 468–479.

Klin, A., Lang, J., Cicchetti, D. V., & Volkmar, F. (2000). Brief report: Interrater reliability of clinical diagnosis and DSM-IV criteria for autistic disorder: Results of the DSM-IV field trial. *Journal of Autism and Developmental Disorders, 30*, 163–167.

Lord, C., Rutter, M., DiLavore, P. C., & Risi, S. (2001). *Autism Diagnostic Observation Schedule (ADOS)*. Los Angeles, CA: Western Psychological Services.

Rutter, M., LeCouteur, A., & Lord, C. (2003). *Autism Diagnostic Interview – Revised (ADI-R)*. Los Angeles, CA: Western Psychological Services.

Volkmar, F. R., Klin, A., Siegel, B., Szatmari, P., Lord, C., Campbell, M., Freeman, B. J., ... & Towbin, K. (1994). DSM-IV autism/pervasive developmental disorder field trial. *American Journal of Psychiatry, 151*, 1361–1367.

Further Reading

Committee on Children with Disabilities (2001). American Academy of Pediatrics: The pediatrician's role in the diagnosis and management of autistic spectrum disorder in children. *Pediatrics, 107*, 1221–1226.

Q15
Are There Reliable Biological Tests to Diagnose ASC?

Roberto Tuchman

The diagnosis of ASC is a clinical diagnosis and not based on any single or multiple medical or neurological laboratory test. Biological testing is done to determine if there is a specific etiology or coexisting biological disorder in the individual being evaluated. Medical and neurological work-ups, as well as biological tests ordered, should reflect the findings on the history and clinical examination that support, or suggest, a specific etiology or coexisting medical condition for the behavioral phenotype of ASC.

Clinical practice parameters addressing the reliability and usefulness of biological testing in children with ASC have been developed both by the Child Neurology Society (CNS) (Filipek et al., 2000) and, more recently, by the American Academy of Pediatrics (AAP) (Johnson & Myers, 2007). There is consensus for assessment of hearing function in all children with ASC and for genetic testing with high-resolution karyotype and DNA for fragile X syndrome. Screening for lead and thyroid testing should be considered in all children with ASC and global developmental delay (GDD) or intellectual disability (ID). In ASC associated with dysmorphic features, GDD or ID, microarray comparative genomic hybridization (CGH) is replacing the high-resolution karyotype as a more informative test (Lintas & Persico, 2009). In addition, in girls with ASC and ID, MECP2 testing (for Rett syndrome) should be carried out.

Despite continued controversy regarding indications for electroencephalogram (EEG) and magnetic resonance imaging (MRI), neither is currently considered part of the routine evaluation of a child with ASC. Clinical indication for an EEG in ASC is a suspicion of clinical seizures or significant regression of language. MRI should be considered if there are specific skin or dysmorphic features, focal neurological findings, or microcephaly or macrocephaly, especially if in association with GDD or ID (Shevell et al., 2003). Recently, there has been increased awareness that metabolic disorders, including mitochondrial disorders, can be associated with GDD/ID and the ASC phenotype (Zecavati & Spence, 2009). The extent of genetic or metabolic testing in children with ASC, with or without ID, depends on clinical findings obtained from the history and clinical examination, as well as on whether the child is being investigated within a clinical versus research setting. The rapid expansion of knowledge on the genetic and biological causes of conditions associated with the phenotype of autism suggests that recommendations for biological testing to diagnose and assess children with ASC are in rapid flux.

References

Filipek, P. A., Accardo, P. J., Ashwal, S., Baranek, G. T., Cook, E. H. Jr., Dawson, G., ... Volkmar, F. R. (2000). Practice parameter: Screening and diagnosis of autism: Report of the Quality Standards Subcommittee of the American Academy of Neurology and the Child Neurology Society. *Neurology, 55*, 468–479.

Johnson, C. P., & Myers, S. M. (2007). Identification and evaluation of children with autism spectrum disorders. *Pediatrics, 120,* 1183–1215.

Lintas, C., & Persico, A. M. (2009). Autistic phenotypes and genetic testing: State-of-the-art for the clinical geneticist. *Journal of Medical Genetics, 46*, 1–8.

Shevell, M., Ashwal, S., Donley, D., Flint, J., Gingold, M., Hirtz, D., Majnemer... Sheth, R. D. (2003). Practice parameter: Evaluation of the child with global developmental delay: Report of the Quality Standards Subcommittee of the American Academy of Neurology and The Practice Committee of the Child Neurology Society. *Neurology, 60*, 367–380.

Zecavati, N., & Spence, S.J. (2009). Neurometabolic disorders and dysfunction in autism spectrum disorders. *Current Neurology and Neuroscience Reports, 9*, 129–136.

Further Reading

Tuchman, R., & Rapin, I. (2006). *Autism: A neurological disorder of early brain development*. London, UK: MacKeith Press.

Q16
What Role Does Comparative Genomic Hybridization (CGH) Play in ASC?

Jonathan A. Bernstein

Array comparative genomic hybridization (CGH) is a method for the identification of regions of the genome that are over- or under-represented in an individual as a result of events respectively called duplications or deletions. It allows the detection of submicroscopic chromosomal changes that were impossible or impractical to assess by previously available diagnostic tests. In recent years, a number of submicroscopic chromosomal deletions and duplications (microdeletions and duplications) have been found to be associated with ASC. Despite the increasing availability of genetic testing (including CGH) with relevance to autism, the diagnosis of an ASC continues to be made through clinical assessment (i.e., by observation or report of the skills and behaviors of an individual). The role of genetic testing, including array-based CGH, is to identify the cause of a developmental disorder rather than its presence or absence.

The identification of a genetic cause, or contributor, to autism can potentially be useful in the prediction of the severity of the condition and the identification of individuals at increased risk of associated complications, such as seizures. It can also be helpful in estimating the risk of recurrence for an ASC in a family. In the future, identification of genetic causes of autism may allow the tailoring of therapies, both medical and behavioral, to the underlying genetic difference or differences in individual patients.

People typically have 23 pairs of chromosomes. A schematic drawing of a set of human chromosomes can be found online at a website produced by the University of Washington Department of Pathology (Adler, 1994). Our genes are carried within these large pieces of DNA. Not long after methods were developed to reliably visualize chromosomes under a microscope in the 1950s, it was recognized that microscopically visible chromosome differences are associated with developmental disorders such as Down syndrome.

In the early 1980s, the technique of fluorescence *in situ* hybridization (FISH) facilitated the recognition that developmental disorders can result from submicroscopic changes in chromosome structure. Examples of such conditions include Williams syndrome, Prader-Willi syndrome, and 22q11 deletion syndrome. During the 1990s, it was recognized that ASC can be associated with submicrocopic chromosomal changes. Such changes are sometimes referred to as copy number variants (CNVs).

The finding of a microduplication, or deletion, in an individual with an ASC can have several implications. It may predict a risk of other health or psychiatric conditions or a significant risk of recurrence of an ASC in a family. However, the effects of a specific genetic change can vary substantially between individuals, even within the same family. It is also increasingly recognized that certain genetic changes are associated with a higher risk of ASC than others.

Array CGH is a valuable tool for the assessment of individuals with ASC. It can provide useful information about an individual's physical and mental health, as well as the risk of recurrence in a family. At present, CGH testing identifies a causative microdeletion, or duplication, in only a small minority of individuals with an ASC. Many research efforts are underway to develop tests that may identify genetic causes or contributors to ASC in a larger number of affected individuals.

References

Adler, D. (1994). *Idiogram album*. Retrieved from http://www.pathology.washington.edu/research/cytopages/idiograms/human/

Further Reading

Kumar, R. A, & Christian, S. L. (2009). Genetics of autism spectrum disorders. *Current Neurology and Neuroscience Reports, 9*, 188–197.
Marshall, C. R., Noor, A., Vincent, J. B., Lionel, A. C., Feulk, L., Skaung, J., ... Scherer, S. W. (2008). Structural variation of chromosomes in autism spectrum disorder. *American Journal of Human Genetics, 82*, 477–488.
Shinawi, M., & Cheung, S. W. (2008). The array CGH and its clinical applications. *Drug Discovery Today, 13*, 760–770.

Q17
Which Diagnoses Might Be Confused with ASC?

Michele Noterdaeme

ASC are complex disorders defined through the presence/absence of abnormalities in early development (A-criterion) and the presence of a list of core symptoms (B-criterion). The A-criterion lists early delays in expressive and receptive language before the age of 3 years as one of the main developmental problems in early childhood. The symptoms (B-criterion) are categorized in 3 core domains: qualitative impairments in communication, qualitative impairments in reciprocal social interaction, and restricted, repetitive, and stereotyped patterns of behavior, interests, and activities. Within ASC, different subtypes are described, mainly based on whether early developmental delays are present (i.e., childhood autism (AUT)) or not (i.e., Asperger syndrome (AS)), the complete clinical picture of ASC is met (i.e., AUT and AS) or not (i.e., atypical autism, pervasive developmental disorders not otherwise specified (PDD-NOS)), and mental retardation is present (i.e., low-functioning AUT) or not (i.e., AS and high-functioning AUT).

Early developmental problems, and most of the core symptoms of ASC, can also be present in a variety of other conditions. In the following sections, the most important differential diagnoses for each of the ASC core domains are discussed. The first section addresses problems in early language development, as well as impairments in communication. The second section presents differential diagnoses relevant to difficulties in social interactions. The third section summarizes differential diagnoses relevant to the presence of repetitive behaviors .

Early Language Development and Communication

Early problems in language and communication development are among the main reasons for referral and diagnostic assessment of young children. The symptoms may vary widely. Reduced babbling, unintelligible speech, no single words at age 2, stagnation/extremely slow development of language skills, no reaction when called by name, and lack of comprehension of simple phrases are just a few of the many concerns listed by parents when they first seek professional advice for their child. Symptoms such as regression, or even loss, of language skills are alarming signs, prompting an immediate referral of the child. These developmental problems can be a central feature of ASC, especially AUT, but also of specific developmental language disorder and mental retardation, as well as sensory impairments, such as deafness. The use of a developmentally oriented, multiaxial diagnostic approach is needed to determine the context in which the developmental delays have to be interpreted. This consists of a comprehensive medical evaluation (i.e., hearing test, neurological examination, including electroencephalogram (EEG), brain imaging as needed (i.e., magnetic resonance imaging), a psychological examination (i.e., expressive/receptive language tests and evaluation of communication skills as well as verbal and nonverbal intellectual functioning), and a psychiatric examination of behavior (i.e., nature of social relatedness, interest in peers, behavioral features, and play skills).

Specific developmental disorders of speech and language are conditions in which the normal patterns of language acquisitions are disturbed from the early stages of development. The disorder is often associated with learning problems and abnormalities in interpersonal relationships, especially in receptive language disorders. Similarities have been described between AUT and the most severe developmental disorders of receptive language. In several studies, the developmental course of a group of autistic children and a group of children with a severe developmental receptive language disorder was described. The follow-up for both groups extended from childhood through adulthood. The results of these studies showed that, although both the autistic children and the children with a receptive language disorder had marked language problems and deficits in social skills, these problems were clearly more pronounced in the autistic group. Deficits in language skills, communication, and social interaction remained particularly stable throughout development in the autistic children but could also be demonstrated in adults with a receptive language disorder. In early adult life, the individuals with a receptive language disorder showed a poor behavioral and social outcome and were particularly likely to be misclassified as having AUT. A comparison of the language abilities between children with autism and children with a specific developmental language disorder shows that there is an overlap in the type of language deficit in both groups. The presence of pragmatic difficulties in a child with communication problems should prompt the clinician to consider a diagnosis of ASC, but it is naïve to assume that all children with pragmatic difficulties have an ASC (Bishop & Norbury, 2002). Since deficits in language/communication and in social interaction are central features in children with autism and in children with a receptive language disorder, the careful assessment of these skills is essential in the diagnostic evaluation and differentiation of both disorders. In many cases, the observation of the child's developmental course over a definite period of time will give important cues on how to weigh specific behavioral features. Studies using standardized instruments (i.e., the Autism Diagnostic Observation Schedule (ADOS) (Lord, Rutter, DiLavore, & Risi, 2001) and the Autism Diagnostic Interview, Revised (ADI-R) (Rutter, LeCouteur, & Lord, 2003) show that both groups can be differentiated but that there is a certain overlap between the two disorders (Noterdaeme, Mildenberger, Sitter, & Amorosa, 2002).

Mental retardation (MR) is described as a condition of arrested or incomplete development of the mind, which is especially characterized by impairments of skills, contributing to the overall level of intelligence. The retardation can be apparent in language performance, motor skills, as well as in social and cognitive abilities. Delays in language acquisition, a reduced vocabulary, and problems in language comprehension have been described in these children. MR can occur with or without any other mental (e.g., ASC, hyperkinetic disorder) or physical conditions (e.g., genetic syndromes, such as fragile X or Rett syndrome). There is a robust association between ASC and MR. It is assumed that about 55% of individuals with ASC also have MR. Not every individual with MR has an ASC, however. Therefore, it is important to determine whether a delay in early language acquisition has to be interpreted in terms of an ASC (with or without an associated MR) or an isolated MR without psychiatric comorbidity. According to several studies, the use of standardized instruments (ADOS, ADI-R) allows for a reliable distinction between ASC with and without MR, and ASC and MR. Children with MR mostly show a fairly homogeneous profile of cognitive functioning on IQ-test batteries, with a consistently reduced performance on verbal and nonverbal scales of intelligence tests, whereas children with ASC typically exhibit a spiky subscale profile. The language impairment in children with MR is mainly quantitative. Even though social communication can be reduced when language problems are severe, these tend to be compensated by nonverbal communication. There is no qualitative impairment in social communication in MR alone.

Hearing impairment/deafness is a complex condition associated with comorbid medical and social aspects. ASC, especially AUT, and deafness share delays in language acquisition and impairments in communication. As some young children with AUT do not develop active language and do not react to being called by their names or to simple instructions, hearing impairments have to be excluded in the diagnostic assessment of ASC. Although there is a certain amount of cooccurrence of ASC and deafness, they do not always overlap. ASC in deaf persons resembles ASC in hearing persons. Learning-disabled, nonautistic, deaf individuals do not resemble individuals with ASC. The two disorders can be reliably distinguished (Roper, Arnold, & Monteiro, 2003).

Language regression. Delays in early language acquisition have to be distinguished from a loss of previously acquired skills. A loss of early language skills occurs in two different ways. About ¼ of the parents of autistic children report the development of a vocabulary of up to 20 meaningful words until the age of 18 months, at which time the vocabulary then gradually declines and disappears. In these regressive cases of ASC, the vocabulary is usually very small and the words are only present for short periods of weeks or months. When parents report that a child loses more than just a few words, and especially when the loss of language occurs after the age of 2, conditions other than ASC must be considered. Loss of language skills in addition to social withdrawal and mental regression after a period of entirely normal development could be an indication of childhood disintegrative disorder. In girls, Rett syndrome might be likely.

Acquired aphasia with epilepsy (Landau-Kleffner syndrome) is characterized by a loss of predominantly receptive language skills, but social skills and cognitive functioning are usually preserved.

Social Interaction

Severe problems in social interaction are the most prominent and persistent feature of ASC and dominate the clinical phenotype in all its forms. Nevertheless, several other psychiatric disorders are associated with problems in the social domain. In school-aged children of normal intelligence, there may be confusion between externalizing disorders (e.g. attention-deficit/hyperactivity disorder (ADHD, conduct disorder (CD), and oppositional defiant disorder) and ASC, as well as internalizing disorders (e.g., social anxiety disorders and elective mutism).

ADHD is characterized by the presence of inattentive, hyperactive, and impulsive behaviors. Social problems are not explicitly listed, but checking the symptom catalogue immediately points to the social implications of the above-mentioned behaviors . As a matter of fact, a sizeable proportion of children with ADHD have problems in developing appropriate peer relationships. The leading symptoms of CD involve a persistent pattern of dissocial, aggressive, or defiant conduct. Again, the symptoms listed in the classification manuals show at least some overlap with symptoms typically occurring in children with ASC (temper tantrums, annoyed by others, etc.). Standardized diagnostic instruments show that individuals with ASC have significantly higher scores on all the behavior scales of the ADI-R and the ADOS than individuals with CD. Despite the social impairments of children with CD, they do not show the patterns of difficulties in social communication and interaction (particularly features of social interaction related to joint attention and the integrated use of verbal and nonverbal communication) that are evident in individuals with ASC (Gilchrist, Green, Burton, Rutter, & Le Couteur, 2001).

Social anxiety disorders of childhood are characterized by a wariness of strangers and social apprehension or anxiety when encountering new, strange, or socially threatening situations. The fears arise during the early years of development. The absence of communication problems and repetitive behaviors allows for a clear distinction from ASC.

Elective mutism is characterized by a marked, emotionally determined selectivity in speaking, such that the child demonstrates a language competence in some situations but fails to speak in other situations. The disorder is often associated with marked personality features such as social anxiety, withdrawal, sensitivity, or resistance to change. Again, the absence of pervasive communication problems in all situations and the absence of repetitive behaviors point to diagnoses other than ASC.

In young adolescents and adults, *personality disorders* can be confused with ASC, especially with high-functioning ASC (AS or AUT). Personality disorders appear in late childhood or adolescence and persist into adulthood. They show deeply engrained behavior patterns in the form of inflexible responses to a broad range of personal and social situations. *Schizoid personality disorder* is characterized by withdrawal from affectionate and social contacts, with a preference for fantasy, solitary activities, and introspection. There is also a limited capacity to express feelings and to experience pleasure. If information about early development is not available, the distinction between ASC and schizoid personality disorder can be problematic.

2

Repetitive Behaviors

Stereotypic, restricted, repetitive behaviors can be prominent in certain subtypes of ASC but are also present in other mental disorders. They can be found in mentally retarded children, with additional sensory impairments (i.e., blindness, deafness) and in children living in disturbed and neglecting psychosocial conditions. These behaviors can also be found in children with ADHD, obsessive-compulsive disorder (OCD), or tic disorder (Harris, Mahone, & Singer, 2008). Stereotyped motor behavior can be confused with *tic disorders*, especially when complex motor tics, such as jumping, hopping, or hitting oneself are present. Restricted pattern of interests and preoccupation with strange fantasies are found in schizoid personality disorders and in psychotic disorders. A compulsive adherence to specific routines or rituals is one of the symptoms of ASC and is also found in *OCD*. However, individuals with OCD find the rituals distressing and try to resist them, whereas individuals with ASC often enjoy the stereotyped behaviors, without offering any kind of resistance. A comparison of individuals with ASC and OCD reveals that the OCD group usually displays a higher severity of the symptoms and that very few subject with ASC fulfill the criteria for OCD (Ruta, Muog, D'Arrigo, Vitello, & Mazzone, 2010).

References

Bishop, D., & Norbury, C. (2002). Exploring the borderlands of autistic disorder and specific language impairment: A study using standardised diagnostic instruments. *Journal of Child Psychology and Psychiatry, 43*, 917–929.

Gilchrist, A., Green, J., Burton, D., Rutter, M., & Le Couteur, A. (2001). Development and current functioning in adolescents with Asperger syndrome. *Journal of Child Psychology and Psychiatry, 42*, 227–240.

Harris, K., Mahone, E., & Singer, H. (2008). Nonautistic motor stereotypies: Clinical features and longitudinal follow-up. *Pediatric Neurology, 38*, 267–272.

Lord, C., Rutter, M., DiLavore, P. C., & Risi, S. (2001). *Autism Diagnostic Observation Schedule (ADOS)*. Los Angeles, CA: Western Psychological Services.

Noterdaeme, M., Mildenberger, K., Sitter, S., & Amorosa, H. (2002). Parent information and direct observation in the diagnosis of pervasive and specific developmental disorders. *Autism, 6*, 159–168.

Roper, L., Arnold, P., & Monteiro, B. (2003). Co-occurrence of autism and deafness: Diagnostic considerations. *Autism, 7*, 245–253.

Ruta, L., Muog, D., D'Arrigo, V., Vitello, B., & Mazzone, L. (2010). Obsessive-compulsive traits in children and adolescents with Asperger syndrome. *European Journal of Child and Adolescent Psychiatry*, 19, 17–24.

Rutter, M., LeCouteur, A., & Lord, C. (2003). *Autism Diagnostic Interview, Revised (ADI-R)*. Los Angeles, CA: Western Psychological Services.

2 Further Reading

Volkmar, F., & Lord, C. (2007). Diagnosis and definition of autism and other pervasive developmental disorders. In F. R. Volkmar (Ed), Autism and Pervasive Developmental Disorders (pp. 1–31). (2nd ed.), Cambridge, UK: Cambridge University Press.

Section 3

Frequency

3

Q18
How Frequent Are ASC in the General Population?

Eric Fombonne

3

The epidemiology of ASC consists mainly of prevalence or cross-sectional studies. Prevalence surveys are studies of a given population at one point in time, and, typically, provide estimates of the proportion of the population that suffers from a given disorder. These studies are useful to provide a picture of the magnitude of the health problem at the population level and to guide the decisions of policy makers and administrators on service planning and development.

A recent review (Fombonne, 2009) of prevalence surveys conducted since 1966 (i.e., the date of the first published epidemiological study) identified 57 studies published between 1966 and 2009. Of these studies, 47 provided data on autistic disorder (AD) and 12 on Asperger disorder, 11 yielded rates of childhood disintegrative disorder (CDD). In addition, 23 studies provided estimates for ASC as a group of disorders. The studies have been conducted in different countries, with a majority coming from the UK and the US. The studies vary in the size of the population surveyed, which is typically around 50,000 subjects. The design of prevalence surveys is not standardized, and, therefore, authors have not used a uniform definition of the disorders or comparable methods to identify cases in their studies. Comparison of prevalence proportions across surveys must, therefore, be performed with extreme caution.

The review of the 47 studies informative for AD indicated that the best current estimate for the narrow definition of AD is 22 / 10,000. Studies of AD have consistently found an excess of males (average male:female ratio of 4.3:1). The proportion of subjects with AD with associated mental retardation is high, typically in the 60–75% range.

Epidemiological surveys of Asperger syndrome are more recent. Due to the use of variable diagnostic criteria and algorithms in different studies, there is a huge variability in the prevalence estimates for this subtype of ASC. An average figure of 10 per 10,000 is emerging from recent studies, with Asperger syndrome being considerably less frequent than AD in surveys which assessed both subtypes simultaneously.

CDD is a very rare condition. In 11 surveys that reported its occurrence, the prevalence of CDD was around 0.2 per 10,000 children, with a strong male overrepresentation. CDD is 120 times less frequent than AD.

When the prevalence of the whole spectrum of ASC was reviewed, 23 surveys (mostly performed since 2000) provided useful information. As a group of disorders, ASC are more frequent with many studies providing estimates around 60–70 per 10,000 children, which translates into 1 child in 150 affected in the underlying population. For ASC, there is an overrepresentation of males (5.5:1) and the association with mental retardation is less than that found for AD, with an average of 45% of children with ASC having some cognitive impairment. The variability of prevalence estimates of the spectrum of ASC is noticeable, with rates varying from 30 to 180 per 10,000 (a 6-fold variation). Several recent surveys have yielded rates varying between 1% and 1.2%.

3

Time Trends and Their Interpretation

The rates of autism and ASC have increased over time, raising the hypothesis of the possibility of environmental risk factors triggering an epidemic of autism. However, many of the studies documenting the increase in rates of children diagnosed with autism are based on statistics derived from service providers, and, therefore, may reflect increased use of services over time, rather than a true change in the incidence of the condition. Studies have been performed to evaluate whether children in the past were misdiagnosed and labeled with other psychiatric diagnoses. There is substantial evidence that this happened with respect to mental retardation and language disorders. Another factor that may explain the increasing prevalence of ASC lies in the fact that there has been a broadening of the case definition and the diagnostic criteria used over time together with improved case ascertainment techniques in most countries. This followed changes in social policy and heightened awareness about the condition quite closely.

It is, therefore, possible that the increase in ASC rates reported in recent surveys reflects the changes in methods used to document the population rate of the condition. However, it cannot be ruled out that, in addition to these factors, there has also been a true change in the incidence of the condition. It is, therefore, important to keep monitoring the rate of ASC in future years. Many countries have developed surveillance programs that should shed light on this question in the next decade.

References

Fombonne, E. (2009). Epidemiology of pervasive developmental disorders. *Pediatric Research, 65*, 591–598.

Q19
Does the Frequency of ASC Vary Depending on Region, Ethnicity, or Socioeconomic Status?

3

Li-Ching Lee

Reports from population-based studies have shown that the prevalence rate of ASC is greater than 1% in Japan, Sweden, the UK, and the US. Estimated prevalence rates from population-based studies that use comparable diagnostic criteria are not yet available in other regions or countries. A study of parent-reported diagnosis of ASC among children in the US indicated that ASC rates are not significantly different across geographic regions.

Evidence regarding racial/ethnic differences in ASC prevalence is inconclusive. A possible explanation for the mixed results on racial differences is the variation in the age of identification, as well as disparities in diagnostic practices and access to health care. To date, no evidence has proven that racial differences are due to biology or genes.

Reports from US national studies indicate that higher ASC rates are linked to higher parental education level (e.g., greater than high school) and single mother households, but not related to family income.

Further Reading

Kogan, M. D., Blumberg, S. J., Schieve, L. A., Boyle, C. A., Perrin, J. M., Ghandour, R. M., … van Dyck, P. C. (2009). Prevalence of parent-reported diagnosis of autism spectrum disorder among children in the US, 2007. *Pediatrics, 124*, 1395–1403.

Mandell, D. S., Wiggins, L. D., Carpenter, L. A., Daniels, J., DiGuiseppi, C., Durkin, M. S., … Kirby, R. S. (2009). Racial/ethnic disparities in the identification of children with autism spectrum disorders. *American Journal of Public Health, 99*, 493–498.

Q20
Is There an Epidemic of ASC

Sven Bölte

3

Studies on the prevalence (frequency) of ASC in the general population before the year 2000 indicated that such conditions were quite rare. In a review from this time, Fombonne (1999) reported an average rate of 0.052% for autism and 0.187% for the entire spectrum. For a long time, most experts had agreed on these figures, although some studies had also found strikingly higher rates. Due to the problem of comparing studies using different methodologies, however, occasional higher prevalence reports received little attention or their validity was questioned. This changed markedly around the millennium shift, as published prevalence studies since then rather consistently suggest significantly higher rates of autism and of the spectrum as a whole than most previous studies. According to the newer studies, the prevalence of autism is perhaps 0.2%, and it is 0.6% for the whole spectrum. Some of the more recent studies have reported prevalence rates as high as 1.16% (Baird et al., 2006) and high values of autism traits in up to 2.7% of the general population (Posserud, Lundervold, & Gillberg, 2006). Therefore, awareness has grown that ASC are surely not very rare and a major challenge for society and health services.

The fact that ASC are probably more prevalent than formerly presumed generated an immediate need for explanation. No one doubts that there must be a reason for the consistently higher prevalence rates and that something must have happened that can account for the new situation. However, the pivotal question to answer is whether there is an epidemic of ASC (i.e., truly more affected individuals) or rather an "epidemic" of diagnosing ASC (i.e., simply more people receiving the diagnosis), with these two potential reasons having dramatically different roots and implications. At the moment, the available scientific data is neither rich nor hard enough to answer this question conclusively, but, based on the existing evidence and clinical experience, the vast majority of ASC experts is convinced that there is no ASC epidemic.

To conclude that a real epidemic underlies the change in reported ASC rates, a true increase in the prevalence of the disorder over time and an environmental factor that caused the increase would have to be identified. At the moment, there is no hint of either. Although the prevalence estimates are higher for more recent studies than for older ones, the studies are simply incomparable. Particularly, the concept of ASC used in each study and the way individuals were assessed may account for a large proportion of the differences in reported prevalence rates. To draw conclusions from prevalence studies in terms of a true increase, the methodology must be held constant over birth years. The few studies that did so failed to detect a true increase or concluded that the increase was likely to be connected to better recognition and improved services, rather than to an environmental factor. Where increase was found, the rate of autism plateaued in more recent years, implying a stabilization or end of a process of any kind. The latter would be unlikely for an (ongoing) epidemic. While referral statistics from governmental centers appear to show a dramatic increase in cases, conclusions are limited, since the statistics do not take into account changes in diagnostic practice over the years.

The history of diagnosing ASC is a history of broadening its definition. For a long time, Leo Kanner's description of the clinical picture of autism dominated the concept of the disorder. In practice, this meant that autism was considered a very severe and rare diagnosis and the differentiation of autism and normality was clearcut. Today, the autism spectrum concept is widely accepted, which indicates a lower diagnostic threshold for clinically relevant ASC. Higher functioning, milder cases of ASC are increasingly diagnosed. In addition, (early) detection of ASC has been significantly improved and services for affected children and their families have been expanded. Thus, changes in diagnostic practices, public and expert awareness, and availability of professional help are likely to be mainly responsible for the higher prevalence data.

Although this may seem to be an inadequate explanation for the higher prevalence data, the history of psychiatry is filled with comparable events. As long as there are no 100% valid psychological or biological markers for mental disorders, such processes may occur. For instance, several studies on diagnostic routines in psychiatry show that not only the frequency of ASC diagnoses, but also those of bipolar disorder, anxiety disorder, and ADHD have increased in the last decade, while others have decreased.

Even without sufficient evidence to assume a real ASC epidemic, there have been numerous claims concerning possible environmental factors causing increased referrals (or a true epidemic). One of them, the combined measles, mumps, and rubella (MMR) vaccine, has raised the greatest concern. Fortunately, research has responded swiftly and the alleged association has been examined fairly carefully in recent years. So far, studies have found no trends in MMR intake, and neither a frequency of autism. A huge population-based study in Denmark (Madsen et al., 2002) compared vaccinated and unvaccinated children (birth years 1991–1998) regarding the prevalence of ASC. The difference in rates of autism between the groups was negligible. Finally, a journalist at the London *Sunday Times* found out that the first author of the study to which the MMR hypothesis of autism could be traced had received substantial sums to claim that vaccinations cause ASC (for a summary, see briandeer.com/mmr/lancet-summary.htm).

References

Baird, G., Simonoff, E., Pickles, A., Chandler, S., Loucas, T., Meldrum, D., & Charman, T. (2006). Prevalence of disorders of the autism spectrum in a population cohort of children in South Thames: The Special Needs and Autism Project (SNAP). *Lancet, 368*, 210–215.

Fombonne, E. (1999). The epidemiology of autism: A review. *Psychological Medicine, 29*, 769–786.

Madsen, K. M., Hviid, A., Vestergaard, M., Schendel, D., Wohlfahrt, J., Thorsen, P., ... Melbye, M. (2002). A population-based study of measles, mumps, and rubella vaccination and autism. *New England Journal of Medicine, 347*, 1477–1482.

Posserud, M. B., Lundervold, A. J., & Gillberg, C. (2006). Autistic features in a total population of 7-9-year-old children assessed by the ASSQ (Autism Spectrum Screening Questionnaire). *Journal of Child Psychology and Psychiatry, 47*, 167–175.

Further Reading

Bölte, S., Poustka, F. & Holtmann, M. (2008). Autism spectrum disorders in Germany: National trends in the inpatient diagnoses in children and adolescents. *Epidemiology, 9*, 519–520.

Eagle, R. S. (2004). Commentary: Further commentary on the debate regarding increase in autism in California. *Journal of Autism and Developmental Disorders, 34*, 87–88.

Fombonne, E. (2003). Epidemiological surveys of autism and other pervasive developmental disorders: An update. *Journal of Autism and Developmental Disorders, 33*, 365–382.

Gillberg, C., Steffenburg, S., & Schaumann, H. (1991). Is autism more common now than 10 years ago? *British Journal of Psychiatry, 158*, 403–409.

Wazana, A., Bresnahan, M., & Kline, J. (2007). The autism epidemic: Fact or artifact? *Journal of the American Academy of Child and Adolescent Psychiatry, 46*, 721–730.

Section 4

Development and Outcome

4

Q21
Why Are ASC Defined as Developmental Disorders?

Sven Bölte

In DSM-IV-TR and ICD-10, disabling ASC are classified under the label of "pervasive developmental disorders" (PDD). This concept summarizes conditions that all are characterized by developmental delay or deviance in a multitude of basic functions, such as play, motor development, attention, adaptive behavior, and particularly social reciprocity, as well as verbal and nonverbal communication. The abnormal development in PDD is, for the most part, apparent from early childhood on. For instance, a diagnosis of autism can only be made if abnormal development becomes obvious before age 3. PDD must not be confused with specific developmental disorders, such as those of speech and language (i.e., expressive, receptive), scholastic skills (i.e., mathematics, reading, and spelling), and motor coordination. As can be judged by the name, these conditions selectively affect one area of functional development, sparing others. Some PDD, including a substantial minority of ASC cases, also experience developmental regression (i.e., a child's mental or physical development stops and begins a reverse cycle) (Werner & Dawson, 2005).

In order to understand the notion of PDD, one has to be familiar with typical development and its natural variation. Leo Kanner, who first described autistic behaviors, explicitly based his observations on behavior he recognized as clearly deviant from normal developmental trajectories. Today, it is known that autistic children show an atypical development from early on. For instance, infant research has shown that autistic children, as opposed to typically developing children, do not show a preference for socially salient visual and acoustical stimuli in their environment, such as faces, voices, or biological motion (e.g., Klin, 1991; Klin, Lin, Gorrindo, Ramsay, & Jones, 2009). Retrospective home video analyses of birthday parties of 1-year-olds, who were later diagnosed with autism, showed that these children spent significantly less time watching others and hardly responded when their names were called (Osterling, Dawson, & Munson, 2002).

In the first years of life, many skills are acquired during typical development, which form the basis of sophisticated social interaction, such as imitation, joint attention, attachment, play, gesturing, and all aspects of language. Autistic children show delays and deviances in many of these areas (Klin, Volkmar, & Sparrow, 1992) or remain in an early stage of development. For instance, play behaviors typically start stereotypically, even in normal development. Therefore, stereotypic play can be viewed as totally normal during infancy, but only if it is gradually supplemented and replaced by imaginative and social play. It is often a striking feature of ASC that individuals remain on early or immature levels of development throughout their lives. Even people with very high-functioning ASC may behave in a manner obviously naive and inexperienced, particularly regarding social cognition and the understanding and necessity of social norms and conventions.

Delays in language development are often among the most prominent reasons for first specialist consultancy and suspicion of autism. About ½ to ¾ of the children diagnosed with autism show delayed appearance of first word (> 24 months) or 2–3 word phrases (> 33 months). Some severely affected children with autism remain mute during their entire lives. Verbal individuals with an ASC, such as those with Asperger syndrome, show no delay in language development. Nevertheless, they frequently show other unusual language features, such as neogolisms (newly coined words) or idiosyncrasy (unusual use of language).

On balance, it would be false to assume that individuals with ASC have no potential for development, as the concept of PDD may convey. Even for the core disabling domains of communication and socialization, it has been demonstrated that low-functioning children with ASC elaborate their social behaviors in later childhood and form definite attachments with caregivers (Sigman & Mundy, 1989).

References

Klin, A. (1991). Young autistic children's listening preferences in regard to speech: A possible characterization of the symptom of social withdrawal. *Journal of Autism and Developmental Disorders, 21,* 29–42.

Klin, A., Volkmar, F., & Sparrow, S. (1992). Autistic social dysfunction: Some limitations of the theory of mind hypothesis. *Journal of Child Psychology and Psychiatry, 33,* 861–876.

Klin, A., Lin, D. J., Gorrindo, P., Ramsay, G., & Jones W. (2009). Two-year-olds with autism orient to non-social contingencies rather than biological motion. *Nature, 459,* 257–261.

Osterling, J. A., Dawson, G., & Munson, J. A. (2002). Early recognition of 1-year-old infants with autism spectrum disorder versus mental retardation. *Developmental Psychopathology,* 14, 239–251.

Sigman, M. & Mundy, P. (1989). Social attachments in autistic children. *Journal of the American Academy of Child and Adolescent Psychiatry, 28,* 74–81.

Werner, E. & Dawson, G. (2005). Validation of the phenomenon of autistic regression using home videotapes. *Archives of General Psychiatry, 62,* 889–895.

Q22
Do Children With an ASC Develop Normally During Early Childhood?

Lonnie Zwaigenbaum & Viviana Enseñat

4

Many of the basic social behaviors that are impaired in children with ASC emerge early in life in typical development. For example, a child with ASC may have poor eye contact, not orient to their parents' voices, and rarely respond with a smile when a parent smiles at them, whereas the child's 3-month-old sister is likely to be highly responsive, have excellent eye contact, and share her enjoyment during social interaction with a beaming smile. Not surprisingly, it is often after the birth of a typically developing younger sibling that parents of children with ASC realize how effortful it was to sustain playful interaction when their child with ASC was younger. What is less clear from parents' recollections is how early in infancy these social differences are first apparent. Anecdotally, some parents believe they knew there was something different about their child from the earliest weeks of life (e.g., due to underreactivity and/or irritability, feeding difficulties, etc.), and several studies that have investigated parents' earliest concerns in retrospect (i.e., after the child is referred or diagnosed) report that as many as 30 to 50% of children with ASC are described as having atypical development in the first year of life. Likewise, analyses of home videos have helped document behavioral evidence of ASC in children as young as 9–12 months. One example is the classic Osterling and Dawson (1994) study, analyzing children's social behavior at their first birthday parties, finding that reduced orienting to faces distinguished children later diagnosed with ASC from those with typical development at this early age. Thus, parents' recollections and early home videos suggest that developmental differences associated with ASC are present, at least in some children, by 12 months of age. Notably, few retrospective studies have systematically addressed the question of when these signs first become apparent; that is, whether social behavior is typical or atypical earlier in the first year of life.

There are also children with ASC who are described as having typical development in the first 12–24 months, only to lose skills and develop symptoms leading to a diagnosis of ASC. This subgroup of children, as many as 30–40% of all children with ASC, is described as having "regressive onset," as opposed to "early onset," which implies that development of symptoms was not accompanied by loss of skills. Regression is most frequently defined by loss of language skills and is described by parents as occurring, on average, around the age of 18 months (e.g., Lord, Shulman, & DiLavore, 2004). As with other early manifestations of ASC, regression has mainly been studied using retrospective parental reports after the child has been diagnosed. However, analyses of home videos confirm that children with ASC reported as having regressed in the second year of life show more typicality in their social behaviors at age 12 months (e.g., social smiling, early joint attention behaviors) than those reported as having early onset, whereas both groups demonstrate clear ASC symptoms at 24 months (Werner & Dawson, 2005). That being said, there was considerable overlap, even at 12 months, between the "early onset" and "regressive onset" groups; for example, in relation to difficulty orienting to name (Werner & Dawson, 2005). There are 2 important implications: First, some children with ASC reported as having regressive onset may not have been entirely typical earlier in development. Second, there may be greater continuity between early onset and regressive onset than the dichotomy in terminology implies. Notably, some parents relate regression to a specific psychosocial or medical event, such as vaccination, but epidemiological studies have not revealed any such associations.

Recent longitudinal studies of infants at increased risk (i.e., younger siblings of children with ASC) have shed further light on onset patterns in ASC. By following these infants from the earliest months of life through the preschool years and beyond, the timing and characteristics of early behavioral indicators of ASC can be systematically obtained. Findings from "infant sibling" studies have been consistent with parental reports that early indicators of ASC can be identified by 1 year of age. However, these studies have provided more precise information about when these behaviors first become apparent. Zwaigenbaum et al. (2005) reported that while infants later diagnosed with ASC had reduced eye contact, reciprocal smiling, and social engagement at 12 months compared to typically developing infants, no differences were detected at 6 months. Similarly, Ozonoff et al. (2010) reported that high-risk infants later diagnosed with ASC had similar frequency of gaze to faces, social smiles, and directed vocalizations at age 6 months, but that all of these social behaviors significantly declined in the ASC group between ages 6 and 12 months. Thus, there is growing evidence that children with ASC, at least those who have an older sibling with the disorder, may have relatively typical development of early social behaviors in the first 6 months of life, with emergence of clear symptoms such as reduced eye contact and social smiling by the first birthday. This period of early symptom emergence coincides with the onset of accelerated head growth in children with ASC, as reported in some studies (Hazlett et al., 2005), potentially linking symptom onset to processes underlying atypical brain growth and development.

References

Hazlett, H. C., Poe, M., Gerig, G., Smith, R. G., Provenzale, J., Ross, A.,... Piven, J. (2005). Magnetic resonance imaging and head circumference study of brain size in autism: Birth through age 2 years. *Archives of General Psychiatry, 62*, 1366–76.

Lord, C., Shulman, C., & DiLavore, P. (2004). Regression and word loss in autistic spectrum disorders. *Journal of Child Psychology and Psychiatry, 45*, 936–955.

Osterling, J., & Dawson, G. (1994). Early recognition of children with autism: A study of first birthday home videotapes. *Journal of Autism and Developmental Disorders, 24*, 247–257.

Ozonoff, S., Iosif, A. M., Baguio, F., Cook, K. C., Moore Hill, M., Hutman, T., ... Young, G. S. (2010). A prospective study of the emergence of early behavioural signs of autism. *Journal of the American Academy of Child and Adolescent Psychiatry, 49*, 256–266.

Zwaigenbaum, L., Bryson, S., Rogers, T., Roberts, W., Brian, J., & Szatmari, P. (2005). Behavioral manifestations of autism in the first year of life. *International Journal of Developmental Neuroscience, 23*, 143–152.

4

Further Reading

Ozonoff, S., Heung, K., Byrd, R., Hansen, R., & Hertz-Picciotto, I. (2008). The onset of autism: Patterns of symptom emergence in the first years of life. *Autism Research, 1*, 320–328.

Rogers, S. J. (2008). What are infant siblings teaching us about autism in infancy? *Autism Research, 2*, 125–137.

Werner, E., & Dawson, G. (2005). Validation of the phenomenon of autistic regression using home videotapes. *Archives of General Psychiatry, 62*, 889–95.

Q23
When Do ASC Become Apparent?

Lonnie Zwaigenbaum & Viviana Enseñat

4

There is growing evidence that behavioral signs of ASC can emerge as early as the first year of life. Both retrospective studies (i.e., parents' descriptions of early symptoms and analyses of early home videos) and prospective studies (i.e., follow-up of high-risk infants, such as younger siblings of children with ASC) suggest that atypical social behavior associated with ASC is often present by 12 months of age. Prospective studies, particularly those that have more systematically examined social development over the first year, have found that features, such as reduced social smiling and directed vocalizations, are detectable at 12 months but not at 6 months of age (Ozonoff et al., 2010). There have been case reports that have described earlier, albeit somewhat nonspecific, difficulties with regulation of emotion (e.g., behavioral irritability) and/or physical functions, such as feeding and sleeping, in children later diagnosed with ASC. However, even in these cases, relatively typical social behavior has been described around the age of 6 months, only to worsen by 12 months of age (e.g., Dawson, Osterling, Meltzoff, & Kuhl, 2000). Notably, among the small but growing number of children with ASC whose social development has been followed closely from early infancy to the time of diagnosis age (2–3 years), the age at which initial symptoms were detected has varied, ranging from prior to 12 months to 18 months or later (e.g., Bryson et al., 2007). Early symptoms noted by parents, observed in early home videos and further documented in recent prospective studies of high-risk infants, include delayed verbal language and use of gestures, reduced or atypical social communication (e.g., eye gaze, social smiling, and orienting to name) and play behaviors (e.g., repetitive actions with toys, absence of pretend play), as well as atypical patterns of visual attention (e.g., prolonged visual inspection of toys, and reduced preference for gazing towards faces) and extremes of behavioral reactivity (see review by Zwaigenbaum et al., 2009).

While this body of research has been highly informative (and indeed, has helped guide current practice), the translation of observations from individual children with ASC to community-wide early detection and screening strategies is a complex process. There is considerable variability in symptom severity and language and intellectual ability among children with ASC, which likely influences early symptom expression (Bryson et al., 2007). In fact, symptom profiles differ considerably across children with ASC early in development, and some symptoms that are associated with ASC are not entirely specific to the disorder (e.g., irritability and reduced sharing of positive emotion can be observed in children with other developmental disorders and/or within normal variation in temperament among non-delayed children). This has important implications for the potential sensitivity and specificity of early screening and resulting mis-classification (i.e., children who truly have an ASC but are not identified by a screen or children who exceed the cut-off score on a screen despite not having an ASC). Efforts continue toward development and evaluation of effective ASC screening tools for very young children, even as some professional bodies, such as the American Academy of Pediatrics, have taken the step of recommending universal screening (Myers & Johnson, 2008). Recent data suggest that screen-ing using standardized parent questionnaires may identify children as young as 18 months with ASC that might not be independently flagged by their com-munity physicians and/or spontaneous expression of concern by parents (e.g., Robins, 2008).

As we learn more about the earliest behavioral expression of ASC and about the underlying biological processes (e.g., through advances in genetic and brain imaging research), we may identify new markers of ASC that may make it possible to identify at-risk infants at an even earlier age than is currently pos-sible. Thus, there is hope that ongoing research advances may allow ASC to be detected even earlier in life, although this remains to be shown through future work.

References

Bryson, S. E., Zwaigenbaum, L., Brian, J., Roberts, W., Szatmari, P., Rombough, V., & McDermott, C. (2007). A prospective case series of high-risk infants who developed autism. *Journal of Autism and Developmental Disorders, 37*, 12–24.

Dawson, G., Osterling, J., Meltzoff, A. N., & Kuhl, P. (2000). Case study of the devel-opment of an infant with autism from birth to two years of age. *Journal of Applied Developmental Psychology, 21*, 299–313.

Myers, S. M., Johnson, C. P., & American Academy of Pediatrics Council on Children with Disabilities. (2007). Management of children with autism spectrum disorders. *Pediatrics, 120*, 1162–1182.

Ozonoff, S., Iosif, A. M., Baguio, F., Cook, K. C., Hill, M. M., Hutman, T., ... & Young, G. S. (2010). A prospective study of the emergence of early behavioural signs of autism. *Journal of the American Academy of Child and Adolescent Psychiatry, 49*, 256–266.

Robins, D. L. (2008). Screening for autism spectrum disorders in primary care settings. *Autism, 12*, 537–556.

Zwaigenbaum, L., Bryson, S., Lord, C., Rogers, S., Carter, A., Carver, L., ... Yirmiya, N. (2009). Clinical assessment and management of toddlers with suspected au-tism spectrum disorder: Insights from studies of high-risk infants. *Pediatrics, 123*, 1383–1391.

Further Reading

Dawson, G. (2008). Early behavioral intervention, brain plasticity, and the prevention of autism spectrum disorder. *Developmental Psychopathology, 20*, 775–803.

Elsabbagh, M., & Johnson, M. H. (2010). Getting answers from babies about autism. *Trends in Cognitive Science, 14*, 81–87.

4

Do the Characteristics of ASC Change Across a Lifetime?

Joachim Hallmayer, Antonio Hardan, Wes Thompson, & Ruth O'Hara

Diagnosis and Symptoms

4

Clinical accounts of the life course of individuals with ASC describe huge variations in symptom development; some children lose skills over time, others seem to reach a plateau in adolescence, and still others improve into adulthood. However, the developmental course of the cognitive and behavioral symptoms of autism from early childhood into adolescence and young adulthood has rarely been described for the same individual.

The majority of cases diagnosed in childhood continue to meet the criteria for autism in early adulthood (Billstedt, Gillberg, & Gillberg, 2007; Howlin, Goode, Hutton, & Rutter, 2004). McGovern and Sigman (2005) found evidence for "both continuity and change in the developmental trajectory of children with autism from early childhood to late adolescence." However, of 44 individuals with a diagnosis of autism in childhood, only 4 showed sufficient lessening of symptoms by adolescence/young adulthood to no longer meet criteria for autism or the autism spectrum on the Autism Diagnostic Observation Schedule (*ADOS*; Lord, Rutter, DiLavore, & Risi, 2001). Speech before age 6 and an IQ above 50 at diagnosis are predictors of better outcomes later in life.

Studies comparing the ratings of current behavior on the Autism Diagnostic Interview (revised version, *ADI-R*; Rutter, LeCouteur, & Lord, 2003) with retrospective ratings of symptoms during early childhood found that parents describe improvements in social interaction and repetitive and stereotyped behaviors. The largest of these studies (Seltzer et al., 2003) assessed 405 adolescents and adults with autism and found that only about half of the participants still fulfilled criteria for autism, and at least 20% of those who manifested clinically significant lifetime symptoms were reported to be asymptomatic in adolescence and adulthood. The authors concluded that "symptoms of autism appear to be different at different stages of life". In a more detailed analysis of symptom patterns 13–22 years after diagnosis, Billsted et al. (2007) found that while 15 out of 22 symptoms in the social interaction category were reported to be present in at least half of individuals, far fewer symptoms were reported in the communication domain and the "behavioral/imagination" domain.

General Cognitive Abilities

Studies over time suggest that the longitudinal trajectories of performance vary across different domains of cognitive functioning (for review see Seltzer, Shattuck, Abbeduto, & Greenberg, 2004). More recent follow-up studies generally report overall changes in abilities among children with ASC. Gains have been found in Verbal IQ, whereas losses have been noted in Performance IQ (Howlin et al., 2004).

Theory of Mind (ToM)

By 4 years of age, children develop the ability to understand mental states (e.g., beliefs, desires, and intentions of others and self), also called theory of mind (ToM). Typically, lower-functioning individuals with autism fail basic ToM tasks. Many higher-functioning individuals with autism perform well on these basic ToM tests but fail more advanced ToM tasks, such as the Eyes Test. Only a handful of longitudinal studies have been conducted to investigate change in performance on ToM tasks over time. Some have found limited to no improvement in the performance on these tasks over time, but others suggest that, while children with ASC do score lower than typically developing children, they can improve over time in critical aspects of social communication and development of mental state concepts (Steele, Joseph, & Tager-Flusberg, 2003). More research is needed to determine whether these children continue to develop with respect to their ToM abilities, albeit at a slower pace, or whether these skills reach a plateau.

Verbal Abilities

Many studies have shown that language skills of preschool children improve over time. The largest and most comprehensive longitudinal study (Anderson et al., 2007) followed 172 children, 130 with a diagnosis of an ASC (84 autism; 46 PDD-NOS) and 42 nonspectrum children, from the age of diagnosis, before 2 years of age, until age 9. Children with autism showed little improvement in language abilities over time compared with children in the other groups. However, contrary to expectations, there was far greater variability in the outcomes for the autism cohort, despite the much lower mean verbal ability score at age 9 (48 months) than the PDD-NOS (82 months) or non-spectrum (67 months) groups. More individuals in the autism group were clustered at the high and low ends. A larger number of children with autism than with nonspectrum disabilities were near or above age norms by age 9. Improvements in verbal abilities began to level off before age 9 for the non-spectrum group, whereas both ASC groups continued to improve through age 9 without slowing. This strongly suggests that verbal abilities among children with ASC continue to change and can improve into adolescence.

Although the literature to date is limited, the evidence suggests that, in individuals with autism, many of the symptoms in the verbal and restrictive and repetitive behavior domains improve over time, whereas other symptoms, especially in the social domain, are more stable.

In a recent study, Taylor & Seltzer (2010) examined the impact of exiting high school on rates of change in autism symptoms and maladaptive behaviors in 242 youths with ASC by collecting data before and after exiting high school. They found overall improvement of autism symptoms and internalized behaviors over time, but these rates slowed following departure from high school. The authors proposed that adult day activities for individuals with ASC may not be as intellectually stimulating as educational activities in school and that this was reflected by less phenotypic improvement after high school finished. This has important implications for potential strategies to enhance symptom improvement over the lifespan in individuals with ASC.

This study also found several key factors that impacted rate of change. Youths who did not have an intellectual disability evidenced the greatest slowing in improvement while lower family income was associated with less improvement. Not only does future research need increased numbers of longitudinal studies of these issues, we also need to consider a broader range of variables that may either enhance or impede cognitive and behavioral symptom improvement in individuals with ASC over time. Few studies, for example, have considered whether the pattern of longitudinal cognitive change in autism differs between males and females.

References

Anderson, D. K., Lord, C., Risi, S., DiLavore, P. S., Shulman, C., Thurm, A., ... Pickles, A. (2007). Patterns of growth in verbal abilities among children with autism spectrum disorder. *Journal of Consulting and Clinical Psychology, 75*, 594–604.

Billstedt, E., Gillberg, I. C., & Gillberg, C. (2007). Autism in adults: Symptom patterns and early childhood predictors. Use of the DISCO in a community sample followed from childhood. *Journal of Child Psychology and Psychiatry, 48*, 1102–1110.

Howlin, P., Goode, S., Hutton, J., & Rutter, M. (2004). Adult outcome for children with autism. *Journal of Child Psychology and Psychiatry, 45*, 212–229.

Lord, C., Rutter, M., DiLavore, P. C., & Risi, S. (2001). *Autism Diagnostic Observation Schedule (ADOS)*. Los Angeles, CA: Western Psychological Services.

McGovern, C. W., & Sigman, M. (2005). Continuity and change from early childhood to adolescence in autism. *Journal of Child Psychology and Psychiatry, 46*, 401–408.

Rutter, M., LeCouteur, A., & Lord, C. (2003). *Autism Diagnostic Interview, Revised (ADI-R)*. Los Angeles, CA: Western Psychological Services.

Seltzer, M. M., Krauss, M. W., Shattuck, P. T., Orsmond, G., Swe, A., & Lord, C. (2003). The symptoms of autism spectrum disorders in adolescence and adulthood. *Journal of Autism and Developmental Disorders, 33,* 565–81.

Seltzer, M. M., Shattuck, P., Abbeduto, L., & Greenberg, J. S. (2004). Trajectory of development in adolescents and adults with autism. *Mental Retardation and Developmental Disabilities Research Reviews, 10,* 234–247.

Steele, S., Joseph, R M., & Tager-Flusberg, H. (2003). Brief report: Developmental change in theory of mind abilities in children with autism. *Journal of Autism and Developmental Disorders, 33,* 461–467.

Taylor, J. L., & Seltzer, M. M. (2010). Changes in the Autism Behavioral Phenotype During the Transition to Adulthood. *Journal of Autism and Developmental Disorders, 40,* 1431–1446.

4

Q25
Are ASC Chronic Conditions?

Digby Tantam

The question about the chronicity of ASC can be broken down into 3 subsidiary questions:

- Do people with an ASC ever change into healthy/neurotypical people over time?
- Do people with an ASC become disordered or stop being disordered over the course of their lives?
- Are there kinds of ASC such that people with one kind of ASC become disordered and others do not?

Several recent studies have suggested that rates of ASC do fall with age (Yeargin-Allsopp et al., 2003; Moss, Magiati, Charman, & Howlin, 2008), and it has been estimated that up to a quarter of children with an ASC may recover (Helt et al., 2008). "Recovery" in these studies means that the current diagnostic criteria no longer fully apply, but since DSM-IV-TR/ICD-10 criteria require "clinically significant impairments in social, occupational, or other important areas of functioning," it is probable that these people are on the autism spectrum but have, fortunately, reached an improved level of adaptive functioning in everyday life. It may remain unclear whether people with ASC turn into healthy/ neurotypical people until it is known what the essential physical differences are between ASC and neurotypicality, particularly in brain function and structure, as well as how the brain changes with age in everyone, since it appears likely that it does much more than was once thought.

In a recent survey, Balfe, Chen, and Tantam (2005) made intensive efforts to locate adolescents and adults with Asperger syndrome in Sheffield, the fourth largest city in the UK. Only 2.4 per 10,000 or 0.024% came forward, compared to the almost 20 per 10,000 that would have been expected from surveys of children with Asperger syndrome (Williams, Higgins, & Brayne, 2006). Of course this might have been our methods, or an unwillingness to be involved. However, it may also reflect my own clinical impression that many people with an ASC can adapt better to adult life than to being a child. This may be due to the increasing pressures of schooling and to the very high risk of bullying to which schoolchildren with ASC are exposed.

If people with an ASC become neurotypical, then they would not be more at risk of later difficulties. However, if people persist in having an ASC, even though they no longer formally have a disorder according to DSM-IV-TR/ICD-10, then it is likely that they have adapted to one particular social environment. But as for an Eskimo who moves to live at the Equator, a change in social environment might provide a new "episode" of a disorder and that person may become unwell having been healthy previously. Of course, it is not change in the physical environment that challenges the adaptation of people with an ASC, but rather change in the social and, more rarely, in the psychological environment. Clinically speaking, these challenges often coincide with major social transitions: First going to school, going from infant to primary school, going to secondary school (which often coincides with puberty in neurotypicals), leaving school, getting a first job, and, for some people who marry, coping with older and more challenging individuals and also negotiating the transition from the first flush of love to the more settled stage of intimacy and reciprocity.

It is well known that people with an ASC find rapid social change, role ambiguity, large group networking, and many unstructured social interactions particularly stressful. So these may be considered likely to provoke overt disorder in a person with an ASC. Anxiety, and many emotional problems that cause anxiety, may be enough to provoke a disorder in some people with an ASC. Whether there are other kinds of psychological or neurological challenges that can provoke a disorder is currently unknown. However, it seems possible that progressive conditions, like epilepsy or tuberous sclerosis, may provoke more autistic symptoms as they worsen. But this is to stress the negatives, something that psychiatrists may have done too often in the past. The positive is that many adolescents, who are able to overcome their anxieties, and who find a relatively stable and fulfilling social environment, can expect their ASC to become, to all intents and purposes, no longer of significance. They may still have an ASC but not a disorder.

References

Balfe, M., Chen, T., & Tantam, D. (2005). *Sheffield survey of health and social care needs of adolescents and adults with Asperger syndrome.* [ScHARR report. No. 13]. Sheffield, UK: School of Health and Related Research.

Helt, M., Kelley, E., Kinsbourne, M., Pandey, J., Boorstein, H., Herbert, M., & Fein, D. (2008). Can children with autism recover? If so, how? *Neuropsychology Review, 18,* 339–366.

Moss, J., Magiati, I., Charman, T., & Howlin, P. (2008). Stability of the autism diagnostic interview-revised from pre-school to elementary school age in children with autism spectrum disorders. *Journal of Autism and Developmental Disorders, 38,* 1081–1091.

Williams, J. G., Higgins, J. P., & Brayne, C. E. (2006). Systematic review of prevalence studies of autism spectrum disorders. *Archives of Diseases in Childhood, 91,* 8–15.

Yeargin-Allsopp, M., Rice, C., Karapurkar, T., Doernberg, N., Boyle, C., & Murphy, C. (2003). Prevalence of autism in a US metropolitan area. *Journal of the American Medical Association (JAMA), 289,* 49–55.

Further Reading

Tantam, D. (2009). *Can the world afford autistic spectrum disorder?* London, UK: Jessica Kingsley.

4

Q26
Can People With ASC Live Independently as Adults?

William M. McMahon & Megan A. Farley

4

Yes, people with ASC can live independently in adulthood. However, only about 15% of those diagnosed in childhood achieve a fully independent, or even a mostly independent, adult lifestyle (Farley et al., 2009; Howlin, Goode, Hutton, & Rutter, 2004; Kobayashi, Murata, & Yoshinaga, 1992; Marriage, Wolverton, & Marriage, 2009). Measures of independence include employment, housing, and interpersonal relationships. Direct comparisons across published studies are difficult, because different measures have been used across studies. For example, there is a difference of almost 10 years in the mean age of participants at follow-up in two major outcome studies (Howlin et al., 2004; Kobayashi et al., 1992). Fortunately, a few broad results have been found repeatedly and can guide expectations. Approximately 15% to 48% of adults with ASC achieve relatively good outcomes (employment, independent or mostly independent housing, and one or more reciprocal relationship, such as a spouse, partner, or friend). Most individuals who achieve adult independence had a childhood IQ in the average range (i.e., IQ ≥ 70) and used meaningful phrase speech by age 6. Unfortunately, many people with an average childhood IQ and early phrase speech achieve limited adult outcomes. Thus, other prognostic factors may also be important, but none have been identified thus far. Some studies (Howlin et al., 2004; Kobayashi et al., 1992) suggest that people with ASC and intellectual disability (ID), like other people with ID, usually require external supports to help organize their lives. Such supports include direct supervision of hygiene and diet as well as recreation and occupational activities.

Parents of today's children have reason to hope that the outcome for their children may be better than the results in published studies. There are several reasons for such hope. First, diagnostic criteria for ASC are broader now than they were for the previous generation. Many people receiving diagnoses under the current criteria have fewer or less severe impairments than those diagnosed in the early 1990s. In addition, more parents are now aware of the signs of autism, and more professionals are equipped to reliably diagnose ASC. Consequently, many children are being reliably diagnosed and referred for intervention at an early age. Third, current interventions and accommodations are better supported by research evidence and, in turn, more accessible than 20 years ago. Early diagnosis means that many children receive condition-specific services at a young age, and early gains may be a foundation for future independence (Dawson et al., 2010). A fourth reason for optimism relates to the ages of adults in published outcome studies. Age ranges are usually broad, running from the late teenage years to around the age of 40. Results from one study suggested that outcomes among an older subset of adult participants were much better than among a subset of younger adults (Marriage et al., 2009). The authors speculated that individuals with ASC may develop independence at a later age compared to adults without ASC.

Historically, advocacy efforts have targeted children with ASC. Efforts are now being directed towards developing services that will support adults with ASC. The National Autistic Society in Britain, Advancing Futures for Adults with Autism in the US, and the international Autistic Self-Advocacy Network are examples of organizations that are marshalling resources to improve the lives of adults with ASC. These groups include adults with autism in their membership and seek to improve employment, residential, leisure, self-care, social, and self-determination resources for adults with ASC.

Answers to many important questions about ASC adult outcome will require ongoing research. Such questions relate to the likely multiple genes and environmental influences that affect outcome. It can be argued that there is not one "autism," but many "autisms," each with a different course over time. More information about the relationship between ASC and other psychiatric comorbidities, such as depression, will be useful to adults with ASC and those who care for them. It is also important to understand the lifetime costs associated with autism and which environmental features provide the best support to adults with ASC. Unfortunately, claims of "miracle cures" based on personal testimonials or unscientific reports have caused confusion and the waste of resources and hope. Adults with ASC and their families are best served by research involving rigorous application of the scientific method. Otherwise, we risk repeating "miracle" interventions for adults that misuse family and community resources without assisting adults with ASC toward a better quality of life.

References

Dawson, G., Rogers, S., Munson, J., Smith, M., Winter, J., Greenson, J., ... Varley, J. (2010). A randomized, controlled trial of an intervention for toddlers: The Early Start Denver Model. *Pediatrics, 125*, e17–23.

Farley, M., McMahon, W., Fombonne, E., Jenson, W., Miller, J., Gardner, M., ... Coon, H. (2009). Twenty-year outcome for individuals with autism and average or near-average cognitive abilities. *Autism Research, 2*, 109–118.

Howlin, P., Goode, S., Hutton, J., & Rutter, M. (2004). Adult outcome for children with autism. *Journal of Child Psychology and Psychiatry, 45*, 212–229.

Kobayashi, R., Murata, T., & Yoshinaga, K. (1992). A follow-up study of 201 children with autism in Jyushu and Yamaguchi areas, Japan. *Journal of Autism and Developmental Disabilities, 22*, 395–411.

Marriage, S., Wolverton, A. & Marriage, K. (2009). Autism spectrum disorder grown up: A chart review of adult functioning. *Journal of the Canadian Academy of Child and Adolescent Psychiatry, 18*, 322–328.

Further Reading

Howlin, P. (2002). Autistic Disorders. In P. Howlin (Ed.), *Outcomes in neurodevelopmental and genetic disorders* (pp. 136–168). New York, NY: Cambridge University Press.

4

Q27
Which Factors Can Predict Outcome of ASC in Adulthood?

Patricia Howlin

For many parents, the first questions they ask after their child has been diagnosed with autism or ASC are: What will happen to him (or her) when they grow up? Will they live independently, find a job, and get married? Or will problems become worse with age? Studies of people with ASC who have been followed up from early childhood to adulthood provide the best source of information to answer these questions. Some of these studies have involved individuals with very mixed levels of ability – from severe cognitive impairment to average or above average IQ. Others have focused specifically on individuals with Asperger syndrome or high functioning autism. The overall finding from such studies is that outcome for individuals with ASC has, generally, improved over recent decades. In particular, there has been a significant decrease in the numbers of adults spending their lives in institutional care. Follow-up studies into adulthood have also revealed certain factors that seem to be related to outcome.

On the whole, individuals who show greater severity of autistic symptomatology in childhood have a poorer outcome as adults, as do those with additional medical problems, such as epilepsy. There is some evidence that women tend to do less well than men, although the number of females in most studies is so small that it is difficult to draw any firm conclusions about the role that gender may play. The two variables that seem to be most closely related to outcome are IQ and language. Thus, the failure to develop useful language by 5–6 years of age and having an IQ below 50 are highly predictive of poor outcomes in adulthood. Very few individuals of this level of severity achieve independence in adulthood. It is much more difficult, however, to make predictions about outcomes for people who are of higher ability, and although intellectual level and language development are positively associated with outcome, they are clearly not the only important factors.

For example, in a study of 68 adults with autism, aged on average 30 years and all with a childhood IQ of above 50 (Howlin, Goode, Hutton, & Rutter, 2004), only around 20% had obtained formal qualifications at school, just over 30% were in work (either independent or supported, but mostly low-paid), and only 10% were reported to be living independently or even semiindependently.

Eight individuals remained in hospital care as adults, because no other suitable place could be found for them. Only one individual with a childhood IQ below 70 was rated as having a good outcome, but even among those individuals with an IQ above 100, only 40% were rated as having a good outcome. Howlin et al. (2004) found that early language ability was also significantly related to subsequent outcome, but unlike performance IQs, which had generally remained very stable over time, verbal abilities often showed much greater change. Thus, almost half of those who had been unable to score on verbal tests at age 5–7 years went on to show significant improvements in their communication skills over time.

It is evident from other recently published follow-up studies that although some individuals do remarkably well as adults, the majority do not. In particular, high levels of stereotyped and ritualistic behaviors, and the anxiety that can arise if these behaviors are disrupted in any way, can have a very negative impact and sometimes counteract the positive effects of a high IQ (Howlin et al., 2004). Mental health problems in adolescence or adulthood are also common (probably occurring in at least 30% of individuals with ASC) and can also negatively affect functioning (Hutton, Goode, Murphy, Le Couteur, & Rutter, 2008). Perhaps the most crucial factor influencing outcome, at least among individuals with an IQ in the normal or borderline range, is the amount and adequacy of the support available to them as they make the transition from childhood to adulthood. The importance of environmental factors, and especially access to appropriate educational, occupational and social support networks, has been noted since the earliest follow-up studies of Kanner (1973) himself.

A recent follow-up study by Farley et al. (2009) provides additional evidence for the importance of environmental factors. They report on the outcome for 41 adults (age 22 to 46 years, with an average IQ in the normal range), originally diagnosed with autism as children. Compared with previous follow-up studies of individuals of similar age and IQ, rates of tertiary education were higher (39%), as were rates for full-time employment (27%), friendships (52%), close sexual relationships (20%; 12% were or had been married and 7% had children of their own), and independent or semi-independent living (27%). It is significant that, in this study, all but 3 individuals belonged to the Church of Jesus Christ of Latter-Day Saints (LDS) in Salt Lake City. The LDS church and community provide a highly exceptional level of support for their members, and it may have been this, rather than any other factor, that was responsible for the unusually positive outcome in this sample.

Another major factor limiting social integration for many individuals with ASC is the lack of employment opportunities for them. Although supported employment schemes have been shown to have a significant impact on individuals' ability to find and maintain employment (Howlin, Alcock, & Burkin, 2005), such schemes are unfortunately few and far between.

References

Farley, M. A., McMahon, W. M., Fombonne, E., Jenson, W. R, Miller, J., Gardner, M., ... Coon, H. (2009). Twenty-Year Outcome for individuals with autism and average or near-average cognitive abilities. *Autism Research, 2*, 109–118.

Howlin, P., Goode, S., Hutton, J., & Rutter, M. (2004). Adult outcomes for children with autism. *Journal of Child Psychology and Psychiatry, 45*, 212–229.

Howlin, P., Alcock, J., & Burkin, C. (2005). An 8-year follow-up of a specialist supported employment service for high-ability adults with autism or Asperger syndrome. *Autism, 9*, 533–549.

Hutton, J., Goode, S., Murphy, M,, Le Couteur, A., & Rutter M. (2008). New-onset psychiatric disorders in individuals with autism. *Autism, 12*, 373–390.

Kanner, L. (1973). *Childhood psychosis: Initial studies & new insights*. New York, NY: Wiley.

Further Reading

Howlin, P. (2004). *Autism and Asperger syndrome: Preparing for adulthood*. London, UK: Routledge.

Q28
Is Mortality Increased in Individuals With ASC?

Svend Erik Mouridsen

4

Standardized mortality ratio (SMR) is frequently used to measure excessive mortality. The SMR is the quotient of the observed to the expected numbers of deaths, and an SMR of 1 indicates that the observed number of deaths is not different from what would be predicted for the general population: An SMR value greater than 1 indicates that the observed mortality exceeds expectations in the group under study.

Only two systematic follow-up studies specifically dealing with mortality and causes of death in individuals with ASC have been published so far. Shavelle, Stauss, and Pickett (2001) and Pickett, Paculdo, Shavelle, and Stauss (2006) reported mortality and causes of death in 13,111 people with ASC who were receiving services from the California Department of Developmental Services between 1983 and 2002. The overall SMR was 2.4, indicating a mortality rate more than twice as high as that for the general population. The increase in mortality was larger in females than in males and more pronounced for school age years. Mortality was associated with mental retardation with an SMR of 3.1 for participants with moderate to profound mental retardation, whereas the SMR was 1.4 for individuals with no or only mild mental retardation. Epilepsy was strongly associated with death risk. Suffocation or drowning were also noted to be frequent specific causes of death. Similar results were obtained in a Danish study (Isager, Mouridsen, & Rich, 1999; Mouridsen, Bronnum-Hansen, Rich, & Isager, 2008) in which an overall SMR of 1.9 was reported in a nationwide cohort of 341 individuals with ASC observed between 1960 and 2007. Again, the SMR was particularly high in females. Epilepsy and infectious diseases were among the most common causes of death.

Prevention efforts to decrease mortality in people with ASC need to address the conditions that are the immediate causes of death (i.e., accidents, infectious diseases, and epilepsy). However, the symptoms that define ASC often make medical care difficult and can lead to exacerbations in the state of somatic illness or diagnostic delay, eventually leading to death causing illness (Larsen & Mouridsen, 1997; Mouridsen et al., 2008).

Assessing pain and discomfort in a cognitively impaired, nonverbal patient is difficult. The best pain assessment by proxy is that provided by caregivers or family members who know the patient well. Only they can identify changes from a patient's baseline behavior that may signify pain and discomfort. Patients may be uncooperative or combative if they do not understand the need for help. It is important to realize that many people with ASC react badly to any change in their environment and, therefore, a visit to a general practice or a hospital can be very alarming for them. In some patients, conventional postoperative management is impossible. Likewise, blood sampling, initiation, or change of medical treatment can be difficult to carry through. Since epilepsy is strongly associated with death risk, careful monitoring of antiepileptic treatment is essential in those ASC individuals with known epilepsy.

To conclude, mortality is increased in ASC. However, increased understanding of the most common causes of death can help parents and professionals focus on reducing risks and, ultimately, the rate of mortality among individuals with ASC.

4

References

Isager, T., Mouridsen, S. E., & Rich, B. (1999). Mortality and causes of death in pervasive developmental disorders. *Autism, 3*, 7–16.

Larsen, F. W., & Mouridsen, S. E. (1997). The outcome in children with childhood autism and Asperger syndrome originally diagnosed as psychotic: A 30-year follow-up study of subjects hospitalized as children. *European Child and Adolescent Psychiatry, 6*, 181–190.

Mouridsen, S. E., Brønnum-Hansen, H., Rich, B., & Isager, T. (2008). Mortality and causes of death in autism spectrum disorders: An update. *Autism, 12*, 403–414.

Pickett, J. A., Paculdo, D. R., Shavelle, R. M., & Strauss, D. J. (2006). 1998–2002 Update on "Causes of Death in Autism." *Journal of Autism and Developmental Disorders, 36*, 287–288.

Shavelle, R. M., Strauss, D. J., & Pickett, J. (2001). Causes of death in autism. *Journal of Autism and Developmental Disorders, 31*, 569–576.

Section 5

Causes and Risk

5

Q29
Are ASC Genetic Disorders?

Joachim Hallmayer

Autism was once considered to have little, if any, genetic component in its etiology. However, on the basis of family and twin studies, autism is now considered to be the most heritable of all multifactorial child psychiatric disorders. In studies utilizing direct assessment, estimates of the prevalence of autism in the siblings of individuals with autism have been between 1% and 6%. These figures may underestimate the true recurrence risk, as some parents of children with a diagnosis of autism may decide to have no more children or have just one more child. Even though the recurrence rate in siblings is modest, it is considerably above the general population prevalence. In one of the few population-based studies, Lauritsen, Pedersen, and Mortensen (2005) reported a 22-fold increase in risk for siblings of an autistic child to develop autism compared to the risk in the general population.

Twin studies strongly suggest that the risk increase in siblings of a child with autism is best explained by genetic factors. There are 3 general population-based twin studies of autism, all of which show a much higher monozygotic than dizygotic concordance. A study carried out in Scandinavia (Steffenburg et al., 1989) is the only one with nearly complete ascertainment of twins. The authors reported twin concordance rates of 90% in monozygotic (MZ) twins and of 0% in dizygotic (DZ) twins. A more recent study (Bailey et al., 1995) is an extension of an earlier study by Folstein and Rutter (1977), in which concordance rates were 73% in MZ twins, compared with 0% in DZ twins. Taken together, these studies argue for a substantial MZ to DZ concordance ratio. Based on these family and twin studies, the heritability has been estimated to be greater than 90%, with environmental factors playing a modifying role.

However, in the interpretation of these results, one has to take into account the small number of twin pairs investigated. The total number of twin pairs in the Scandinavian study is 22 (11 MZ and 10 DZ), and in the British study this number is 45 (23 MZ pairs, 1 triplet counted as 2 pairs, and 20 DZ pairs), or a combined total of 66 multiples. The concordance rate in the DZ twins was 0%. The study by Croen, Grether, and Selvin (2002) identified 150 twin pairs, 33 of which are concordant for the autism phenotype. Of the pairs concordant for autism, 7 are sex-discordant DZ twins. These suggest that previous studies may have underestimated the concordance rate in DZ twins and overestimated the concordance rate in MZ twins. Twin concordance rates are also strongly influenced by how autism is defined. Using a broader definition of the autism phenotype, 2 recent twin studies estimated the concordance rate for autism in DZ twin pairs to be much higher, in the range of 20–40% (Rosenberg et al., 2009; Taniai, Nishiyama, Miyachi, Imaeda, & Sumi, 2008). Newer, larger twin and family studies are urgently needed to obtain a better and more reliable estimate of the heritability of autism.

Several twin studies have investigated the heritability of autistic traits in the general population. The impetus for these studies was the observation that there are many children who have autistic-like features that are not severe or wide-ranging enough to merit a diagnosis of autism. The label "Asperger syndrome" was coined for high-functioning cases where the child's language milestones are normal but there is social impairment and stereotyped behaviors and interests. "Pervasive developmental disorder – not otherwise specified" (PDD-NOS) is another label given to children who meet fewer than the 6 diagnostic criteria needed for a diagnosis of autistic disorder. The term "autism spectrum condition" (ASC) is frequently used to include those with autism, Asperger syndrome, and PDD-NOS. First-degree relatives of individuals with autism show a higher rate of these autistic-like features, suggesting that the genetic risk is not so much for the full autistic syndrome as for the characteristically social and cognitive deficits. Different scales have been developed to measure these milder symptoms more accurately. The most widely used scale is the Social Responsiveness Scale (SRS). In a large twin study (Constantino & Todd, 2003) additive genetic effects were estimated to account for 76% of the variance in boys and 40% in girls. An even larger study, based on parent report, was conducted in the UK (Childhood Asperger Syndrome Test – Ronald et al., 2006). The investigators found that extreme autistic-like traits are etiologically similar to autism. The researchers also found that, based on their modeling, the triad of impairments defining autism (i.e., social impairments, communication impairments, restricted repetitive behaviors and interests) are genetically heterogeneous, i.e. that they are influenced by different genetic factors.

The validity of twin studies has been questioned. Several studies reported that the rate of twins in their samples of affected sibling pairs was highly overrepresented (Greenberg, Hodge, Sowinski, & Nicoll, 2001), and, therefore, autism occurs at a higher frequency in twins than in singletons. However, population-based studies did not find support for the notion that being a twin confers a risk for autism (Hallmayer et al., 2002), and the most likely explanation for the finding in twins is that autism is indeed strongly influenced by genetic factors.

References

Bailey, A., Le Couteur, A., Gottesman, I., Bolton, P., Simonoff, E., Yuzda, E., & Rutter, M. (1995). Autism as a strongly genetic disorder: Evidence from a British twin study. *Psychological Medicine, 25*, 63–77.

Constantino, J. N., & Todd, R. D. (2003). Autistic traits ind the general population: A twin study. *Archives of General Psychiatry, 60,* 524–530.

Croen, L. A., Grether, J. K., & Selvin, S. (2002). Descriptive epidemiology of autism in a California population: Who is at risk? *Journal of Autism and Developmental Disorders, 32,* 217–224.

Folstein, S., & Rutter, M. (1977). Infantile Autism: A genetic study of 21 twin pairs. *Journal of Child Psychology and Psychiatry, 18,* 297–321.

Greenberg, D. A., Hodge, S. E., Sowinski, J., & Nicoll, D. (2001). Excess of twins among affected sibling pairs with autism: implications for the etiology of autism. *American Journal of Human Genetics, 69,* 1062–1067.

Hallmayer, J., Glasson, E. J., Bower, C., Petterson, B., Croen, L., Grether, J., ... Risch, N. (2002). On the twin risk in autism. *American Journal of Human Genetics, 71,* 941–946.

Lauritsen, M. B., Pedersen, C. B., & Mortensen, P. B. (2005). Effects of familial risk factors and place of birth on the risk of autism: A nationwide register-based study. *Journal of Child Psychology and Psychiatry, 46,* 963–971.

Ronald, A., Happé, F., Bolton, P., Butcher, L. M., Price, T. S., Wheelwright, S., ... Plomin, R. (2006). Genetic heterogeneity between the three components of the autism spectrum: A twin study. *Journal of the American Academy of Child and Adolescent Psychiatry, 45,* 691–699.

Rosenberg, R. E., Law, J. K., Yenokyan, G., McGready, J., Kaufmann, W. E., & Law, P. A. (2009). Characteristics and concordance of autism spectrum disorders among 277 twin pairs. *Archives of Pediatric and Adolescent Medicine, 163,* 907–914.

Steffenburg, S., Gillberg, C., Hellgren, L., Andersson, L., Gillberg, I. C., Jakobsson, G., & Bohman, M. (1989). A twin study of autism in Denmark, Finland, Iceland, Norway and Sweden. *Journal of Child Psychology and Psychiatry, 30,* 405–416.

Taniai, H., Nishiyama, T., Miyachi, T., Imaeda, M., & Sumi, S. (2008). Genetic influences on the broad spectrum of autism: Study of proband-ascertained twins. *American Journal of Medical Genetics Part B Neuropsychiatric Genetics, 7B,* 844–849.

5

Q30
What is the Broader Autism Phenotype?

Jeremy Parr & Ann Le Couteur

ASC are common neurodevelopmental disorders characterized by impaired reciprocal social communication and repetitive, rigid, and stereotyped behaviors and interests. Twin and family studies suggest that the behavioral phenotype extends beyond the clinical diagnoses to include related milder behaviors or personality traits in relatives of individuals with ASC. These autism-related behaviors have been termed the "extended or broader autism phenotype" (BAP) (Bolton et al., 1994). Researchers have defined the BAP behaviorally through interview and questionnaire methods and neuropsychological testing (Dawson et al., 2002). To date, the term BAP has only been used in relation to the behaviors and personality traits of relatives of individuals with ASC. In contrast, some researchers have focused on identifying ASC traits through general population samples (Constantino & Todd, 2003). Whether individuals with these social communication difficulties but without an ASC relative should be considered to have the BAP is not known. Unlike autism and other ASC described in ICD-10 and DSM-IV-TR, BAP is not a defined diagnosis. However, in practice, parents and siblings of individuals with ASC may themselves note similarities between their relative's ASC and their own behavior.

At present, there is no gold standard method of assessing the BAP. Studies have shown that individuals with the BAP are likely to have social difficulties (e.g., qualitative impairments in friendships and social reciprocity, difficulty showing affection, and problems recognizing and responding to emotional cues). Communication may also be impaired, with difficulties in reciprocal conversation and pragmatics. In addition, affected individuals often show rigid, inflexible behavior. There may also be a tendency toward obsessive behaviors (Parr et al., in preparation). Individuals with the BAP might have reduced awareness and insight into the impact of their behaviors and traits. This may lead to relationships becoming strained or breaking down, and cause conflict with friends or in the workplace. Psychiatric disorders (most frequently depression and/or anxiety) are experienced more commonly by individuals with the BAP as compared to controls.

Many aspects of the BAP remain poorly understood. The extent of functional impairment caused by BAP traits in relatives of individuals with ASC requires further study. At present, there are no definite criteria for defining the boundary between the BAP and "normal" behavioral variation within the general population. Therefore, individuals cannot be categorized as "having the BAP," as thresholds (or cut-off scores) on an interview or questionnaire scale do not exist. Most clinicians are able to identify qualitative impairments in social communication in some individuals who do not meet ASC criteria, but clinically they do not categorize these individuals as having the BAP. For families, the label "BAP" is rarely helpful in allowing them to access support through education services and social care. Clinicians are probably better advised to describe an individual's skills and their significant social communication difficulties, which are similar to those seen in individuals with ASC. When making recommendations in written reports, clinicians should outline that support is required to help the individual in social and educational settings.

References

Bolton, P., Macdonald, H., Pickles, A., Rios, P., Goode, S., Crowson, M., ... Rutter, M. (1994). A case-control family history study of autism. *Journal of Child Psychology and Psychiatry, 35*, 877–900.

Constantino, J. N., & Todd, R. D. (2003). Autistic traits in the general population: A twin study. *Archives of General Psychiatry, 60*, 524–530.

Dawson, G., Webb, S., Schellenberg, G. D., Dager, S., Friedman, S., Aylward, E., & Richards, T.(2002). Defining the broader phenotype of autism: Genetic, brain, and behavioral perspectives. *Development and Psychopathology, 14*, 581–611.

Parr, J., et al., & the International Molecular Genetic Study of Autism Consortium (IIMGSAC). Characterising the Broader Autism Phenotype: Using the revised Family History Interviews with relatives from multiplex ASD families. Manuscript in preparation.

Further Reading

Bailey, A., Palferman, S., Heavey, L., & Le Couteur, A. (1998). Autism: The phenotype in relatives. *Journal of Autism and Developmental Disorders, 28*, 369–392.

Le Couteur, A., Bailey, A., Goode, S., Pickles, A., Robertson, S., Gottesman, I., & Rutter, M. (1996). A broader phenotype of autism: the clinical spectrum in twins. *Journal of Child Psychology and Psychiatry, 37*, 785–801.

Losh, M., & Piven, J. (2007). Social-cognition and the broad autism phenotype: Identifying genetically meaningful phenotypes. *Journal of Child Psychology and Psychiatry, 48*, 105–112.

Q31
Can ASC Be Caused by Environmental Factors?

Irva Hertz-Picciotto

For several decades, it has been established that environmental factors can cause ASC. Monozygotic twins, who share 100% of their inherited genes, do not show complete concordance (i.e., one twin can have autism and the other not, or the two can be extremely different in the severity of their symptoms). These discordant twin pairs demonstrate that genes alone cannot tell the whole story: The environment must explain part of the causal process in the neuropathology of these disorders. Evidence also derives from specific environmental exposures that confer a greatly increased risk for autism. An epidemic of rubella in the late 1960s revealed that congenital exposure was associated with dramatically elevated incidence rates, as high as 1 in 25 exposed children, as compared with the prevailing rates in the population during that same time period. Further research has supported a role for maternal viral infections. Microbes may act on the developing central nervous system (CNS), or they may produce an inflammatory reaction in the mother, which then acts upon the fetal CNS. Other examples include valproic acid and thalidomide, which, when used medically during pregnancy, induce autistic behaviors in the offspring. Several studies now suggest a potential contribution from pesticide exposures to autism and related disorders but are not consistent with regard to which chemical classes are of concern. Overall, the fact that both viral and pharmacologic agents are capable of giving rise to the same syndrome of behaviors known as ASC suggests that the potential causes and their pathways are likely to be quite diverse.

Thus, environmental factors must be broadly understood to encompass all that is not inherited and spans the chemical, microbiological, physical, and social world in which we live, work, play, and reproduce. Besides reports on specific exposures, a number of investigations implicate suboptimal conditions of the neonate as a risk factor for autism. Several studies observed associations with low APGAR scores (health rating system of the newborn at delivery using appearance, pulse, grimace, and activity as markers), while others found breech presentation or fetal distress to have occurred more commonly in children who later developed autism. Thus, a variety of prenatal stressors are suspects as environmental influences. Parents of children with autism are, on average, older than parents of those who develop typically, and age can be a marker for a wide range of changes: Poorer quality gametes, lower fertility and, hence, greater use of assisted reproductive technology, higher incidence of chronic or autoimmune conditions, more interventions and diagnostic procedures and interventions during the pregnancy, and the accumulation of chemical exposures or the damage they produce. Moreover, even where chromosomal rearrangements, mutations, and copy number variants are identified in the genome of persons with ASC, these alterations are often de novo events and, therefore, may be attributable to upstream environmental insults that could occur prenatally or during infancy.

Much attention has focused on vaccines as potential causes of autism. Several different hypotheses have been proposed. No rigorous study has found a link either with the measles, mumps, rubella (MMR) vaccine or with vaccines containing the preservative thimerosal. Nevertheless, the studies of thimerosal have been noted to have methodological problems that would have reduced their ability to validly test the theory, underscoring the need for stronger science on this question.

The complexity of autism etiology is currently well accepted. The environmental factors identified at an earlier point (congenital rubella and thalidomide) cannot account for more than a few isolated cases of autism today. With regard to genetic research, the last decade has produced a phenomenal amount of information and has uncovered linkages with regions on virtually every chromosome, indicating that multiple genes, including common polymorphisms, contribute to autism risk, with each conferring a small increment in susceptibility. It is likely that the field of environmental health research will similarly identify a multitude of exposures, each accounting for a relatively small percentage of cases. Thus, any expectation that a single cause will explain most autism cases is misplaced and simplistic. Multifactorial etiology means that the causes of autism are numerous, and this is true, not only at the population level, but also for each individual. Similar to so many other chronic conditions, most autism cases can be expected to have both genetic and environmental underlying causes.

Further Reading

Daniels, J. (2006). Autism and the environment. *Environmental Health Perspectives, 114*, A396.

Hertz-Picciotto, I. (2010) Large scale epidemiologic studies of environmental factors in autism. In D. G. Amaral, G. Dawson, & D. H. Geschwind (Eds.), *Autism Spectrum Disorders*. Oxford, UK: Oxford University Press.

Newschaffer, C. J., Croen, L. A., Daniels, J., Giarelli, E., Grether, J. K., Levy, S. E., ... Windham, G.C (2007). The epidemiology of autism spectrum disorders. *Annual Review of Public Health, 28*, 235–258.

Q32
Can Prenatal Factors Cause ASC?

Mina Hah

A recent scientific review of 64 separate studies looking at 40 different prenatal characteristics found several statistically significant risk factors (Gardener, Spiegelman, & Buka, 2009). Women who experienced bleeding or infections during pregnancy, as well as those who suffered from gestational diabetes, were more likely to have autistic children. Autism was also associated with older parents, including women over the age of 30. Children born abroad also had higher instances of autism. The review of the various studies also found that first-born children in families with two children, as well as children born third or later in larger families, were more likely to have autism. Factors not found to be associated with autism were previous miscarriage, preeclampsia, proteinuria, maternal hypertension and maternal edema. Several other studies have found that infants with low APGAR scores had higher rates of autism diagnoses, as did those delivered by cesarean and those whose mothers received epidural medication. In evaluating these factors, it is worth noting that both low APGAR scores and emergency cesarean delivery often arise in infants already suffering from hypoxia, a lack of oxygen. Induced labors, short labors, and no labors (as seen in elective cesarean delivery) have also been associated with autism.

Maternal stress and anxiety has also been linked to autism. One study found that mothers of autistic children reported more family discord than those without autism (Ward, 1990). In that study, mothers of autistic children experienced more prenatal stressors than mothers of children with Down syndrome or mothers of children without any neurodevelopmental delay. The study also found the autistic mothers reported significantly more stressors at 21–32 weeks of gestation than other mothers. This time coincides with the period when scientists believe the abnormal brain development associated with autism occurs.

Scientists have studied a possible connection between stress caused by natural disasters and autism. In one study of mothers affected by hurricanes or tropical storms, investigators found that the closer a woman lived to the disaster, the more likely she had a child with autism (Kinney, Miller, Crowley, Huang, & Gerber, 2008). The rate of autism was higher in women who were in their 5th–6th or 9th–10th month of pregnancy. The investigators noted that 19–26 weeks, a period corresponding to the 5th–6th month, is when the placental barrier becomes more permeable to levels of the maternal stress hormones. Stress has also been found to cause abnormal social interactions in animal models of both rodents and monkeys.

Research has investigated whether fetal exposure to certain medicines presents a risk of autism. Several medications and drugs that have been associated with increased prevalence of autism include valproic acid, misoprostol, psychiatric medications, hormones, alcohol, cocaine, smoking, and thalidomide. The latter has been studied extensively in regards to its relationship to autism. Thalidomide is a sedative-hypnotic used to help induce sleep in the 1950s. Thalidomide has been found to cause autism between the 20th and 25th day of gestation. During this gestational period, cranial nerve motor nuclei and the ears are being formed, and the children who developed autism after prenatal use of thalidomide all had ear malformations and cranial nerve dysfunction. Ear malformations and cranial nerve dysfunction were also supported by neuroanatomical findings both in the brains of people with autism and in animal models after thalidomide exposure (Rodier, Ingram, Tisdale, & Croog, 1997).

The possible role of environmental toxins in contributing to autism is a subject of extreme interest to the public and the scientific community. Many toxins have not been fully researched in relationship to autism, but those that have been studied include pesticides, heavy metals, trichloroethylene (TCE) and polyvinyl chloride (PVC). One California study looked at the use of agricultural pesticides and found the risk of autistic spectrum disorders increased with the amount of pesticide used in a given area. The study found that the risk for having a child with autism decreased the further the pregnant mother lived from the sites treated with pesticides. Another study found a possible association between autism and air polluted with the metals mercury, cadmium, nickel, trichloroethylene (TCE; an organic solvent used to degrease metals, extract oils from vegetables, soy, and coconut, and to decaffeinate coffees), and vinyl chloride, which is used to produce polyvinyl chloride (PVC). A Swedish study found that flooring made with polyvinyl chloride (PVC), found in many plastics, is also associated with autism.

There is an ongoing debate about whether higher mercury exposure is connected with autism. Some believe there are some similarities between mercury poisoning and autism, while others feel the symptoms are vastly different (Bernard, Enayati, Roger, Binstock, & Redwood, 2002; Nelson & Bauman, 2003). One study found that there was an increase in autism rates with power plant emissions of mercury, and that the risk of being diagnosed with autism decreased the further a child lived from a power plant. Another study in San Francisco found an association between heavy metals, including mercury, in the ambient air and autism prevalence. However, other studies have failed to find a connection between mercury and autism. A large study examined 7,375 participants and found no adverse effects from maternal dental fillings prenatally and the child's birth outcome in association with autism. A recent study from the Childhood Autism Risk from Genetics and the Environment (CHARGE) Study group examined mercury levels in 452 children aged 2–5 years divided into three groups: Those with autism and autism spectrum disorders, those with developmental delay without autism, and typically developing children (Hertz-Picciotto et al., 2009). They found no difference in mercury levels between the autistic population and the typically developing children. This study measured mercury level post diagnosis, so did not necessarily address whether mercury might cause autism, however, it does speak to how mercury could be metabolized and stored in children with autism.

Ethylmercury is the type of mercury in thimerosal, a preservative previously commonly found in vaccines. Research has shown that children who received vaccines containing thimerosal had increased mercury blood levels. Preterm infants had an increase from 0.54 to 7.36 ug/l, and term infants had an increase from 0.04 to 2.24 ug/l. These results clearly show that both preterm infants and full term infants have increased blood levels of mercury after a single dose of the hepatitis B vaccine, and, furthermore, the mercury levels in preterm infants were 3 times higher than in the full term infants. The finding that mercury levels were much higher in preterm infants may indicate that preterm infants might be more susceptible to mercury than term infants. This study is also noteworthy because, prior to this study, most of the guidelines for maximum recommended levels of mercury were based on adult studies.

Concern over thimerosal exposure and risk of autism drove researchers to conduct several epidemiologic studies examining autism and the use of thimerosal. Epidemiologic studies in Sweden and Denmark found that the incidence of autism continued to rise, despite the removal of thimerosal from vaccines. Additionally, a research study conducted in the UK, in which children were followed after they received vaccines containing thimerosal found no harmful outcomes and no link with autism.

In summary, at this time there is no substantive proof that thimerosal-containing vaccines cause autism. However because mercury is a known toxin, the environmental protection agency (EPA), the world health organization (WHO), the US Agency for Toxic Substances and Disease Registry (ATSDR), and the US Food and Drug Administration (FDA) have guidelines for safe mercury levels. Prior to the removal of thimerosal from most vaccines, some infants were receiving up to 200ug of mercury with the standard immunization schedule. This was higher than the EPA recommended guideline but not higher than the WHO, ATSDR, or FDA guidelines for safe mercury levels. The EPA has a 10-fold safety factor built into the limits, and these limits are meant to be a starting point for evaluating toxicity. Even though there was no evidence of significant adverse reports associated with vaccinations, the American Academy of Pediatrics and the US Public Health Service filed a joint statement in July 1999 calling for the removal of thimerosal from vaccines because there was an increase in mercury levels after vaccinations and there was concern of a possible cumulative effect. Currently most vaccines no longer contain thimerosal.

Autism etiology is believed to be multifactorial and heterogeneous. The role of genetics in the etiology of autism is scientifically well established. Now there is emerging evidence that there are environmental contributors to the illness, most likely during early development. In synthesizing the information, we can conceptualize the information into several areas. There are medications that cause abnormal fetal development, such as thalimidomide, misoprostol, and valproic acid, that could cause autism. There could be a role of environmental toxins that may interfere with normal development *in utero* or even after a child is born. This could explain why there are some cases of regression seen in children with ASC. There could be a genetic predisposition to develop autism and some environmental factor(s) could trigger the development of autism. Since autism is a very heterogeneous disease with many different presentations, it may be likely that autism is the final pathway of numerous different etiologies. As research continues, we continue to find more evidence to support some environmental risk factors for the development of autism in addition to the genetic risk factors, which are already better understood and substantiated.

References

Bernard, S., Enayati, A., Roger, H., Binstock, T., & Redwood, L. (2002). The role of mercury in the pathogenesis of autism. *Molecular Psychiatry, 7(Suppl. 2)*, S42–43.

Gardener, H., Spiegelman, D., & Buka, S. L. (2009). Prenatal risk factors for autism: Comprehensive meta-analysis. *British Journal of Psychiatry, 195*, 7–14.

Hertz-Picciotto, I., Green, P. G., Delwiche, L., Hansen, R., Walker, C., & Pessah, I. N. (2010). Blood mercury concentrations in CHARGE study children with and without autism. *Environmental Health Perspectives, 118*, 161–166.

Kinney, D. K., Miller, A. M., Crowley, D. J., Huang, E., & Gerber, E. (2008). Autism prevalence following prenatal exposure to hurricanes and tropical storms in Louisiana. *Journal of Autism and Developmental Disorders, 38*, 481–488.

Nelson, K. B., & Bauman, M. L. (2003). Thimerosal and autism? *Pediatrics, 111*, 674–679.

Rodier, P. M., Ingram, J. L., Tisdale, B., & Croog, V. J. (1997). Linking etiologies in humans and animal models: Studies of autism. *Reproductive Toxicology, 11*, 417–422.

Ward, A. J. (1990). A comparison and analysis of the presence of family problems during pregnancy of mothers of "autistic" children and mothers of normal children. *Child Psychiatry and Human Development, 20*, 279–288.

5

Q33
How Do Genetic and Environmental Factors Interact in ASC?

Irva Hertz-Picciotto

The development of the central nervous system (CNS) requires the orchestration of an exceedingly complex series of events in which timing is critical: Cells must divide, differentiate, migrate correctly, form synapses, communicate with other cells through signaling mechanisms, organize themselves into units, such as the mini-columns of the cerebral cortex, produce a protective myelin sheath, and much more. These processes are regulated by genes but depend on a supportive milieu, including energy sources, methyl donors, and specific hormones at critical time windows. Genes showing associations with ASC have a wide range of functions, for instance, involvement in neuronal development (*PLAUR, EN2*), directing cell migration and/or synaptogenesis (*NRXN1, NLGN3, NLGN4, RELN*) and neural connectivity (*RELN, MET*), regulation of neurotransmitters and their receptors (*MAOA, GRIK2*), immune development or function (*MET, PLAUR, PTEN, HLA-DRB1*), and conjugation in xenobiotic metabolism (*GSTM1*). However, not all studies have confirmed associations with these or other genes.

Environmental factors could potentially interfere with the orderly development of the CNS through numerous mechanisms, such as direct action on neuronal tissue at various stages of early development, disruption of cell signaling, and up or down regulation of the expression of genes that regulate brain development. Other actions might include alteration in cell energy metabolism through mitochondrial dysfunction, disruption of thyroid hormone homeostasis or sex steroid production/activity, and induction of inflammatory or autoimmune responses. At present, these are largely hypothetical, yet quite plausible.

Although genes are inherited from the previous generation, their transcriptional expression (i.e., the production of the mRNA for which the gene encodes) will vary by organ or tissue, stage of development, and in response to other genes, environmental chemicals, and epigenetics. Epigenetics refers to changes in the conformational structure of the DNA that are not in the core DNA coding sequence. These changes include modification of the chromatin by histone complexes and methylation of the DNA itself, and they play a major regulatory role of cell functions and development through control of gene expression and signaling. Epigenetics, therefore, is at the interface of genetic and environmental influences on health, disease, and development. Nutritional factors and aging appear to alter epigenetics of an individual, and this has been observed both in animal models and in humans.

Interestingly, many of the gene loci linked to autism are near, or overlap with, regions that are subject to genomic imprinting, a form of epigenetics in which the gene's expression differs according to whether it was inherited from the mother or from the father. The most common linkage is to chromosome 15q11-13. A role for epigenetics in autism is also supported by the cooccurrence of ASC in several syndromes having known epigenetic contributions: fragile X, Rett, Angelman, and Prader-Willi.

Early in embryonic development, the entire genome undergoes demethylation followed by reestablishment of the pattern of methylation. This suggests a potential window of heightened susceptibility to factors governing the attachment of methyl groups to DNA sites. Indeed, some researchers have placed the origins of autism quite early in gestation. More recently, a case-control study investigating environmental contributors to autism found that maternal supplementation with prenatal vitamins during the 3 months prior to conception and the first month of pregnancy can significantly reduce risk for autism. Since folate is a methyl donor for key metabolic reactions, epigenetics provides a plausible explanation for the protective association. Furthermore, the effect of inadequate folic acid intake on autism risk was dramatically increased in children with the COMT *472 AA* genotype, which regulates conversion of methionine to homocysteine through the addition of a methyl group. Folate is involved in methylation of not only DNA but also neurotransmitters and proteins.

At present, few studies have attempted to directly examine interactions of genes with environment as joint causal factors for ASC. Yet the findings that common polymorphisms are associated with relatively modest elevations in risk suggest that vulnerability may be contingent on other factors, environmental ones being prime candidates. This is a wide open area in need of in-depth research, which, rather than yielding a "smoking gun," may ultimately reveal a minefield.

Further Reading

Bartlett, C. W., Gharani, N., Millonig, J. H., & Brzustowicz, L. M. (2005). 3 autism candidate genes: A synthesis of human genetic analysis with other disciplines. *International Journal of Developmental Neuroscience, 23*, 221–234.

Schmidt, R. J., Hansen, R. L., Hartiala, J., Allayee, H, Schmidt, L. C., Tancredi, D. J., ... Hertz-Picciotto, I. (2010). *Maternal prenatal vitamin supplements, functional gene variants in folate, methionine, and transmethylation pathways, and risk for autism in the CHARGE Study.* Submitted for publication.

Wassink, T. H., Brzustowicz, L. M., Bartlett, C. W., & Szatmari, P. (2004). The search for autism disease genes. *Mental Retardation and Developmental Disabilities Research Reviews, 10*, 272–283.

Wilson, A. (2008). Epigenetic regulation of gene expression in the inflammatory response and relevance to common diseases. *Journal of Periodontology, 79*, 1514–1519

Q34
Is the Immune System Involved in ASC?

Ruth O'Hara, Rabindra Tirouvanziam, Antonio Hardan, & Joachim Hallmayer

Despite decades of research, the etiology of ASC remains unclear, and multiple possible pathophysiological pathways have been postulated to subserve this disorder. One area that has garnered particular attention in recent years is the immune system. Animal and human studies document that immune response plays a central role in the modulation of neural systems, particularly in early developmental periods (Boulanger, 2009). An expanding literature suggests that dysfunctional immune response may play a key role in ASC, but whether it is involved in the etiology and development of this disorder or whether it is yet another symptomatic manifestation of this illness remains unclear. Further, the literature on immune functioning and autism is extremely varied and complex, and synthesizing the findings into a more comprehensive picture of how immune function might subserve or exacerbate ASC has proven difficult. This likely reflects the fact that the immune system itself is a highly complex physiological system with critical influence on multiple central and peripheral nervous system physiological functions. Advances in this field will be instrumental in increasing our understanding of the role that the immune system plays in the pathophysiology of autism.

The function of the immune system is to protect the body against pathogens (e.g., against bacteria and viruses) and foreign substances from the environment (e.g., toxins), as well as from dysfunctional cells (e.g., cancer cells) within the body itself. Most broadly, the immune system is comprised of innate and adaptive immune responses. The innate immune system is the first-line response to pathogens and foreign substances and comprises several functions. These include a) secretion of molecular mediators, called cytokines and chemokines, at the site of injury, leading to the recruitment of cells from blood which act as "inflammatory cells," b) detection and killing/removal of pathogens and foreign substances by these inflammatory cells, c) activation of scavenging cascades to remove exhausted inflammatory cells and resolve inflammation, and d) activation of the adaptive immune system. The adaptive immune response leads to the build-up of responses, most notably, antibodies that are tailored to specific features of the offending pathogen or foreign substance. It forms the basis for vaccine approaches to pathogen protection. Common dysfunctions of the immune system include an overzealous proinflammatory response and autoimmune disorders, which occur when the immune system mistakenly targets nonpathogens or attacks healthy cells. Both have been implicated in ASC.

To date, the most consistent evidence suggests that ASC is associated with impaired cytokine profiles, increased neuroinflammation, altered cellular immunity, exacerbated autoimmune response, and altered sensitivity to environmental toxins. Specifically, dysregulated immune function in ASC includes evidence of brain reactive antibodies, skewed T lymphocyte (a form of white blood cell) responses to mitogens, altered function of monocytes, natural killer (NK) cells and altered levels of inflammatory mediators in the brain, cerebrospinal fluid, and blood (Goines & Van de Water, 2010). Nowhere has the relationship between ASC and immune system gained more attention and controversy than around the issue of vaccinations (see Q35). Here we describe the 2 main aspects of immune dysfunction speculated to be involved in ASC: Proinflammatory response and autoimmune dysfunction.

Proinflammation

It has been suggested that immune dysfunction results in the generation of localized or systemic inflammation or release of immunomodulatory molecules that influences, alters, or modifies neurodevelopment and/or neuronal function, especially during critical periods of brain development (Ashwood, Wills, & Van de Water, 2006). Cytokines are proteins that control the intensity and duration of an immune response. Cytokines can significantly impact neuronal development. Several studies suggest that individuals with ASC have aberrant cytokine profiles. In general, studies observe increased levels of proinflammatory cytokines, including interleukin (IL)-12, interferon (IFN), and tumor necrosis factors (TNF) in ASC relative to typical developing children, suggesting that there is an overactivation of the immune response in ASC (Goines & Van de Water, 2010). However, some have observed lower levels of these cytokines in ASC, with Jyonouchi, Geng, Ruby, & Zimmerman-Bier (2005) observing increased IL-12 but decreased IL-10 production in ASC patients with gastrointestinal symptoms. Transforming growth factor β (TGF-β) has also been linked to ASC. TGF-β is involved in diverse aspects of development, including neuronal cell migration, apoptosis (programmed cell death) and regulation in the immune and central nervous system. Ashwood et al. (2008) replicated several studies when they observed lower TGF-β in ASC and found lower TGF-β to be correlated with increased behavioral symptoms. Postmortem studies of brain tissues indicate a significant increase in proinflammatory cytokines in ASC relative to age- and education-matched controls (Li et al., 2009), providing evidence for a direct impact on the brain that may explain some of the core cognitive and behavioral symptoms of this disorder. It may be that overactivation of the immune response, as suggested by findings of increased levels of proinflammatory markers and failure to mount an adequate immune response, indicated by reduced levels of some inflammatory cytokines, represent 2 different phenotypic manifestations of ASC.

Impaired Autoimmune Response

Although findings are mixed, epidemiological and case-control studies suggest individuals with autism also have an increased family history of autoimmune disease (Mouridsen, Rich, Isager, & Nedergaard, 2007). In an investigation of maternal immune abnormalities during pregnancy, Croen et al. (2008) found that mothers diagnosed with asthma or allergies during the second trimester were significantly more likely to have a child with autism. Antibodies that target brain tissues have been described in both ASC patients and their mothers. Anti-CNS antibodies found in autism include antibodies to myelin basic protein, neuron axon filament protein, and nerve growth factor among others. NK cells are integral to autoimmune response, and several studies suggest the function of these cells may be impaired, displaying reduced activity in individuals with ASC relative to controls (Enstrom, Van de Water, & Ashwood, 2009a). Abnormal immunoglobulin (Ig) levels have also been observed in autism. Immunoglobulins are gamma globulin proteins that are found in blood or other bodily fluids and are used by the immune system to identify and neutralize foreign objects, such as bacteria and viruses. Enstrom et al. (2009b), recently found significantly increased levels of IgG4 in children with autism compared to both children who were developmentally delayed and healthy controls. Overall, these findings suggest that abnormalities in autoimmune response may play an important role in ASC, yet their real impact remains unknown. Findings implicating antibodies with particular specificities are not always replicated, or they are also implicated in other developmental or immune disorders, making it difficult to ascertain the extent to which the presence and impact of such antibodies are specific to ASC.

Despite the bourgeoning interest in immune dysfunction in ASC, the literature is still limited by several factors. In addition to methodological issues, such as small sample sizes, lack of appropriate controls, variability in the diagnosis, and differences in age and gender distributions, many studies investigate very different components of the immune system. A further complexity is that the immune system does not operate alone, but interacts with multiple physiological processes. For example, the immune system is not only triggered by exogenous stimuli, but it also senses multiple damage-associated molecular pattern molecules that originate from our own body under oxidative stress. Impaired stress response is implicated in ASC, and stress-immune regulatory loops may be particularly important in this disorder, but few studies have investigated such potential synergistic relationships in ASC. Thus, there is, as yet, insufficient evidence to reach a clear consensus regarding the specific involvement and impact of immune dysfunction in ASC, since these abnormalities have also been reported in other neuropsychiatric disorders, such as schizophrenia. Despite these challenges, as Goines and Van de Water (2010) conclude in their excellent review of this issue, continued and effective exploration of the immunological features of ASC presents a significant opportunity to increase our understanding of the etiology of this disorder and may eventually point the way to novel therapeutic solutions.

References

Ashwood, P., Wills, S., & Van de Water, J. (2006). The immune response in autism: A new frontier for autism research. *Journal of Leukocyte Biology, 80*, 1–15.

Ashwood, P., Enstrom, A., Krakowiak, P., Hertz-Picciotto, I., Hansen, R. L., Croen, L. A., ... Van de Water, J. (2008). Decreased transforming growth factor beta1 in autism: A potential link between immune dysregulation and impairment in clinical behavioral outcomes. *Journal of Neuroimmunology, 204*, 149–153.

Boulanger, L. M. (2009). Immune proteins in brain development and synaptic plasticity. *Neuron, 64*, 93–109.

Croen, L. A., Braunschweig, D., Haapanen, L., Yoshida, C. K., Fireman, B., Grether, J. K., ... Van de Water, J. (2008). Maternal mid-pregnancy autoantibodies to fetal brain protein: The early markers for autism study. *Biological Psychiatry, 64*, 583–588.

Enstrom, A. M., Van de Water, J. A., & Ashwood, P. (2009a). Autoimmunity in autism. *Current Opinion in Investigational Drugs, 10*, 463–473.

Enstrom, A., Krakowiak, P., Onore, C., Pessah, I. N., Hertz-Picciotto, I., Hansen, R. L., ... Ashwood, P. (2009b). Increased IgG4 levels in children with autism disorder. *Brain Behavior Immunology, 23*, 389–395.

Goines, P., & Van de Water, J. (2010). The immune system's role in the biology of autism. *Current Opinions in Neurology, 23*, 111–117.

Jyonouchi, H., Geng, L., Ruby, A., & Zimmerman-Bier, B. (2005). Dysregulated innate immune responses in young children with autism spectrum disorders: Their relationship to gastrointestinal symptoms and dietary intervention. *Neuropsychobiology, 51*, 77–85.

Li, X., Chauhan, A., Sheikh, A. M., Patil, S., Chauhan, V., Li, X. M., ... Malik, M. (2009). Elevated immune response in the brain of autistic patients. *Journal of Neuroimmunology, 207*, 111–116.

Mouridsen, S. E., Rich, B., Isager, T., & Nedergaard, N. J. (2007). Autoimmune diseases in parents of children with infantile autism: A case-control study. *Developmental Medicine and Child Neurology, 49*, 429–432.

5

Q35
Can Vaccinations Cause ASC?

Susan E. Folstein

In the late 1990s, parents of autistic children became concerned that vaccines could cause autism. This occurred for two completely separate reasons. The first was related to the use of tiny amounts of thimerosal, or ethyl mercury, as a preservative for many vaccines. If several doses of these vaccines are provided in the same container, a preservative is needed to prevent contamination once the vial is opened. Because of parent concerns, not because of any evidence that thimerosal was toxic, these vaccines are now sold only in single-dose vials in most countries. In the 1990s, the number of vaccines given during the first year of life increased considerably, and at the same time, the number of reported cases of autism was increasing. This correlation of these two events was interpreted by some people to mean that one caused the other. However, correlation does not mean causation. For example, there was also a correlation between the number of reported autism cases and the use of the internet, but use of the internet cannot be assumed to be the cause of autism in any individual.

The second event that raised concern was the publication in 1998 of a paper in the prestigious journal *The Lancet* that suggested that the combined vaccine for measles, mumps, and rubella (MMR) may cause autism. MMR vaccine is given between the ages of 12 and 18 months. At this same time, autism symptoms may first appear after relatively normal development in the first year of life (regression). For many others, autism comes to parents' attention at this time because of the appearance of repetitive behaviors and because the "expected language explosion" does not occur. At about 12–18 months, children start to learn new words very fast. Again, the cooccurrence of MMR vaccination and the worsening of symptoms invited the conclusion that one caused the other. In the case of MMR, the claim was made by a pediatric gastroenterologist who was seeing autistic children with GI complaints. He surmised that autistic children with GI symptoms were more likely to have autism with regression and that the regression was caused by the MMR vaccine. This work, and subsequent studies based on it, has since been shown to be so flawed – indeed false claims were made – that the journal has withdrawn the article (see also Q20).

Researchers took these concerns very seriously. Although evidence overwhelmingly points to genetic causes, only a few of the relevant genes have been identified, and there is always the possibility that environmental factors may also be causal, either alone or in concert with genes. A fair number of studies have been done to test the hypotheses that thimerosal and MMR vaccine, separately or together, had some causal role in autism.

Before describing examples of these studies, let us first discuss the reasons that autism is being diagnosed so much more frequently than in the past. This is important because the increasing number of cases being diagnosed was the main rationale for the concern that some new environmental etiologies must be operating. However, the increase in diagnosis has other more mundane causes. First, the diagnostic criteria changed in such a way that many more cases met the criteria, and an aven larger number met the criteria for the similar but milder pervasive developmental disorder – not otherwise specified (PDD-NOS). A telling example is a study by Wing and Gould (1979), published years before the concerns about vaccines arose. Using data from the British National Health System, they identified all the children in one county that had an IQ of less than 70, which qualified them as "mentally handicapped." If they used Kanner's criteria, they found about 4.9 autistic persons per 10,000 population, the expected number. However, if they broadened the criteria slightly, the number rose to 2.1 per 1,000. If they had included children with an IQ in the normal range, that would have added even more cases. Another factor that has led to more cases being diagnosed is the way in which the broadened diagnostic criteria are now applied. In the past, children with very low IQs, dysmorphic features, or specific medical diagnoses, such as fragile X syndrome or tuberous sclerosis, were not included. Now all children who meet the behavioral criteria are included. A third factor that increased the number of cases concerns the methods used to find affected children in surveys. In the past, only cases already diagnosed were counted, and cases were sought only in schools for the handicapped. More recent surveys have done much more thorough screening. The only country with a longstanding, thorough screening program is Japan, and higher rates than in other countries have always been reported there. The final reason for the increase in cases is the age at which autism is diagnosed. This alone has caused the prevalence to nearly double (Parner, Schendel, & Thorsen, 2008). Interestingly, as the diagnosis of autism has increased, the diagnosis of mental retardation has decreased. This is partly driven by the broadened criteria for autism and partly because the better services provided to children with autism in some localities leads clinicians to diagnose cases even where evidence for the diagnosis is slim (Shattuck, 2006). So in aggregate, these various changes in diagnostic criteria, diagnostic practices, better survey methods, and earlier diagnosis are responsible for a huge increase in cases. This means that there is no necessity to postulate new causes in order to explain these additional cases.

Nevertheless, there could be some small increase or decrease in autism that could not be noticed because of all the diagnostic changes that were taking place at the same time. It could be related to some environmental change. Therefore, several different types of studies were done to test the hypothesis that there was a change in autism frequency that could be attributed specifically either to thimerosal or to MMR vaccines.

One type of study tracked changes in autism frequency at the time that MMR was introduced and at the times that the formula of one of the components was changed. Each of these events, the introduction and the formula changes, took place at about the same time throughout the US, and nearly all children in the appropriate age range were vaccinated. Therefore, the change in autism frequency should have been large and abrupt, if it was related to MMR. However, there was no change either in cases with regression or in cases without regression. Studies carried out in different countries all yielded the same results (Fombonne & Cook, 2003).

Thimerosal was similarly studied from several perspectives. For example, child development was studied in populations where the diet was very high in fish, particularly large fish such as tuna since large fish accumulate considerable amounts of mercury over their lifespan as they eat smaller fish. One of the studies occurred in the Seychelles Islands. Mothers' mercury levels were measured during pregnancy, and the children's levels were tracked over time. Not only was there no increased rate of developmental delays in this population, but the children who ate the most fish and had the highest mercury levels actually scored better on the various tests. Their mercury levels, and those of their mothers during pregnancy, were much higher than the levels seen just after a vaccination. Later, a specific study of autism was carried out in the Faroe Islands, whose population has a similar high-fish diet, since it was possible that studying general developmental problems might have missed some cases. Again, the frequency of autism was the same as in other populations, where the same diagnostic criteria were used (Ellefsen, Kampmann, Billstedt, Gillberg, & Gillberg, 2007).

Several studies were done in Scandinavian countries, where all autistic children are registered with the health service so that it is easy to get accurate data. In a Danish study, there was no difference in the frequency of autism in children who did and did not receive vaccinations containing thimerosal, and there was no relationship between the dose of thimerosal received (based on the number of vaccinations each child received) and the frequency of autism. Even though Danish children received, in total, less thimerosal in their vaccines than did American children, the prevalence of autism was the same in both countries. Thimerosal was removed from all vaccines in the US in 1992. At that time, autism prevalence was rising there for the reasons described above. The rates continued to increase after thimerosal was removed, leading researchers to conclude that it was unrelated to the increased diagnosis of autism.

In conclusion, there is general agreement that autism is more frequent than was once thought. This is due to better ways of finding all the cases, broadened criteria and the application of these criteria to children without regard to medical diagnoses, and earlier diagnosis of autism. Numerous high-quality studies have tested the hypotheses that MMR vaccine or thimerosal in vaccines play a role in the increased number of cases. These studies have been uniformly negative. Thus, while there could be small fluctuations due to unknown environmental causes, the evidence is clear that MMR vaccine and thimerosal do not play a causal role.

References

Ellefsen, A., Kampmann, H., Billstedt, E., Gillberg, I., & Gillberg, C. (2007). Autism in the Faroe Islands. An epidemiological study. *Journal of Autism and Developmental Disorders, 37*, 437–444.

Fombonne, E., & Cook, E. H. (2003). MMR and autistic enterocolitis: Consistent epidemiological failure to find an association. *Molecular Psychiatry, 8*, 133–134.

Parner, E., Schendel., D., & Thorsen, P. (2008) Autism prevalence trends over time in Denmark: Changes in prevalence and age at diagnosis. *Archives Pediatric Adolescent Medicine, 162*, 1150–1156.

Shattuck, P. T. (2006). The contribution of diagnostic substitution to the growing administrative prevalence of autism in US special education. *Pediatrics, 117*, 1028–1037.

Wing, L., & Gould, J. (1979). Severe impairments of social interaction and associated abnormalities in children: Epidemiology and classification. *Journal of Autism and Developmental Disorders, 9*, 11–29.

Further Reading

Fombonne, E. (2009). Epidemiology of pervasive developmental disorders. *Pediatric Research*, 65, 591–598.

5

Appendix

Recommended vaccinations in childhood and beyond

Birth
Hep B: Hepatitis B vaccine (HBV); recommended to give the first dose at birth, but may be given at any age for those not previously immunized.

1–2 months
Hep B: Second dose should be administered 1–2 months after the first dose.

2 months
DTaP: Diphtheria, tetanus, and acellular pertussis vaccine
Hib: Haemophilus influenzae type b vaccine
IPV: Inactivated poliovirus vaccine
PCV: Pneumococcal conjugate vaccine
Rota: Rotavirus vaccine

4 months
DTaP
Hib
IPV
PCV
Rota

6 months
DTaP
Hib
PCV
Rota

6 months and annually
Seasonal influenza: Influenza vaccine is now recommended every year for children older than 6 months. Children under 9 who get an influenza vaccine for the first time will receive it in 2 separate doses a month apart. Although young toddlers (from 6 months to 5 years old) are still considered the group of kids who need the influenza vaccine the most, updated guidelines from the Centers for Disease Control and Prevention (CDC) now recommend that all older children and teens also get it (as long as enough is available). It's also especially important for high-risk children to be vaccinated. High-risk groups include, but are not limited to, children with asthma, heart problems, sickle cell anemia, diabetes, and human immunodeficiency virus (HIV). It can take up to 2 weeks after the shot for the body to build up protection against influenza (see also http://kidshealth.org/parent/infections/immunizations/vaccine.html).
H1N1 (Swine) Influenza: All children 6 months and older should receive this vaccine in addition to the seasonal flu vaccine. Kids under 9 will receive the

vaccine in 2 separate doses (a month apart), while older kids will receive just one dose. Following the 2009–2010 flu season, recommendations for this vaccine may change, so talk to your doctor about what's recommended for your child.

6–18 months
Hep B
IPV

2–15 months
Hib
MMR: Measles, mumps, and rubella (German measles) vaccine
PCV
Varicella (chickenpox) vaccine

12–23 months
Hep A: Hepatitis A vaccine; given as 2 shots at least 6 months apart

15–18 months
DTaP

4–6 years
DTaP
MMR
IPV
Varicella

11–12 years
HPV: Human papillomavirus (HPV) vaccine, given as 3 shots over 6 months. It's recommended for girls ages 11 or 12, and also recommended for girls ages 13–18, if they have not yet been vaccinated. The vaccine also may be given to boys ages 9–18. *Tdap:* Tetanus, diphtheria, and pertussis booster *MCV:* Meningitis vaccine; should also be given to 13- to 18-year-olds who have not yet been vaccinated. Children between the ages of 2 and 10 who have certain chronic illnesses will also need this vaccine, with a booster shot a few years later, depending on the age at which the first dose was given.

College entrants
MCV: Meningitis vaccine; recommended for previously unvaccinated college entrants who will live in dormitories. One dose will suffice for healthy college students whose only risk factor is dormitory living.

Q36
Is the Structure of the Brain of Individuals With ASC Different?

Nancy Minshew

The short answer to this question is yes, but the details are complicated, because the brain is highly complex and because there is much that is not yet known about the intricacies of its structure in ASC. Autism and related conditions are characterized as neurologic disorders, because their signs and symptoms have been demonstrated to be the result of alterations in brain structure and function. The characterization of these alterations, and the resulting understanding of what they mean about how ASC occur, have evolved as advances in diagnostic procedures for ASC and in the technology for studying the brain have evolved. Although much remains to be discovered about autism, a great deal is now known about the fundamental alterations in the brain. ASC are now considered disorders of the development of the connectivity of the neurons of the cerebral cortex which results in disturbances in the highly specialized connections that provide for uniquely human abilities. The characterization of autism as a disorder of cortical connectivity was confirmed and extended by the recent discovery of 20 to 25 mostly rare genes that cause 15 to 20% of ASC cases and that share chemical signaling pathways at the synapse involved the development of neuronal connections. The effects of these genes are mediated by messenger RNA (mRNA) and expressed as proteins that act on these cellular signaling pathways. The discovery of these genes and signaling pathways marked the beginning of a molecular pathophysiology for ASC. The next phase of ASC research will define connectomes (all the connections of a single neuron), mRNA expression profiles, and protein expression profiles for different areas of cortex at different ages in ASC to determine, in greater detail, the molecular mechanisms of action of these genes, which is the key to designing neurobiologic interventions.

The earliest brain imaging studies in childhood psychoses and infantile autism reported a number of brain abnormalities, but the individuals diagnosed in that era (1950s–1980s) often had underlying infectious, genetic, metabolic, and neurologic disorders causing their ASC. These structural abnormalities of the brain were ultimately traced to the associated conditions and not to the ASC. The same was true of the rare early autopsy brain studies in ASC. Thus, clinical practice guidelines developed at the end of the 20th century recommended that brain imaging not be undertaken routinely in ASC in the absence of a specific neurologic indication. Since the current clinical trend is to, again, not differentiate between those with and without underlying conditions when diagnosing ASC, it is important to develop new indications for clinical imaging in ASC that identify those individuals who are likely to have associated conditions and visualizable structural imaging abnormalities that will alter diagnosis and/or treatment if defined. Collation of scan outcome and impact on diagnosis and intervention will inform physicians and families of the contribution of clinical imaging to the care of children and adults with ASC, and thus inform future practices.

The first neuropathologic or postmortem examination of a brain in an autism case not caused by an associated condition was reported by Bauman and Kemper (1985). After completing 10 additional cases using the whole brain, serial section method over the next decade (Bauman & Kemper, 2005), 3 common findings emerged: First, brain weight was slightly increased in the children and slightly decreased in the adults; second, neuron or brain cell size was smaller and the cells' packing density increased in selected small, compact, forebrain limbic structures at all ages (golgi staining of the neurons in one of these brain structures revealed underdevelopment of the neuronal dendritic tree which provides enormous contact area for incoming connections); and third reduction in the number of Purkinje cells (brain cells in the cerebellum or hind brain) without retrograde gliosis (scarring) of the inferior olivary nuclei in the brainstem, to which the Purkinje cells are connected, indicating that the Purkinje cell loss occurred prenatally. These findings suggested that autism was the result of disturbances in neuronal organization, the complex developmental sequence of events that takes place between 5 months prenatally and several years postnatally, and results in the elaborate circuitry unique to the human brain. These events include the establishment and differentiation of subplate neurons, lamination of the cortex, outgrowth of dendrites and axons, synaptogenesis, cell death and selective elimination of processes and synapses, and glial proliferation and differentiation (Volpe, 2008). In a later report on 6 cases, Bailey et al. (1998) emphasized cortical dysgenesis in 4 of the 6 cases (i.e., increased cortical thickness, increased neuronal density, irregular layering pattern, and neurons in the molecular layer (i.e., neurons had not migrated to their final destination). However, the significance of these findings in implicating developmental neurobiologic mechanisms in ASC was largely overlooked at the time.

Scientific thinking about ASC shifted dramatically when it was demonstrated that head circumference (HC), a proxy for brain size, of individuals with ASC was 60–70% of population norms, with 15–20% of those individuals having lifelong macrocephaly (HC > 97%) that developed by 4–5 years of age but was not present at birth. Studies of toddlers presenting with symptoms of autism and infants with older siblings with autism, who were themselves later diagnosed with ASC, defined the onset of the *accelerated* rate of head growth in autism as beginning at about 6 months of age with a peak at 12 months of age, coinciding with the emergence of signs and symptoms of ASC. Because the premature brain overgrowth in ASC corresponds to the onset of symptoms, it may represent an ineffective or failed attempt to achieve the cortical connectivity needed to support these emerging higher order abilities. This period of overgrowth of the brain in ASC is followed by a plateau in growth, at which time typically developing children make gains in brain growth. Regardless of the specifics of the mechanism, the generalized overgrowth made focal brain theories and single primary deficit theories no longer tenable as causes of autism. This overgrowth phenomenon also attracted the attention of developmental neurobiologists and geneticists, who immediately recognized it as a sign of a disturbance in developmental brain mechanisms under genetic programming from conception through life. Studies of brain and structure size later in childhood and adulthood in ASC show further evidence of dysregulated growth patterns.

There is a caveat to this overgrowth story. A large multisite study of HC in individuals with ASC and their family members revealed that, although HC > HT (HT, height) was the most common finding in those with ASC, their parents, and siblings, the most striking characteristic of the ASC population was the wide distribution of HC measurements, consistent with heterogeneity among the underlying molecular mechanisms disrupting the development of cortical connectivity (Lainhart et al., 2006). This wide distribution of head growth profiles suggests that some of the underlying genetic and molecular mechanisms might result in an increase in the amount of brain tissue, whereas others might not, though the end result would still be underdevelopment of connectivity.

Magnetic resonance imaging (MRI) studies of ASC confirmed that the increase in HC was the result of increased total brain volume. Imaging studies of toddlers (Hazlettet al., 2005; Sparks et al., 2002) (mean age 2.7 years) with autism found enlargement of cerebral white matter (axonal projections of neurons that connect with dendrites of other neurons), cerebral cortical gray matter (multilayered surface of the brain where neuron cell bodies reside in a complex matrix of circuitry) with disproportionate enlargement of the amygdala (bilateral structures associated with emotion) and the hippocampus (bilateral structure associated with memory and learning). This enlargement was also apparent at 5 years of age and not detectable after 7 years of age. In addition, one of the toddler studies observed enlargement of the caudate nucleus, but not the cerebellum in 2-year-olds with ASC, whereas several other toddler studies reported enlargement of the cerebellum but no data on the caudate nucleus. Further analysis of cortical regions in the toddlers revealed either a diffuse increase in volume throughout the cerebral cortex or an increase in the frontal, temporal, and parietal cortex, but not in the occipital cortex. Imaging studies after age 7 have been inconsistent in reporting differences on structural MRI, though diffusion tensor imaging (DTI) of fiber pathways is likely to prove more revealing. Imaging studies of infants with an older sibling with autism are in progress to define the sequence of events between birth and age 2: These studies are critical to determining which changes in brain connectivity are primary (resulting directly from ASC) and which are secondary to not receiving ordinary input of connections. The imaging studies in ASC, so far, make it clear that findings are age-dependent, that brain development in ASC follows an altered trajectory across the life span, and that it is important to control for the effect of IQ and gender when doing neuroanatomic studies. Longitudinal imaging studies will play a vital role in delineating the evolving sequence of changes in the brain from birth to adulthood in ASC.

These findings dramatically changed the scientific conceptualization of autism. In the face of a very early, generalized increase in total brain volume, theories that had proposed regional brain dysfunction or a single deficit as the cause of autism, which were the majority of theories, were no longer tenable. A broader conceptualization of autism was required. This broader involvement has been supported by the emerging results of studies of infants with an older sibling with autism, who present at 9 months of age with sensory signs, motor signs, and unusual interests (Rogers, 2009). The increase in white matter highlighted the key role of developmental alterations in neuronal connectivity in producing the signs and symptoms of ASC. The diffuse increased thickness of the cortical gray matter in toddlers emphasized the role of cerebral cortex.

One neuropathological finding offered an integration of the gray and white matter findings. The cerebral cortex (gray matter) has a 6-layered horizontal structure as well as a vertical minicolumn structure. Casanova, Buxhoeveden, Switala, and Roy (2002) and Casanovo et al. (2006) reported an increased packing density and increased number of mini-columns; neuronal density within the minicolumns was increased, and the size of the neurons was reduced. Casanova et al. (2002; 2006) proposed that the increased number of neurons in the mini-columns and increased number of minicolumns would necessitate a multifold increase in white matter projections to maintain cortical connectivity, but the small size of the nuclei of these neurons was compatible with local connections (u-fibers), not longer, interregional connections. Regardless of the specifics of the mechanism by which these alterations in connectivity arise, the major point of these and supporting findings is that the key disturbance in ASC is at the level of the cortical neuron, not the gray matter or the white matter. DTI studies will be able to address this specific hypothesis regarding selective underdevelopment of cortico-cortical fibers. Two specific issues related to connectivity in ASC have drawn particular attention. Emphasis in the literature has been placed on underconnectivity of the frontal cortex as the major site of brain dysfunction in ASC. However, this emphasis may well reflect its role as polymodal integratory cortex with strong connections to all cortical regions and affected forebrain structures in ASC in combination with the dependence fMRI studies on high functioning individuals. This explanation is supported by the diffuse increase in gray and white matter volume in toddlers and very young children with ASC who are more affected. In addition, connectivity issues in frontal cortex alone will not readily explain the ASC in individuals with severe and profound intellectual disability (ID). ID is not a cooccurring or comorbid disorder, but rather part and parcel of the cognitive impairment of ASC, which involves information processing that disproportionately impacts higher order information and spares simpler information processing abilities (Williams, Goldstein, & Minshew, 2006).

The second issue pertains to the corpus callosum, a broad band of white matter that connects the two halves of the brain and is associated with interhemispheric information processing. The reduction in the size (or absence of an increase in proportion to the increase in the size of the rest of the brain) of the corpus callosum in ASC suggests that it is not impacted by the same perturbed

5

developmental process impacting intrahemispheric white matter. This suggests that the reduction in the size of the corpus callosum is secondary to decreased intrahemispheric connectivity, which is consistent with correlations between intrahemispheric functional connectivity measures and area of the corpus callosum (Just, Cherkassky, Keller, Kana, & Minshew, 2007).

Two reports have implicated other important developmental events: Neuronal migration and neuronal proliferation. First, Strauss et al. (2006) reported a syndrome of focal epilepsy, mental retardation, and autism in association with the mutant contactin-associated protein-like 2 (CNTNAP2) gene. These Old Order Amish children presented with focal epilepsy, language regression, mental retardation, and macrocephaly; about 70% have an ASC. Neuropathological examination revealed cerebral cortical dysplasia, disturbances in lamination, and nests of gray matter in the white matter, evidence of neuronal migrational disturbances. The second example is a report of ASC in 8% of surviving extremely premature infants (born at or before 28 weeks gestation) (Johnson et al., 2010). These infants also have cerebral palsy. At 28 weeks, the neurons that are destined for the cerebral cortex are adjacent to the lateral ventricles (i.e., fluid-filled spaces in the center of each half of the brain) in the premature infant's watershed area (subject to loss of perfusion when blood pressure drops), and thus vulnerable to hypoxic-ischemic damage. This association suggests that symptoms and signs of ASC are associated with neuronal proliferation and/or after coming developmental events.

In order to differentiate between these developmental neurobiologic mechanisms and primary and secondary effects of disturbed connectivity, studies are in progress to examine the developmental aspects of gyrification (cortical folding) patterns, cerebral cortical thickness, and cortical surface, such as cortical areas and gyral and sulcal curvatures (Hardan, Jou, Keshavan, Varma, & Minshew, 2004; Hardan, Muddasani, Vemulapalli, Keshavan, & Minshew, 2006; Hardan, Libove, Keshavan, Melhem, & Minshew, 2009). For example, subplate neurons provide temporary connections for thalamocortical connections while the multilayered cerebral cortex is developing (Volpe, 2008). Without this intermediate support structure, these vital connections for sensory processing will be disrupted. Every event in brain development is dependent on preceding events and sets the stage for subsequent events.

In summary, studies of brain structure have implicated multiple events in prenatal and postnatal brain development, particularly neuronal organizational events. The generalized enlargement of the brain, resulting from premature overgrowth, attests to the broadness of the involvement of the brain, precluding focal brain theories and single primary deficit theories. The discovery of 20 to 25 mostly rare genes that act on synaptic signaling pathways involved in the development and maintenance of neuronal and synaptic connections have reinforced the centrality of disruption of cortical connectivity in ASC. Considerable research remains to be done in order to specify the molecular pathophysiology of ASC for the genes discovered and define the links to the connectivity disturbances, as well as the specific links to behavior differences in ASC, which will provide powerful entry points to future treatments. The molecular mechanisms for the remaining 80% of cases remain to be discovered.

References

Bailey, A., Luthert, P., Dean, A., Harding, B., Janota, I., Montgomery, M., ... Lantos, P. (1998). A Clinicopathological Study of Autism. *Brain, 121*, 889–905.

Bauman, M. L., & Kemper, T. L. (2005). Neuroanatomic Observations of the Brain in Autism: A review and future directions. *International Journal of Developmental Neuroscience, 23*, 183–187.

Bauman, M. L., & Kemper, T. L. (1985). Histoanatomic observations of the brain in early infantile autism. *Neurology, 35*, 866–874.

Casanova, M. F., Buxhoeveden, D. P., Switala, A. E., & Roy, E. (2002). Minicolumnar pathology in autism. *Neurology, 58*, 428–432.

Casanova, M. F., van Kooten, I., Switala, A. R., van Engeland, H., Heinsen, H., Steinbusch, H. W., ... Schmitz, C. (2006). Abnormalities of cortical minicolumnar organization in the orefrontal lobes of autistic patients. *Clinical Neuroscience Research, 6*, 127–133.

Hardan A. Y., Jou, R. J., Keshavan, M. S., Varma, R., & Minshew, N. J. (2004). Increased frontal cortical folding in autism: a preliminary MRI study. *Psychiatry Research, 5*, 263–268.

Hardan, A. Y., Libove, R. A., Keshavan, M. S., Melhem, N. M., & Minshew, N. J. (2009). A preliminary longitudinal magnetic resonance imaging study of brain volume and cortical thickness in autism. *Biological Psychiatry, 66*, 320–326.

Hardan, A. Y., Muddasani, S., Vemulapalli, M., Keshavan, M. S., & Minshew, N. J. (2006). An MRI study of increased cortical thickness in autism. *American Journal of Psychiatry, 163*, 1290–1292.

Hazlett, H. C., Poe, M., Gerig, G., Smith, R. G., Provenzale, J., Ross, A., Gilmore, J., & Piven, J. (2005). Magnetic resonance imaging and head circumference study of brain size in autism: Birth through age 2 years. *Archives of General Psychiatry, 62*, 1366–1376.

Johnson, S., Hollis, C., Kochhar, P., Hennessy, E., Wolke, D., & Marlow, N. (2010). Autism spectrum disorders in extremely premature children. *Journal of Pediatrics, 156*, 525–531.

Just, M. A., Cherkassky, V. L., Keller, T. A., Kana, R. K., & Minshew, N. J. (2007). Functional and anatomical cortical underconnectivity in autism: Evidence from an fMRI study of an executive function task and corpus callosum morphometry. *Cerebral Cortex, 17*, 951–961.

Lainhart, J. E., Bigler, E. D., Bocian, M., Coon, H., Dinh, E., Dawson, G., & Deutsch, C. K. (2006). Head circumference and height in autism: A study by the collaborative programs of excellence in autism. *American Journal of Medical Genetics Part A, 140A*, 2257–2274.

Rogers, S. J. (2009). What are infant siblings teaching us about autism in infancy? *Autism Research, 2*, 125–137.

Sparks, B. F., Friedman, S. D., Shaw, D. W., Aylward, E. H., Echelard, D., Artru, A. A., Maravilla, K. R., Giedd, J. N., Munson, J., Dawson, G., & Dager, S. R. (2002). Brain structural abnormalities in young children with autism spectrum disorder. *Neurology, 59*, 184–192.

Strauss, K. A., Puffenberger, E. G., Huentelman, M. J., Gottlieb, S., Dobrin, S. E., Parod, J. M., ... & Morton, D. H. (2006). Recessive symptomatic focal epilepsy and mutant contactin-associated protein-like 2. *New England Journal of Medicine, 354*, 1370–1377.

Volpe, J. J. (1998). Brain Development Unit. In *Neurology of the Newborn* (5th ed., pp. 3–118). (5th ed.), Philadelphia, PA: Saunders-Elsevier.

Williams, D. L., Goldstein, G., & Minshew, N. J. (2006). Neuropsychologic functioning in children with autism: Further evidence for disordered complex information-processing. *Child Neuropsychology, 12*, 279–298.

Further Reading

Abramson, B. S., & Geschwind, D. H. (2008). Advances in autism genetics: On the threshold of a new neurobiology. *Nature Reviews, 9*, 341–355.

Amaral, D. G., Schumann, C. M., & Nordahl, C. W. (2008). Neuroanatomy of autism. *Trends in Neuroscience, 3*, 137–145.

Mosconi, M., Zwaigenbaum, L., & Piven, J. (2006). Structural MRI in autism: Findings and future directions. *Clinical Neuroscience Research, 6*, 135–144.

Zoghbi, H. Y. (2003). Postnatal neurodevelopmental disorders: Meeting at the synapse? *Science, 302*, 826–830.

5

Q37
What Is Known About Brain Functions in Individuals With ASC?

Isabel Dziobek

Functional brain imaging using magnetic resonance imaging (fMRI) and positron emission tomography (PET) can be employed to study the neuronal mechanisms underlying cognitive processes and to document changes in the organization of these processes throughout development. Early functional imaging studies in ASC in the late 1990s have focused on a priori regions of interest that have been implicated in social functioning or repetitive behaviors or that have been identified as deviant by structural imaging studies in ASC. More recently, as new technology in image analysis has been developed, the patterns of activation and synchronization of activation across cortical networks recruited to perform various cognitive tasks have attracted the attention of brain researchers (Williams & Minshew, 2007).

The social impairments, verbal and nonverbal communication deficits, and repetitive behaviors that are defining behaviors in ASC are thought to reflect neuropsychological abnormalities in social cognition (e.g., face processing, theory of mind – ToM), executive functions (e.g. planning, cognitive flexibility), and central coherence (e.g., detail-focus). Consequently, those neuropsychological frameworks have been applied in functional neuroimaging studies aimed at characterizing the neural substrates underlying the core ASC behaviors.

The pronounced impairment in social cognition found in neuropsychological studies of ASC suggests involvement of certain brain areas known to mediate social and emotional behavior, such as the amygdala, medial prefrontal cortex, and parts of the temporal lobe. Activity in those regions has, indeed, been reported deviant, employing tasks of face recognition, gaze processing, and ToM. Reduced activation of the fusiform gyrus (FG) during tasks that demand the processing of faces is probably the most replicated functional imaging finding in ASC (Schultz et al., 2000). Interestingly, there is evidence that autistic individuals recruit brain areas during face processing more typically associated with object recognition, such as the inferior temporal gyrus. However, a number of recent studies that failed to find differences in FG activation between individuals with and without ASC call for a refining of the nature of FG abnormalities. For example, the amount of eye fixation to faces, which is reduced in individuals with ASC but has rarely been controlled for in functional imaging studies, seems an important contributor to FG hypoactivation.

Given that ASC involve reduced eye contact, functional imaging studies have employed paradigms in which individuals with ASC have to engage in gaze processing. Those studies revealed decreased activation in the posterior superior temporal gyrus in autistic individuals compared to controls. The ability to infer mental states, such as beliefs, thoughts, or emotions of others, is referred to as ToM. While typically developed individuals activate a network of brain regions comprising the superior temporal sulcus, medial prefrontal cortex, and temporal pole when engaged in ToM processing, individuals with ASC do not activate this network to the same extent. Findings of activation of the amygdala, a structure identified as atypical by neuropathological studies in ASC, yielded conflicting results in ToM fMRI studies. A recent meta analysis of more than 20 functional imaging studies examining social processes, including face process-ing and ToM tasks, found, however, that individuals with ASC had significantly lower probability of activation in the right amygdala, along with the anterior and posterior cingulate gyrus, anterior insula, and left FG (Di Martino et al., 2009). In contrast, individuals with ASC displayed greater probability of activation in somatosensory regions, such as the postcentral gyrus or inferior occipital gyrus, possibly pointing to alternative strategies that are being used during social cog-nition.

There were reports of reduced activity in the mirror neuron system in the inferior frontal gyrus when individuals with ASC performed tasks of social cog-nition. However, hypoactivation in the same area is also found in nonsocial tasks in autistic individuals. Thus, although mirror neuron dysfunction represents a compelling potential mechanism for the social-emotional deficits in ASC, fur-ther research is needed to verify if activation in the inferior frontal gyrus, in-deed, reflects mirror neuron activity and, if so, to establish its relevance for social functioning and ASC symptomatology.

While impairments in some areas of executive functioning, such as in plan-ning, cognitive control, and flexibility, are frequently reported characteristics of ASC, other areas of executive functions, such as working memory or inhibition, are generally not affected. Although it has been difficult to establish consistent patterns of deviant brain activation in ASC across studies, hypoactivation in areas of the frontal cortex, such as the dorsolateral prefrontal cortex and an-terior cingulate gyrus, has been reported by a number of studies, even when tasks that do not pose problems for autistic individuals were used. In addition, aberrant functional connectivity among brain areas was reported in various stud-ies, and individuals with ASC were shown to recruit different brain areas than controls. This suggests that autistic individuals use different cognitive strategies during executive functioning. Similar conclusions as to divergent strategies can be drawn from a few studies investigating the neuronal correlates of superior focus to detail in ASC. Using The Embedded Figures test, on which individuals with ASC often outperform control individuals, functional imaging studies have found evidence that while controls demonstrate greater activation in prefrontal cortex regions, autistic individuals show a more powerful response in basic sen-sory processing regions in the occipitotemporal cortex.

Given the centrality of language abnormalities in ASC, functional imaging studies in ASC have been concerned among others with sentence comprehension and semantic processing. Findings of those studies indicate that individuals with ASC show reduced Broca's area activation (i.e., an area important for speech production) and increased Wernicke's area activation (i.e., an area important for speech perception) compared to controls. More importantly, functional connectivity between these two fundamental language-processing areas was also reported as reduced. Interestingly, a preference in ASC to process language using visual areas, was demonstrated in a study that employed stimuli that allowed visual imagery during sentence comprehension (Kana, Keller, Cherkassky, Minshew, & Just, 2006). Those results can be taken in support of the notion that in ASC there is a tendency to "think in pictures."

Although functional neuroimaging investigations in ASC have mostly focused on the brain activation to specific cognitive events, some recent studies have investigated the default mode network, a set of neural regions that are highly active in the absence of a task, such as the posterior cingulate cortex, medial prefrontal cortex, and parts of the temporal lobe. Suppression of the default mode network, which facilitates performance of tasks demanding attention, was reportedly impaired in individuals with ASC (Kennedy, Redcay, & Courchesne, 2006). In addition and more consistently shown across studies, ASC involves reduced functional connectivity between the areas of the default mode network.

Taken together, the available evidence suggests that, although some aspects of brain functioning are comparable to that of neurotypical individuals, ASC, nevertheless, involve widespread brain function abnormalities. Autistic individuals seem to recruit different brain regions when performing cognitive tasks, possibly compensating for dysfunctional brain areas. The most striking differences, however, have been reported for the synchronization between cortical regions mediating a wide variety of cognitive functions, such as social cognition, executive functions, or language processing. This supports the disconnection model of ASC, highlighting deviance in functional connectivity between regions, rather than focal abnormalities.

References

Di Martino, A., Ross, K., Uddin, L. Q., Sklar, A. B., Castellanos, F. X., & Milham, M. P. (2009). Functional brain correlates of social and nonsocial processes in autism spectrum disorders: An activation likelihood estimation meta-analysis. *Biological Psychiatry, 65*, 63–74.

Kana, R. K., Keller, T. A., Cherkassky, V. L., Minshew, N. J., & Just, M. A. (2006). Sentence comprehension in autism: thinking in pictures with decreased functional connectivity. *Brain, 129*, 2484–2493.

Kennedy, D. P., Redcay, E., & Courchesne, E. (2006). Failing to deactivate: Resting functional abnormalities in autism. *Proceedings of the National Academy of Sciences USA, 103*, 8275–8280.

Schultz, R. T., Gauthier, I., Klin, A., Fulbright, R. K., Anderson, A. W., Volkmar, F., …
Gore, J. C. (2000). Abnormal ventral temporal cortical activity during face discrimi-
nation among individuals with autism and Asperger syndrome. *Archives of General
Psychiatry, 57*, 331–340.
Williams, D. L., & Minshew, N. J. (2007). Understanding autism and related disorders:
What has imaging taught us? *Neuroimaging Clinics of North America, 17*, 495–509.

Further Reading

Casanova, M. F. (2005) (ed.). *Recent developments in autism research*. New York, NY:
Nova Science Publishers.

Q38
What Are Executive Functions?

Marjorie Solomon

"Executive functions" is a broad term used to describe the set of cognitive processes required to prepare for and execute goal-directed actions. Some individual components of executive functioning include goal representation, action planning, impulse inhibition, organization, self-monitoring, and cognitive flexibility. Given that patients with focal frontal lobe lesions have difficulty in planning future actions and in inhibiting habitual responses, executive functions have been associated with the prefrontal cortex (PFC). Many clinical neuropsychology assessment batteries are premised on this assumption and are designed to test what are believed to be the specific components of executive functioning based on studies of patients with brain lesions.

Impairments in executive functions are among the most consistently reported deficits in individuals with ASC. More specifically, many studies have shown that individuals with ASC have difficulty in shifting their frame of reference in thinking about problems (shifting cognitive set), in shifting how they conceptualize options that are not presented in the immediate environment (extra dimensional set shifting), in shifting the focus of their visual attention, in shifting their attention between sensory modalities like seeing and hearing, and in shifting between sets of rules they have learned (see Hill, 2004, for a review). Executive function deficits are not specific to autism and also are present in many other forms of developmental psychopathology, including ADHD.

As all parents and clinicians know, individuals with ASC have difficulty maintaining reciprocal social relationships, having two-sided conversations, transitioning between activities, and disengaging from their idiosyncratic interests. They also have difficulty inhibiting old behaviors in favor of new, more appropriate ones. Thus, there have been many studies examining the relationship between executive functions and theory of mind (perspective taking), central coherence (understanding and maintaining the "big picture" as opposed to focusing on details), and restricted and repetitive behaviors. However, despite the fact that deficits in executive functions would appear to be directly related to this inflexibility in everyday behaviors, it has been challenging to demonstrate this link empirically using clinical neuropsychology measures (see Geurts, Corbett, & Solomon, 2009). Language abilities may be more important to everyday social functioning than executive functions, theory of mind (ToM), or weak central coherence (Joseph & Tager-Flusberg, 2004). Work in this area continues.

Fortunately, the advent of new technologies, including functional magnetic resonance imaging (fMRI) is helping to advance what we know about brain functioning beyond what could be learned by lesion models. "Cognitive control" is a term evolving in the field of cognitive neuroscience to describe the cognitive processes that traditionally have been thought of as executive functions. The newer cognitive control-based model of PFC function suggests that: (1) the PFC is specialized for the representation and maintenance of context information, (2) context information is maintained in the PFC as a pattern of neural activity, and (3) context representations mediate cognitive control through interactions that modulate the flow of information in other brain systems that more directly support task performance. Proper functioning of this system is required for (a) effective allocation of attention, (b) inhibition of irrelevant responses, (c) appropriate shifting of frame of reference, (d) relating information appropriately over time and space, and (e) adjusting behavior in relation to the evolving environment. For example, when Americans visit London and attempt to cross the street, cognitive control must be engaged to avoid the customary practice of looking to the left for oncoming traffic, in favor of looking to the right. In sum, cognitive control must be engaged when overcoming habitual responses, ignoring irrelevant stimuli, or transforming representations. Cognitive control is not required to perform simple or automatic behaviors, but it must be engaged to guide action in novel, difficult, or rapidly changing conditions. This is especially important when there is strong competition between the potential responses, such as choosing between the ingrained habit of looking left, versus facing the prospect of being run over.

Specific brain regions thought to be involved in the application of cognitive control include the dorsolateral prefrontal cortex (DLPFC), medial frontal cortex (including the anterior cingulate cortex), and parietal cortex. In the cognitive control model, the DLPFC is believed to maintain appropriate context for action. The anterior cingulate cortex is thought to function as part of a "control loop." It detects response conflict and signals the DLPFC to allocate more control-related resources. The parietal cortex is activated when it is necessary to switch attentional focus. It is also thought to act as a repository of learned stimulus-response associations from which the DLPFC "selects" the appropriate response.

In conclusion, it is an exciting time for executive functions research, and we believe that more research in this area will help to advance the understanding of autism. Directions for future executive functions research include:

(1) Studies that help us understand specific aspects of executive functioning that are impaired in autism and how this compares to problems found in other neurodevelopmental disorders.

(2) The field lacks clear hypotheses about the neural mechanisms that are responsible for ASC so that they can be tested and validated. In our lab, we are attempting to test the Miller and Cohen model of cognitive control in ASC, using behavioral tasks (Solomon, Ozonoff, Cummings, & Carter, 2008) and functional neuroimaging (fMRI) studies (Solomon et al., 2009).

(3) The development of measures that enable us to tease apart discrete cognitive processes related to executive functioning are needed.

(4) More ecologically valid measures may help in forging associations between the observed day-to-day behavior and what we are measuring.

(5) Most experimental research has used data analytic models that focus on mean group differences. There has been little consideration of the role of individual differences in areas such as temperament and personality, stress responsiveness, and motivation in studies of executive functions.

References

Geurts, H., Corbett, B., & Solomon, M. (2009). The paradox of cognitive flexibility in autism spectrum disorders. *Trends in Cognitive Science, 13,* 74–82.

Hill, E. L. (2004). Executive dysfunction in autism. *Trends in Cognitive Sciences, 8,* 26–32.

Joseph, R., & Tager-Flusberg, H. (2004). The relationship between theory of mind and executive functions to symptom type and severity in children with autism. *Developmental Psychopathology, 16,* 137–155.

Solomon, M., Ozonoff, S., Ursu, S., Ravizza, S., Cummings, N., Ly, S., & Carter, C. S. (2009). The neural substrates of cognitive control deficits in autism spectrum disorders. *Neuropsychologia, 47,* 2515–2526.

Solomon, M., Ozonoff, S. J., Cummings, N., & Carter, C. S. (2008). Cognitive control in autism spectrum disorders. *International Journal of Developmental Neuroscience, 26,* 239–247.

Further Reading

Russell, J. (1997). *Autism as an executive disorder.* Oxford, UK: University Press

Q39
What is "Weak Central Coherence"?

Francesca Happé

The term "central coherence" was coined by Uta Frith in her influential 1989 book *Autism: Explaining the Enigma* to describe the "neurotypical" (i.e., non-autistic) tendency to put information together in context for meaning, looking for the "big picture." In Frith's words, this drive for coherence "pulls together large amounts of information" like the tributaries of a river, and "without this type of high-level cohesion, pieces of information would just remain pieces, be they small pieces or large pieces" (p. 97). She speculated that the drive for coherence was weaker in people with ASC and offered the novel thought that this would make them *better* than neurotypicals (NTs) at some tasks and tests. In particular, she demonstrated that people with ASC were better than IQ-matched comparison groups on the Block Design Test (see Figure 1) and Embedded Figures Tests, apparently being able to see the parts without being distracted by the whole picture. Indeed it has been a defining feature of the weak coherence account that, in contrast to, say, "theory of mind" or "executive dysfunction, " this theory aims to explain *assets* commonly seen in ASC, emphasizing abilities not just difficulties.

Since Frith's first description of weak coherence, the idea has been refined in several ways, however, the core notion that people with ASC are more detail-focused than NTs remains. It fits with Kanner's first reports of autism (1943) as involving an

> "inability to experience wholes without full attention to the constituent parts... A situation, a performance, a sentence is not regarded as complete if it is not made up of exactly the same elements that were present at the time the child was first confronted with it. If the slightest ingredient is altered or removed, the total situation is no longer the same and therefore is not accepted as such." (p. 246)

It also fits with what very able individuals with ASC tell us about their own experience – for example, Gunilla Gerland (2003) writes *"Every little bit of fact seemed to land in its own compartment in my head and refused to be linked with any other."* (p. 225) Superior attention to, and memory for, detail may help explain puzzling symptoms of ASC, such as "insistence on sameness " (because tiny changes are noticed), and desire for repetition (spinning a coin for hours may not be repetitive if you perceive minute variations). Indeed, a persistent preoccupation with parts of objects is one of the diagnostic criteria for autistic disorder in current international psychiatric classification practice (DSM-IV-TR).

Studies to date suggest that weak coherence represents a cognitive *style*, not deficit, and may be best conceptualized as an information-processing bias towards local or featural information. This bias can be overcome, just as NTs can overcome their preference for meaning to memorise "meaningless" information such as telephone numbers or bank codes. So, for example, people with ASC *can* read text for meaning, but unless asked to do so explicitly, their default approach may be to read a story as if it were just a list of words (e.g, not using context to disambiguate homographs). A natural eye for detail appears to play a part in the unusually high rate of savant skills in ASC (Happé & Vital, 2009), facilitating, for example, absolute pitch as a basis for further musical skills. Even the child with ASC who is terribly distressed by a familiar ornament being moved a fraction of an inch is demonstrating a special skill few NTs possess.

Whether the good eye and memory for detail in ASC comes at the expense of processing the meaning and "bigger picture" is a topic of much debate. Several alternative accounts of superior local processing in ASC (including Laurent Mottron's "enhanced perceptual functioning" and Simon Baron-Cohen's "hyper-systemising" theories) propose that global processing is intact in ASC. Recently, Happé and Booth (2008) have suggested that weak coherence may be the result of two somewhat independent aspects, superior featural processing and poor global processing, with different subgroups within ASC showing only the former, only the latter, or both of these.

Studies to date suggest that detail-focused processing bias is not secondary to so-called executive dysfunction: Impulsivity and poor planning in ADHD, for example, do not result in the characteristic assets or deficits associated with weak coherence in ASC (Booth, Charlton, Hughes, & Happé, 2003). The relationship between weak coherence and theory of mind deficits is less clear, although a degree of independence seems likely as, for example, some fathers of children with ASC show excellent eye for detail without accompanying social difficulties (Happé, Briskman, & Frith, 2001). Weak coherence may also be relevant to other special groups, for example, recent work suggests superior eye for detail in some women with eating disorders.

To date, the brain basis of weak coherence is unclear, although the theory chimes well with suggestions of reduced functional connectivity, stronger local than long-range neural connections, and reduced top-down modulation (e.g., Belmonte et al., 2004). The working hypothesis is that weak coherence is among the features of the "broader autism phenotype" inherited in many cases of ASC. Importantly, ongoing work suggests an overlap between genetic contributions to ASC-like eye for detail and superior skills in maths, music, art, or memory (Happé & Vital, 2009).

An important aim for the future is to develop educational interventions based on the weak coherence hypothesis, helping children with ASC learn to "zoom

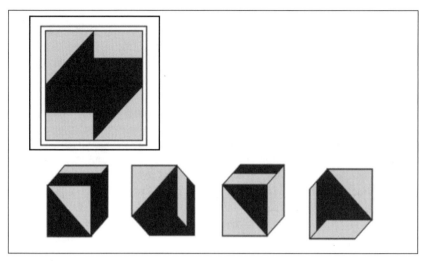

Figure 1. Block design task: The aim is to copy the design using the cubes

out" (using a camera analogy) to see the bigger picture where needed. Education using the natural strength in detail focus is also an important implication of research on weak coherence in ASC.

References

Belmonte, M. K., Allen, G., Beckel-Mitchener, A., Boulanger, L. M., Carper, R. A., & Webb, S. J. (2004). Autism and abnormal development of brain connectivity. *The Journal of Neuroscience, 24*, 9228–9231.

Booth, R., Charlton, R., Hughes, C., & Happé, F. (2003). Disentangling weak coherence and executive dysfunction: Planning drawing in autism and attention-deficit/ hyperactivity disorder *Philosophical Transactions of the Royal Society – Series B, 358*, 387–392.

Frith, U. (1989). *Autism: Explaining the Enigma.* Oxford, UK: Blackwell.

Gerland, G. (2003). A real person: Life on the outside (J. Tate, Trans.). London: Souvenir Press.

Happé, F., & Booth, R. D. L. (2008). The power of the positive: Revisiting weak coherence in autism spectrum disorders. *The Quarterly Journal of Experimental Psychology, 61*, 50–63.

Happé, F., Briskman, J., & Frith, U. (2001). Exploring the cognitive phenotype of autism: Weak "central coherence" in parents and siblings of children with autism. I. Experimental tests. *Journal of Child Psychology and Psychiatry, 42*, 299–307.

Happé, F. & Vital, P. (2009). What aspects of autism predispose to talent? *Philosophical Transactions of the Royal Society – Series B, 364,* 1369–1375.

Kanner, L. (1943). Autistic disturbances of affective contact. *Nervous Child, 2*, 217–250.

5

Further Reading

Happé, F., & Frith, U. (2006). The weak coherence account: Detail-focused cognitive style in autism spectrum disorders. *Journal of Autism and Developmental Disorders*, *36*, 5–25.

Happé, F., & Frith, U. (Eds.). (2010). *Autism and Talent*. Oxford, UK: Oxford University Press.

5

What Is Theory of Mind, and Is It Impaired in ASC?

Simon Baron-Cohen

A theory of mind (ToM) is the ability to infer mental states (i.e., beliefs, desires, intentions, imagination, emotions, etc.). This is a crucial way to help us make sense of behavior, and predict what that person might do next. Deficits in understanding other minds seem to be a core and, possibly, universal deficit among such individuals. Some people with ASC lack almost all signs of a ToM – a form of "mindblindness." More commonly, people with autism have some of the basics of a ToM but have some difficulties in using it at a level that one would expect, having degrees of mindblindness. Note that the terms "ToM, " and "mindreading, " can to some extent be used synonymously. The following is a summary of experimental evidence reviewed by Baron-Cohen (1995), Happé (1996), and Frith (1989).

The *mental-physical distinction* is a fundamental cornerstone of our ToM. 3- to 4-year-old typically developing children can easily make these judgments, whereas children with severe ASC have difficulty making such judgments. Typically developing 3- to 4-year-olds also already know that the brain has a set of mental, as well as physical, functions. In contrast, children with ASC who have a mental age above a 4-year-old level appear to know about the physical functions, but most fail to mention any mental function of the brain. Children from about the age of 4 years are, typically, able to distinguish between *appearance* and *reality* and talk about objects that might have misleading identities. Children with ASC, presented with the same sorts of tests, may not talk about objects in the same way, not capturing the object's dual identity in their spontaneous descriptions. *First-order false belief tests* assess the understanding that different people can have different thoughts about the same situation. Typically developing 4-year-olds can keep track of how different people might think different things about the world. Children with ASC have difficulties in shifting their perspective to judge what someone else might think, instead, simply reporting what they themselves know. Another corner stone of the typically developing child's ToM is understanding where knowledge comes from, so that they can work out who knows what. This underpins appropriate communication and understanding of deception. Typically developing 3-year-olds can understand the *seeing-leads-to-knowing* principle, but children with ASC are virtually at chance on this test.

By the age of 4, typically developing children can also pick out words from a word list that refer to what goes on in the mind or what the mind can do. Children with ASC have much more difficulty in making this judgment. Many studies have also reported a lower frequency of *pretend play* in the spontaneous play of children with ASC. This might express a failure to reflect on one's own imagination – a mindreading difficulty – or a failure to switch attention flexibly from reality mode to pretend mode as a result of some aspect of what is called "executive function," or both. Emotions can be caused by physical events and/or by mental states, such as desires and beliefs. Typically developing 4- to 6-year-olds understand all 3 types of emotional causes. In contrast, children with ASC with this mental age have difficulty with the more complex *causes of emotion* (i.e., mental states). From *gaze-direction,* typically developing children (age 4 years) can work out when someone is thinking about something. Gaze-direction also allows young typically developing children of the same age to work out which of several objects a person wants. Children with ASC, in contrast, are relatively blind to such information from gaze-direction. *Figurative speech*, of course, also requires an understanding of the speaker's intentions, in order to move beyond the literal level of simply mapping words onto their referents. This more advanced mindreading test (pitched at the level of a typically developing 8-year-old) reveals more subtle mindreading difficulties in higher-functioning individuals with ASC. *Pragmatics* is the use of language appropriate to the social context. Almost every aspect of pragmatics involves sensitivity to speaker and listener mental states and, hence, mindreading. Studies of pragmatics in children with ASC have included whether the principles of conversational relevance can be recognized and recognizing when someone said the wrong thing (i.e., faux pas). Both studies suggest that children with ASC have difficulties in this area.

There are no reported cases of individuals with ASC who pass first order ToM tests (i.e., considering one person's thoughts) at the right mental age. A child should be able to pass such tests at 3–4 years of mental age. However, in ASC, on average, a mental age of 9 is needed before the passing of such tests is seen, and the youngest mental age of an individual with ASC passing such tests is 5 ½ years. As a result of a delay in acquiring first order ToM, these individuals often fail *second-order false belief tests*. These involve considering one person's thoughts about another person's thoughts. This corresponds to a 6-year-old mental age level. Some individuals with ASC, who are high functioning and who are usually adults, may pass even second-order false belief tests but have difficulties in more advanced ToM tests, such as inferring complex mental states (e.g., bluff and double bluff), or in decoding complex mental states from the expression in the eye region of the face.

Difficulties in mindreading in ASC appear to be early occurring, starting from at least the end of the first year of life, if one includes joint attention deficits, such as not following what other's are interested in. They also appear to be universal, if one tests for these either at the right point in development or by using sensitive, age-appropriate tests. Clues relating to the brain basis of the ToM difficulties in ASC are being gathered from functional neuroimaging studies.

References

Baron-Cohen, S. (1995). *Mindblindness: An essay on autism and theory of mind*. Cambridge, MA: MIT Press/Bradford Books.

Frith, U. (1989). *Autism: Explaining the enigma*. Oxford, UK: Blackwell.

Happé, F. (1996). *Autism*. London, UK: UCL Press.

Further Reading

Baron-Cohen, S., & Bolton, P. (2009). *Autism and Asperger Syndrome: The Facts*. Oxford, UK: Oxford University Press.

Baron-Cohen, S., Campbell, R., Karmiloff-Smith, A., Grant, J., & Walker, J. (1995). Are children with autism blind to the mentalistic significance of the eyes? *British Journal of Developmental Psychology, 13*, 379–398.

Baron-Cohen, S., Jolliffe, T., Mortimore, C., & Robertson, M. (1997). Another advanced test of theory of mind: Evidence from very high functioning adults with autism or Asperger syndrome. *Journal of Child Psychology and Psychiatry, 38*, 813–822.

Baron-Cohen, S., Tager-Flusberg, H., & Cohen, D. (Eds.). (1993). *Understanding other minds: Perspectives from autism*. Oxford, UK: Oxford University Press.

5

Q41
Can Bad Parenting Cause ASC?

Rita Jordan

ASC are a biological condition (or spectrum of conditions) where failures in social responsiveness at a perceptual and psychological level lead to developmental consequences with characteristic behavioral patterns that form the "symptoms" of the condition. Some of those behaviors will be common to other conditions and to cases of typical children who have had traumatic experiences that have affected development, including "bad" parenting. Before the biological base of autism was understood, judgments were made, based on the behavior alone and influenced by psychodynamic theories of child development, but such views of "refrigerator mothers" causing autism have long been discredited (Gillberg & Coleman, 2000). There is no evidence that bad parenting causes ASC, but bad parenting can cause developmental problems that may be confused with autism, as in the study of the children adopted from Romanian orphanages, some of whom, after severe and prolonged neglect and abuse, met criteria for autism, at least initially (Rutter & ERA study team, 1998).

It is a sad fact that parents of children with ASC have not only had to deal with the difficulties caused to them and their children by the condition, but have also had to fight ignorant attitudes (even displayed by some professionals) that have blamed them for their child's condition. As a result, parents and some professionals have emphasized (understandably) the biology of the condition and have ignored, or even denied, the role of parenting, not in causing ASC, but in influencing its outcome. It is only as knowledge of the biological base has become more secure that it has been acknowledged that, like other children, children with ASC benefit from supportive and facilitatory parenting. The problem is that what constitutes "good" or "bad" parenting of a child with an ASC may not be the same as for typical children. A blind child will need parents who understand the effects of blindness on development and can help the child understand the world in his/her own way; neither child nor parents will flourish if the parents just try to insist on the blind child behaving as if the child were able to see. Of course, in the case of blindness, the differences are recognized, and parents and child usually receive early support because it is not expected that the parents will automatically know how to help. In ASC, development is also different but the child may not even be identified as needing special support until much later, and very few countries offer parents good support in the special parenting skills they need. In fact, the more parents of children with ASC adapt to their child, the "odder" their behavior may seem to ignorant outsiders (e.g., holding their child away from them when the child is sitting on their lap to enable the child to tolerate this position) and the more the parents may be blamed for their child's different behavior.

When parents were blamed, they were often given "treatment," but this was shown to be ineffective, and programs such as Treatment and Education of Autistic and related Communication-handicapped Children (TEACCH; Mesibov, Shea, & Schopler, 2005), achieved far more success in seeing parents as part of the "solution" (i.e., as cotherapists), rather than as the problem. Since then, interventions have largely been directed at "fixing" the child, but this too is an unbalanced approach. Children with ASC, like other children, need to be treated with respect and enabled to develop to be as good as they can be on their own terms, not to have to try to behave in ways that make no sense to them. They need to fit in with the world but as part of its rich variety, not to assume we can, or should, be all the same. At last, interventions are being developed that help parents interact with their children with ASC that are respectful, sensitive, and helpful and these are beginning to show their effectiveness (e.g., Aldred, Green, & Adams, 2004). We need to recognize the value of helping parents and children with ASC understand each other and get pleasure from their interactions. In this way, the child with an ASC will develop socially, communicatively, and flexibly, and parents will learn to love and respect the child they have, while helping him/her to make the most of his/her talents and overcome any difficulties, just as they would for a child without an ASC.

References

Aldred, C., Green, J., & Adams, C. (2004). A new social communication intervention for children with autism: Pilot randomized controlled treatment study suggesting effectiveness. *Journal of Child Psychology and Psychiatry, 45,* 1420–1430.

Gillberg, C., & Coleman, M. (2000). *The Biology of the Autistic Syndromes.* (3rd ed.). Oxford, UK: MacKeith.

Mesibov, G. B., Shea, V., & Schopler, E. (2005). *The TEACCH approach to autism spectrum disorders.* New York, NY: Kluwer Academic/Plenum.

Rutter, M., & ERA study team (1998). Developmental catch-up, and deficit, following adoption after severe global early deprivation. *Journal of Child Psychology and Psychiatry, 39,* 465–476.

Section 6

Treatment of ASC

6

Q42
What Can Be Achieved by Treatment in ASC?

Patricia Howlin

There is a variety of approaches that, whilst not resulting in "cures" for ASC, can bring about improvements in many areas, including communication, social functioning, and behavioral difficulties. Intensive behavioral interventions are among the most widely evaluated, but there is also evidence, from a number of recent randomized control trials, that other nonintensive interventions, particularly those with a focus on communication and joint social interaction, can have a significant and positive impact on children's functioning (see Howlin, Magiati, & Charman, 2009).

Most interventions for ASC focus either on the principal deficits associated with the condition (social and communication impairments and stereotyped and ritualistic patterns of behavior) or the behavioral difficulties that can arise from these fundamental areas of impairment. Many different approaches have been reported as successful. Among the most effective interventions are those involving applied behavioral analysis, functional communication training, and those with a focus on improving communication skills and reciprocal social interactions. There is no evidence that any one type of intervention is *consistently* more effective than any other. Research also indicates that the effects of intervention are often relatively circumscribed. Thus, for example, programs to improve nonverbal communication do just that. They do not, in turn, tend to have a significant impact on verbal skills or broader cognitive functioning.

The focus of some recent research has shifted from attempts to demonstrate that any one program is better than all others (a somewhat naïve aim given the heterogeneity of ASC) to attempts to identify factors that may predict which subgroups of children are most likely to respond to different interventions. For example, within behavioral programs, there is some indication that pivotal response training may be more successful for children who are making more social initiations pre-intervention (Koegel, Koegel, Shoshan, & McNerney, 1999). Ingersoll, Schreibman, and Stahmer (2001), investigating the effects of an inclusive educational group program for toddlers with ASC, found that those with low social avoidance at baseline made more gains than those with initially high social avoidance. Kasari, Paparella, Freeman, and Jahromi (2008) explored the differential effects of training to enhance either joint attention (JA) or symbolic play (SP). Although, overall, JA training had a greater impact on expressive language than SP training, the effect of the JA program was most significant for children with the lowest levels of language pre-treatment. In a study comparing the Picture Exchange Communication System (PECS) with Responsive Education and Pre-linguistic Milieu Training (RPMT), Yoder and Stone (2006) found that, although RPMT significantly enhanced turn taking, joint attention, and initiation, initiations only increased in children with some initial joint attention skills. RPMT also seemed to be more successful when used by mothers showing higher responsivity. Children exposed to PECS, on the other hand, tended to show a greater increase in requesting behavior, although this effect was found only in children with initially low levels of initiation/joint interaction and higher levels of object exploration.

In summary, although behavioral strategies are an important element of many programs (perhaps especially in the early years) other elements that focus more specifically on social development and communication also need to be introduced in order to maximize progress. Moreover, wide variation in child characteristics and in responsiveness to treatment may require a far more individualized approach to intervention than can be delivered using manualized treatment packages (March, 2009).

There are concerns, too, that interventions proven to work in highly controlled experimental settings (efficacy trials) may prove less effective in real life settings. Rogers and Vismara (2008) note that those interventions with the strongest evidence base have been developed and evaluated primarily with children and families from white, often middle-class backgrounds. Their effectiveness for ethnically diverse groups remains untested.

Finally, it is important to remember that ASC persist throughout life. The types of intervention needed in early childhood, which focus mainly on behavior and communication, may be very different to those required in adolescence or adulthood, when social, emotional, and mental health problems may be of greater concern. Thus, there is a need for provision that can both monitor and meet individuals' changing needs over the years. Indeed, the provision of specialized interventions for adults with ASC remains woefully inadequate and constitutes a major challenge for the future.

References

Howlin, P., Magiati, I., & Charman, T. (2009). A systematic review of early intensive behavioural interventions (EIBI) for children with autism. *American Journal of Intellectual & Developmental Disability, 114,* 23–41.

Ingersoll, B., Schreibman L., & Stahmer, A. (2001). Brief report: Differential treatment outcomes for children with autistic spectrum disorder based on level of peer social avoidance. *Journal of Autism and Developmental Disorders, 31,* 343–349.

Kasari, C., Paparella, T, Freeman, S., & Jahromi, L. B. (2008). Language outcome and autism: Randomized comparison of joint attention and play interventions. *Journal of Consulting and Clinical Psychology, 76,* 125–137.

Koegel, L. K., Koegel, R. L., Shoshan, Y., & McNerney, E. (1999). Pivotal response intervention II: Preliminary long-term outcome data. *Journal of the Association for Persons with Severe Handicaps, 24*,186–198.

March, J. S. (2009). The future of psychotherapy for mentally ill children and adolescents. *Journal of Child Psychology and Psychiatry, 50*, 170–179.

Rogers, S. J., & Vismara, L. A. (2008). Evidence based comprehensive treatments for early autism. *Journal of Clinical Child and Adolescent Psychology, 37*, 3–38.

Yoder, P. J., & Stone, W. L. (2006). Randomized comparison of two communication interventions for preschoolers with autism spectrum disorders. *Journal Consulting and Clinical Psychology, 74*, 426–435.

Further Reading

Howlin, P. (2010). Psychological treatments for children with autism spectrum disorders: how good is the evidence base? *Advances in Psychiatric Treatment, 16*, 133–140.

6

Q43
How Can Outcome Be Measured in ASC?

Patricia Howlin

Although there are treatments for ASC that claim to be effective, drawing conclusions about whether one intervention works better than another is made difficult by the fact that outcome can be measured in many different ways. Some interventions simply provide anecdotal accounts of progress, often focusing only on children who have improved during treatment without describing those who have not responded so well. Others rely mainly on parent reports, and although these are very important, parents who have spent a great deal of time, energy, and sometimes money on a particular intervention, may not always be the most objective judges.

Single case reports and small group studies can be valuable in indicating *potentially* effective treatments, but these are not, of themselves, adequate to demonstrate that a particular treatment is successful. For example, children might have made just as much progress had they not had the treatment at all. Comparing separate groups of children, those who have the treatment and those who do not, is more informative, but, unless they are randomly assigned to treatment (i.e., parents cannot choose which intervention their child will get), the findings may be subject to systematic bias. For example, parents who choose the "new" treatment may be better informed, or their children more able, than parents who are willing to accept "treatment as usual. " Therefore, it would not be surprising if children in the latter group made less progress. Randomized control trials, in which children are randomly assigned to one form of treatment or another, are the strongest way of demonstrating the effectiveness of treatment. However, they are difficult and often expensive to run. Carefully controlled studies, in which the children who receive the experimental treatment are well matched with the children who do not, can also provide important data.

Recent reviews of interventions for children with ASC stress that if research and, hence, practice in this area are to improve, a number of specific guidelines need to be followed (Howlin, Magiati, & Charman, 2009; Reichow, Volkmar, & Cicchetti, 2008; Smith et al., 2008). Thus, information on the characteristics of all the children in both the treatment and comparison groups (i.e., age, IQ, language level, severity of autism, etc.) should be collected immediately before treatment starts. Diagnosis should be confirmed, using standardized and objective measures. The age at which children begin treatment, the quality of that treatment, and the duration and intensity of intervention should be documented. Data on the quality/intensity/duration of the alternative treatment(s) should also be collected.

The important issue then is to decide which measures should be used to assess the impact of the treatment on children's progress. As noted, it is not enough to rely on parental reports alone, not just because of possible bias, but also because these reports are too subjective to be used for comparisons between studies. Nevertheless, although it is crucial to use standardized measures, there is no general agreement on which to choose. IQ is often the principal outcome measure chosen, and the most commonly used IQ tests for young children with ASC include the Mullens Scales of Early Learning and the various Wechsler tests (WPPSI, WISC and WASI). However, as tests can vary from study to study and from baseline to follow-up within the same study, these inconsistencies can result in spurious conclusions about the extent of cognitive change. Moreover, IQ tests are not constructed to be particularly sensitive to change, and there is no a priori reason why change in IQ should be the principal goal of intervention. For example, a child may show increases in IQ following treatment without this improving the child's ability to function in social situations or reflecting improvements in behavior or autistic symptomatology. Therefore, it is important to choose measures that directly reflect the specific aims of treatment.

If the goal is to improve language, then communication assessments should be the primary outcome measure. Language can be measured by direct assessment of various different aspects of communication (e.g., the Reynell Scales of Receptive and Expressive Language or the Clinical Evaluation of Language Fundamentals (CELF-4)). Other commonly used measures include the Peabody Picture Vocabulary Test, the British Picture Vocabulary Test, and the Expressive One-Word Picture Vocabulary Test (EOWPVT). However, although the age range for these latter tests is relatively wide (from around 2 years to adulthood), they examine only very circumscribed aspects of language, and basal levels may be too high for very young children with ASC. The MacArthur Communicative Development index (CDI) can be used to assess language abilities in even the youngest or most linguistically impaired children. Although based on parental report, the data from this measure have been found to correlate well with other standardized, direct assessments of language. The Vineland Adaptive Behavior Scales' (VABS; Sparrow, Balla, & Cicchetti, 2000) Communication subscale, also based on parental information, is another potentially useful measure for children who are very young or have limited language. When reporting language outcomes, it is also important to provide age equivalents and standard scores, as raw scores alone are not adequate to make comparisons between different studies.

For some treatments, the main goal is a reduction in behavior problems, in which case a measure that can be given to both parents and teachers, such as the Developmental Behaviour Checklist, can be very useful (Einfeld & Tonge, 1995). Other interventions may have a focus on improving self help and daily living skills. The VABS are among the best standardized measures in this field and have been used to assess outcome in many behavioral intervention programs. They also cover a broad age range (from infancy to adulthood).

Many recent intervention studies have focused on reducing the severity of autistic symptoms and, hence, have used measures such as the Autism Diagnostic Interview-Revised (ADI-R) or the Autism Diagnostic Observation Schedule (ADOS). However, although considered among the most reliable and valid diagnostic measures of ASC, both have some limitations. The ADI-R relies on parental report whilst the structured setting of the ADOS may result in some children (particularly those who are older or more able) failing to show the full range of behaviors that characterize ASC. Moreover, neither instrument was specifically constructed to monitor change and hence they are not necessarily sensitive to changes that have occurred during intervention.

There are, of course, many other standardized measures that can be used to assess change across a wide range of different behaviors, and it is often important to include measures of family functioning (e.g., stress, parental well-being, family support, etc.) in order to monitor the impact of intervention on parents. The choice of which particular measure to use will depend largely on the goal of the intervention involved, but, as far as possible, interventions with a focus on the same area of development should ensure that comparable outcome measures are used across studies. Otherwise, it is not possible to compare one treatment or study with another. If novel treatments are involved, it may be necessary to develop new assessments that reflect the specific aims of the intervention. If this is the case, then it is essential to ensure that progress is recorded in an objective way and that outcome is measured by independent observers, who are *not* involved in the intervention treatment and who do *not* know which treatment the children have received. Video recordings can also help to avoid bias. Individual change can also be measured in an objective way using Goal Attainment Scaling (GAS; Turner-Stokes, 2009), which is a method, developed from health psychology, that allows very specific goals to be set for *individual* children but also allows for statistical analysis on a group level. Finally, of course, it is always necessary to establish the reliability (i.e., agreement between different raters) of the data collected.

References

Howlin, P., Magiati, I., & Charman, T. (2009). A systematic review of early intensive behavioural interventions (EIBI) for children with autism. *American Journal of Intellectual and Developmental Disabilities, 114*, 23–41.

Einfeld, S., & Tonge, B. (1995). The Developmental Behavior Checklist: The development and validation of an instrument to assess behavioral and emotional disturbance in children and adolescents with mental retardation. *Journal of Autism and Developmental Disorders, 25*, 81–104.

Reichow, B., Volkmar, F. R., & Cicchetti, D. V. (2008). Development of the evaluative method for evaluating and determining, evidence-based practices in autism. *Journal of Autism and Developmental Disorders, 38*, 1311–1319.

Smith, T., Scahill, L., Dawson, G., Guthrie, D., Lord, C., Odom, S., ... Wagner, A. (2007). Designing research studies on psychosocial interventions in autism. *Journal Autism and Developmental Disorders, 37*, 354–366.

Sparrow, S., Balla, D., & Cicchetti, D. (2000). *Vineland Adaptive Behavior Scales* (2nd ed.), San Antonio, TX: Pearson.

Turner-Stokes, L. (2009). Goal attainment scaling (GAS) in rehabilitation: A practical guide. *Clinical Rehabilitation, 23*, 362–370.

6

Q44
Are There Any General Criteria for Good Treatments of ASC?

Susanne Nußbeck

An ASC diagnosis encompasses a wide range of individual differences in terms of cognitive and language development, behavior, as well as social and communication skills. Numerous treatments are offered to individuals with ASC. Most of the treatments are passionately promoted by their advocates. Some treatments are controversial, promising rapid, miraculous healing. Some are restricted to the specific problems of individuals with ASC. In wishing the best for their child, parents are typically prone to any treatment irrespective of the absence of scientific grounding. Moreover, many health and educational professionals support unproven practices. Therefore, the question arises if there are any general criteria to separate the wheat from the chaff.

First of all, we have to consider that there is currently no cure for ASC. Some treatments appear to help individuals lead more productive lives by reducing the frequency of challenging behaviors and the severity of problems, facilitating development, as well as enabling greater independence and enjoyment of life. Conventional therapies focus on educational interventions to address skill acquisition to overcome the specific problems associated with ASC. Outcomes of validated treatments, generally, involve increasing these skills in specific areas. Treatments that postulate quick healing or recovery by holding one simple core deficit (e.g., deficiencies in the auditory or visual processing) responsible for the whole range of symptoms are generally suspected to be ineffective. The same applies to treatments that are reported to be appropriate to any disorder across a wide range of conditions regardless of etiology, nosology, and pathology. Good treatments define a target group that benefits from the intervention and rule out boundary conditions. In the case of ASC, the wide variation of behaviors and skills requires that specific target subgroups are defined according to the level of cognitive functioning, communication skills, and challenging behavior. Good treatments take these differences into account.

In order to be empirically testable, the goals of a treatment have to be clearly formulated in terms of specific outcomes. Benefits like "enhanced learning," "increased focus," "improved body awareness," "greater well-being," or "better sense of self" remain vague and stay outside testability. Nevertheless, if these promises hold, fundamental changes should translate readily into observable change of behavior (Smith, 2005). Additionally, the concept of treatment should be recorded carefully and made transparent. Therefore, structured training of the intervention strategies should be available. In sum, the description of a good treatment allows for the prediction of which effects can be expected for which group of individuals caused by which particular techniques. Treatments that are associated with particular "gurus" or single institutions have to be assessed with scrutiny (Herbert, Sharp, & Gaudiano, 2002).

Nearly all newly proposed treatments start with an idea from health or educational practitioners, who are trying out different strategies in the urge of acting and for lack of sound treatments. These new fads and movements are neither good nor bad, per se (Favell, 2005). Usually, their assumed success is disseminated by testimonials, as anecdotes from parents or case reports. They are rapidly promoted as miracle or break-through via web and self-help groups. However, good treatments go beyond that level. Their assumptions are explicitly and unambiguously stated so that anybody with expertise in the field can agree on the meaning. Additionally, the key terms are operationalized (i.e., "translated" into observable and measurable terms) (Newsom & Hovanitz, 2005). These operational definitions allow for the evaluation and verification of treatment success and allow for replication. In short, good treatments are testable for the scientific community. Thus, researchers and practitioners can test if the reported success of a treatment is not confined to one individual with ASC, one practitioner/researcher, or other unique and nonrepeatable set of circumstances. In testing interventions, one will usually find a variety of responses to a treatment, depending on the level of functioning and surrounding conditions. In most cases, there are only small steps of improvement. Exaggerated claims of effectiveness outside the range of established procedures, generally, do not stand up to verification.

6

Good treatments face up to evaluation in controlled studies. These studies do not have to consist of large samples and be quantitative in nature; a set of strongly controlled single case studies may do as well. However, only under controlled conditions can an intervention prove to functionally cause the claimed effects. Scientifically grounded proceeding entails looking for refutation, not for confirmation, and therefore, takes alternative explanations into account. Results comprise probability and doubt, not certainty. Proponents of unsubstantiated fads select empirical data and highlight confirming results while unsupportive results are reinterpreted or simply ignored (Lilienfeld, Lynn, & Lohr, 2003).

Although many empirically validated treatments were initially not derived from scientific theories, they are consistent with known principles about human behavior and physiology. Any treatment needs plausible and scientifically founded explanations of what is supposed to cause the effects. If this is not the case, it must, at least, not contradict established empirically tested theories. Unsubstantiated fads usually rely on implausible theories that cannot be proven false and eclectically select single simplified explanation bound to scientific-like assumptions. Good treatment continues to develop in line with scientific progress, whereas fads usually do not. After all, the effects of any good treatment have to be observable in everyday life with sustained yield.

References

Favell, J. E. (2005). Sifting sound practice from snake oil. In J. W. Jacobson, P. M. Foxx, & J. A. Mulick (Eds.), *Controversial therapies for developmental disablities: Fad, fashion, and science in professional practice* (pp. 19–29). Mahwah, NJ: Erlbaum.

Herbert, J. D., Sharp, I. R., & Gaudiano, B. A. (2002). *Separating fact from fiction in the etiology and treatment of autism: A scientific review of the evidence.* Retrieved from www.quackwatch.com.

Lilienfeld, S. O., Lynn, S. J., & Lohr, J. M. (2003). Science and pseudoscience in clinical psychology: Initial thoughts, reflections, and considerations. In S. O. Lilienfeld, S. J. Lynn, & J. M. Lohr (Eds.), *Science and pseudoscience in clinical psychology* (pp. 1–14). New York, NY: Guilford.

Newsom, C., & Hovanitz, C. A. (2005). The nature and value of empirically validated interventions. In J. W. Jacobson, P. M. Foxx, & J. A. Mulick (Eds.), *Controversial therapies for developmental disablities: Fad, fashion, and science in professional practice* (pp. 31–43). Mahwah, NJ: Erlbaum.

Smith, T. (2005). The appeal of unvalidated treatments. In J. W. Jacobson, P. M. Foxx, & J. A. Mulick (Eds.), *Controversial therapies for developmental disabilities:Fad fashion and science in professional practice* (pp. 45–57). Mahwah, NJ: Erlbaum.

Further Reading

Jacobson, J. W., Foxx, P. M., & Mulick, J. A. (Eds.), (2005). *Controversial therapies for developmental disabilities: Fad fashion and science in professional practice.* Mahwah, NJ: Erlbaum.

Lilienfeld, S. O., Lynn S. J., & Lohr, J. M. (2003). *Science and pseudoscience in clinical psychology.* New York, NY: Guilford.

6

Q45
What Are Evidence-Based Treatments?

Scott O. Lilienfeld & James D. Herbert

By evidence-based treatments, mental health professionals mean interventions that are supported by high-quality research data about what works. Many authors refer to a "3-legged stool" of evidence-based practice, which includes (a) research evidence, (b) clinical experience, and (c) patient preferences and values (APA Task Force on Evidence-Based Practice, 2006). Here, we emphasize the first leg, research evidence, given the vast and often bewildering array of interventions for ASC, only a minority of which is based on solid scientific evidence. The evidence-based practice movement, which originated several decades ago in the field of traditional medicine, is gathering momentum in psychology, psychiatry, social work, and other domains of mental health practice (Spring, 2007).

The scientific support for evidence-based treatments for ASC derives from 2 major types of research designs. The first is the *randomized controlled trial* (RCT). In RCTs, investigators randomly assign some individuals with ASC to receive an intervention, which could be either psychological (e.g., a behavioral intervention) or biological (e.g., a medication) in nature. These individuals constitute the "experimental group." Investigators then randomly assign other individuals with ASC to receive either no treatment or, ideally, a "placebo" treatment (in the case of medication studies, typically a sugar pill that contains no active ingredients), which controls for positive expectations of improvement. These individuals constitute the "control group." By randomly assigning individuals to experimental and control groups, researchers minimize the possibility that preexisting differences between these groups, such as differences in gender or the severity of their conditions, contribute to differences in treatment outcome. If the study was properly conducted, and if individuals in the experimental group improve significantly more than individuals in the control group, we can tentatively conclude that the intervention is effective. If several such studies conducted by independent research teams yield similar findings, we can typically regard the treatment as evidence-based. Although RCTs are generally considered the "gold standard" of research designs, they tend to be expensive and time-consuming to conduct. Perhaps largely as a result, relatively few RCTs have been conducted on ASC, especially for nonmedication treatments.

6

The second type of research design on which evidence-based treatments are based is the *single-subject study*, in which each individual with an ASC serves as "his or her own control." In single-subject studies, investigators systematically observe individuals' behavior when a treatment, such as a behavioral intervention, is absent, as well as when it is present. For example, researchers might administer a treatment for a specific period of time, then withdraw it, then re-administer it, and then withdraw it again, all the while carefully monitoring one or more "target" behaviors (e.g., physical aggression, eye contact with adults). If target behaviors consistently improve when the intervention is delivered, but not when it is removed, a compelling case can be made that the intervention is evidence-based. Although single-subject studies often allow reasonably strong inferences for the individuals tested, they do not permit strong generalizations to other individuals. As a result, it is crucial that such studies be replicated for multiple persons with ASC.

Many parents and teachers, understandably, wonder why RCTs and single-subject studies are needed to determine whether a treatment works. After all, can't we merely (a) administer a treatment, (b) wait a while, say a few weeks, and (c) look to see whether the individual has improved? Although intuitively appealing at first glance, this approach to ascertaining treatment effectiveness is problematic, because the individual may have improved for a host of reasons unrelated to the treatment itself. Putting it a bit differently, improvement *following* a treatment does not necessarily imply improvement *because of* a treatment. For example, individuals with an ASC might get better after a treatment because of (a) spontaneous improvement (i.e., getting better on their own), (b), placebo effects (i.e., improvement resulting merely from the expectation of improvement) or (c), regression to the mean, a phenomenon that refers to the tendency of extreme scores to become less extreme after retesting. Regression to the mean is a particular problem for many symptoms of ASC that often vacillate in severity over brief time periods. If we administer a treatment when a symptom, such as yelling in response to frustration, becomes especially problematic, we may find that this symptom improves shortly thereafter. However, this improvement may merely reflect regression to the mean and be unrelated to the treatment. Another set of problems with looking for changes over time concerns how symptoms are observed and measured. Parents, teachers, and even therapists can sometimes be biased in their observations, noticing apparent improvement in an area, because they expect to see it even when no real improvement occurred. High quality studies, whether RCTs or single-subject studies, use objective, systematic measures to avoid the biases inherent in informal observations.

Because other entries in this volume focus on specific evidence-based treatments for ASC, we do not offer an exhaustive list of such treatments here. Nevertheless, interventions based on applied behavior analysis (ABA) qualify as evidence-based treatments for ASC. Although ABA does not "cure" the core features of these conditions, RCTs and single-subject studies suggest that it yields significant improvements in multiple target domains, including social skills, language, and aggression.

It is equally important for parents, teachers, and clinicians to be aware of which treatments are *not* evidence-based. Non-evidence-based treatments for

ASC fall into two classes: (1) Treatments that have not yet been adequately tested and (2) treatments that *have* been adequately tested and shown not to work. Largely or entirely untested treatments may eventually be shown to be effective in well-controlled studies. However, parents, teachers, and mental health professionals should regard them with caution, because some of them could turn out to be ineffective or even harmful. Such treatments for ASC include art therapy, music therapy, Son-Rise, vision therapy, herbal remedies (e.g., Valerian, Gingko biloba), hyperbaric oxygen treatment, antifungal treatments, and CranioSacral therapy. In rare circumstances, a few of these interventions may be justified when multiple evidence-based treatments have been tried and failed. Nevertheless, when deciding whether to administer these interventions, mental health professionals must carefully weigh the potential costs against the potential benefits and must inform clients (if they are capable of providing informed consent) and their families that these treatments are experimental.

In contrast, some treatments for ASC have been tested repeatedly and found to be largely or entirely ineffective. Examples of these interventions are facilitated communication, auditory integration training, psychoanalytic play therapy, secretin, glutein-free diets, and heavy metal detoxification (chelation therapy) (Herbert, Sharp, & Gaudiano, 2002; Smith, 2008). Such interventions are, at best, a waste of time and resources, and, at worst, potentially harmful. Barring the appearance of new scientific evidence that contradicts previous conclusions, these interventions are not recommended for individuals with ASC.

References

APA Task Force on Evidence Based Practice (2006). Report of the 2005 Presidential Task Force on Evidence-Based Practice. *American Psychologist, 61*, 271–285.

Herbert, J. D., Sharp, I. R., & Gaudiano, B. A. (2002). Separating fact from fiction in the etiology and treatment of autism: A scientific review of the evidence. *Scientific Review of Mental Health Practice, 1*, 25–45.

Smith, T. (2008). Empirically supported and unsupported treatments for autism spectrum disorders. Scientific Review of Mental Health Practice, *6*, 3–20.

Spring, B. (2007). Evidence-based practice in clinical psychology: What it is, why it matters, and what you need to know. *Journal of Clinical Psychology, 63*, 611–631.

6

Q46
Is There a Standard Treatment for All Individuals With ASC?

Wendy Froehlich & Linda Lotspeich

There is no "standard" treatment for all people with ASC. There is no single treatment that is able to address either all the symptoms of autism for some individuals or specific symptoms for all individuals. However, some treatments may help some individuals with various aspects of the disorder. Unlike some medical disorders, where a given condition produces relatively predictable symptoms (e.g., asthma causes breathing difficulties or diabetes causes high levels of sugar in the blood), autism can produce a wide range of varying symptoms in different individuals. Although all children with ASC have some kind of deficit in socialization and either restrictive or stereotyped behaviors, the problem areas within each of these categories and any other accompanying symptoms may be quite different from person to person. Some may have extensive communication difficulties and be completely nonverbal, while others may have "genius" level verbal IQ's and be described as "little professors" because of their extensive vocabularies. Some may become frustrated due to their difficulties establishing and maintaining friendships while others may have no interests in forming friendships at all. Some children may have significant oversensitivities to stimuli, such as sound and touch. Others may have significant undersensitivities. Because each child with autism possesses a unique subset of symptoms, it is important to tailor a treatment program to the individual needs of the child.

With recent advances in technology and the internet, it is easy for information to be disseminated widely using search engines and advertisements. This has both pros and cons. On one hand, parents and providers can readily read about various treatments being tried, success stories, and novel approaches. However, some of these approaches carry dangerous risks and/or can be extremely costly. One must be very careful to examine where information arises from in order to not only avoid becoming the target of scams, but also to avoid inappropriate and dangerous treatments. Even well-intended individuals with personal success stories may not understand the dangers associated with given treatments. Furthermore, it is impossible to pursue every treatment in an effort to find "the best one," and parents and providers may feel overwhelmed not only by the possibilities, but by the guilt of not being able to try every proposed treatment. Therefore, treatment teams should generally begin with scientifically proven interventions when designing treatment plans.

6

Q47
What Are the Best Scientifically Proven Interventions for ASC?

Wendy Froehlich & Linda Lotspeich

In today's society, clinicians, therapists, and educators rely upon what are known as "evidence-based-treatments" to help guide treatment decisions. Evidence-based treatment refers to using well-designed, scientific studies to determine the benefits and risks of treatments. Until recently, there has been little formal guidance as to which treatments for which symptoms of ASC are supported by sound, evidence-based research. However, in the past several years, national organizations have begun to conduct extensive reviews of scientific literature to help guide parents and providers in designing treatment plans appropriate for individual children. Organizations such as the American Academy of Child and Adolescent Psychiatry, the American Academy of Pediatrics, the American Academy of Child Neurology and the National Research Council are all interested in using evidence-based medicine to guide treatment recommendations for autism. While much remains to be learned, these scientific reviews are beginning to help clarify which treatments are scientifically shown to help children with ASC.

The many treatments for autism can *generally* be divided into two main categories: (1) Educational and behavioral treatments, such as educational interventions, developmental and behavioral therapies, communication interventions, social skills interventions, sensory-motor interventions, psychological therapies, and physical therapy; and (2) biologic treatments, including prescription medications, over-the-counter medications, nutritional supplements, and diet changes. The amount of scientific evidence supporting each of these treatments varies greatly. It is also not uncommon for individual studies investigating a specific treatment to have very different findings, depending on the group chosen for the study, the measures used to determine if a treatment was successful, and the statistics used to calculate the results. Typically, the best designed studies use either a single-case design, in which baseline measures of behavior in a given individual are compared to the individual's behaviors after a treatment is given; or a randomized controlled trial that compares a large sample of carefully chosen subjects, who are then randomly assigned to either receive the treatment being studied or not. Once studies are designed, carried out, and completed, the studies are then rigorously reviewed by experts in the field, before being accepted for publication in well-known scientific journals. Unfortunately, recruiting subjects that are representative of all children with autism, making sure treatment and control groups are otherwise equal and being certain that any improvements seen are truly due to the treatment (as opposed to other differences between the groups or misleading statistical methods), can be a near impossible task. Therefore, recommendations based on multiple studies and extensive reviews by experts are key and just beginning to emerge within the field. Unfortunately, however, there is still no one single published review that investigates all the studies on all possible therapies.

Although scientific studies and reviews of multiple scientific studies can help determine which treatments are effective, one must also consider which symptoms (or targets) an intervention is effective in treating. For example, one intervention may be very beneficial for teaching a child appropriate social response, but it may not address impairing rituals or routines. While many of the treatments available have overlapping targets, no one intervention focuses on all possible goals of treatment. Furthermore, most interventions are not exclusive of one another and may be combined into various multi-approach programs that occur throughout various settings, including the home, school, and community. Most importantly, despite the evidence supporting various interventions, because all individuals with ASC are unique, one should not assume that each of the supported treatments will work for every individual with autism or that any treatment will work to the same degree for one individual as another.

Of the main reviews that exist to date, one of the most inclusive for educational and behavioral therapies was recently published by the National Autism Center (2009) in a document known as the National Standards Report. This review was conducted by a panel of experts within the field of autism who examined 775 research studies covering a wide variety of treatment interventions for autism, but not including medications or nutritional supplements. From their findings, they categorized treatments into 11 established treatments (treatments with enough evidence to support favorable outcomes), 22 emerging treatments (treatments with some evidence to support favorable outcomes, but not enough to qualify as established), and five unestablished treatments (treatments with little or no evidence to support the treatment as being effective). The 11 established treatments were all behavior-based interventions. Most behaviorally based treatments involve techniques that can be learned and carried out by parents, caregivers, educators, and/or therapists.

Other large reviews include a report in *Pediatrics* (Myers, Johnson, & the Council on Children with Disabilities, 2007), the journal published by the American Academy of Pediatrics. This report investigated educational interventions and associated strategies (including Applied Behavior Analysis (ABA) therapy), structured teaching (such as the TEACCH model), developmental models (including the Denver Model and relationship-focused intervention models), speech and language therapy, social skills instruction, and occupational and sensory integration therapy. Most of these strategies had some scientific evidence to support their use in treating core symptoms of autism, but the degree to which the studies supported their respective efficacies varied. The review also discussed situations in which biologic treatments for coexisting seizures, gastrointestinal problems, sleep disturbances, and severe symptoms of potentially other coexisting psychiatric diagnoses may be appropriate.

While the aforementioned 2007 report in *Pediatrics* only briefly discussed complimentary and alternative medicines (CAMs), a more in-depth and recent review of CAMs for autism was published by Levy and Hyman (2008). CAMs include a wide variety of health therapies, practices, and products that are typically not considered to be part of conventional medicine. In regards to autism, several CAMs exist that fall into both categories of educational and behavioral interventions, as well as biologic treatments. Levy and Hyman investigated several studies of CAMs including yoga, music therapy, dietary supplements and diets, gastrointestinal medications, hyperbaric oxygen therapy, chelation, immune therapies, antibiotics, antifungal agents, chiropractic therapies, massage therapies, auditory integration, and transcranial magnetic stimulation. In general, none of these treatments had enough evidence to support their use to the same degree as the established treatments from the National Standards Report. Most of the CAM treatments had not been adequately studied to support their use from the standpoint of evidence-based treatment. A few had some evidence to suggest they may be helpful but required further study, and some showed evidence suggesting they should not be recommended as a routine treatment for autism.

Finally, a third large review from the M.I.N.D Institute at the University of California at Davis investigated early intervention treatments for children with autism aged 5 years and younger (Rogers & Vismara, 2008). The review focused mainly on educational and behavioral treatments, but also briefly reviewed the limited studies on medication for children with autism. In their conclusions, they highlighted that, while several different kinds of early treatments targeting the core symptoms of autism do seem to improve abilities and reduce the severity of autistic symptoms, more data is needed to decide which treatments work best for which children and how much improvement can be expected.

In general, most experts and organizations concur that, based on current scientific evidence, the most effective treatments for children with autism include a comprehensive program with educational, developmental, and behavioral strategies. These treatments currently have the most scientific evidence supporting their use in ASC. However, further studies need to be done to help clarify which of these treatments are most efficacious for which children with autism. Biologic treatments may play an additional role for some individuals with ASC in reducing certain symptoms associated with autism. However, medications do not treat the language or social deficits of autism. Similarly, further studies are needed to determine which specific medications work for which children with autism. With all types of treatments, perhaps the most important factor in devising a treatment plan begins with assembling a team of providers who create an accurate assessment of the individual's capabilities, needs, and reasonable short-term and long-term goals. In addition to parents and the child with autism, the team making treatment decisions should consist of multiple professionals trained in autism. It may include several different disciplines, such as teachers, behavior therapists, speech and language therapists, occupational and physical therapists, child psychiatrists, pediatricians, psychologists, and others.

From a purely scientific standpoint, those treatments with the most evidence to support their use should be implemented first. However, other treatments should be considered in certain cases where the most established treatments are deemed ineffective or inappropriate by the decision-making team. Research evidence should not be the only determinant in selecting a treatment program. It is crucial to consider the individual values and preferences of parents, service providers, and the person with autism. Per the expert panel from the National Standards Report (National Autism Center, 2009), "Treatment selection is complicated and should be made by a team of individuals who can consider the unique needs and history of the individual with an ASC along with the environments in which he or she lives." (p. 25)

References

Levy S. E., & Hyman S. L. (2008). Complementary and alternative medicine treatments for children with autism spectrum disorders. *Child and Adolescent Psychiatric Clinics of North America, 17*, 803–820.

National Autism Center. (2009). *National Standards Report: The national standards project – addressing the need for evidence-based practice guidelines for autism spectrum disorders*. Randolph, MA: National Autism Center. Retrieved from http://www.nationalautismcenter.org

Myers, S. M., Johnson C. P., & the Council on Children with Disabilities (2007). Management of children with autism spectrum disorders. *Pediatrics, 120*, 1162–1182.

Rogers, S. J., & Vismara, L. A. (2008). Evidence-based comprehensive treatments for early autism. *Journal of Clinical Child and Adolescent Psychology, 37*, 8–38.

6

Q48
Which ASC Treatments Are Ineffective or Lack a Sound Evidence Base?

Patricia Howlin

The internet abounds with promises of "miracle cures" for ASC. These cover a vast range, including pet therapies, psychoeducational therapies, such as the Waldon or Son-Rise programs, facilitated communication, cranial osteopathy, special diets, vitamin supplements, wearing tinted spectacles or listening to tapes of filtered sounds, clay baths, hyperbaric oxygen tents and salt crystal lamps to name but a few.

A valuable source of up-to-date information on commonly used treatments is the Research Autism website (www.researchautism.net), associated with the UK National Autistic Society. Over 100 interventions are currently listed, and the quality of evidence, both favorable and unfavorable, is rated by independent experts. The site covers developmental, educational, psychological, pharmacological, and "alternative" or "complementary" therapies (e.g., pet therapies, special diets, and vitamin supplements).

Unfortunately, as soon becomes clear, systematic, scientific evaluations indicate that claims of success are rarely substantiated, and, for most treatments, the evidence base is nonexistent. That is not to say that some of these therapies may not be helpful for *some* children. Interventions such as the Waldon or Son-Rise program, for example, incorporate educational and behavioral components that may certainly have some value. Sensory integration therapy may be helpful for children who show oversensitivity to specific sensory stimuli, and art and music are clearly important components of any good educational curriculum. However, it is the *claims* that are made for these therapies that are the main problem. *No* therapy works for all children, and, as far as can be established given the lack of sound research, the effects, if any, are much more circumscribed than their advocates would have us believe. It is difficult to understand, for example, how wearing tinted spectacles or undergoing 10 sessions of listening to tapes of filtered sound could have any major impact on the severity of ASC symptoms more widely.

Recent reviews indicate that 50–75% of parents try some form of alternative therapy at one time or another, and often several different interventions may be combined (Hanson et al., 2007; Levy & Hyman, 2005; Wong & Smith, 2006). Diets and/or vitamin supplement treatments are particularly popular, and their use is based on the premise that the symptoms of ASC may be caused by nutritional deficiencies that can be overcome by altering the dietary intake. Some diets involve increasing the intake of substances such as essential fatty acids, probiotics, vitamins, and minerals. Others involve a reduction in, or avoidance of, particular substances (e.g., Feingold Diet; gluten-, casein- or yeast-free diets, ketogenic diet, low salicylate diet) (see Adams, 2007). However, the theories underlying most dietary/vitamin treatments are generally weak and unproven. For example, there is no evidence that children with ASC, as a group, are deficient in basic vitamins or minerals. Thus, despite the positive claims, there is little scientific evidence of the effectiveness of such interventions. It is also important to note that special dietary and vitamin treatments can involve significant expense and inconvenience to families. Special or exclusion diets, for example, often impose strict limitations on what the individual can eat and this can give rise to major difficulties, especially in the case of children who already have very rigid or limited dietary habits.

It is understandable that families who want to do their best for their child are tempted by the optimistic promises made for many current therapies. Although many interventions for which there is no evidence, in themselves, may not do direct harm, damage can occur if pursuing ineffective and inappropriate treatments reduces the child's opportunity to profit from intervention approaches that are more effective. Some of the more intensive therapies (e.g., Son-Rise) also incur significant financial costs, as well as being very disruptive to family life. The challenge for professionals is to help parents look beyond the enthusiastic claims and impressive websites and to support them in identifying treatments that may best suit, not only their child, but their own needs as a family.

References

Adams, J. B. (2007). *Summary of Biomedical Treatments for Autism*. San Diego, CA: Autism Research Institute.

Hanson, E., Kalish, L. A., Bunce, E., Curtis, C., McDaniel, S., Ware, J., & Petry, J. (2007). Use of complementary and alternative medicine among children diagnosed with autism spectrum disorder. *Journal of Autism and Developmental Disorders, 37*, 628–636.

Levy, S. E., & Hyman, S. L. (2005). Novel treatments for autistic spectrum disorders. *Mental Retardation and Developmental Disabilities Research Reviews, 11*, 131–142.

Wong, H., & Smith, R. (2006). Patterns of complementary and alternative medical therapy use in children diagnosed with autism spectrum disorders. *Journal of Autism and Developmental Disorders, 36*, 901–909.

Further Reading

National Autism Center (2009). *National Standards Report- Addressing the need for evidence-based practice guidelines for autism spectrum disorders*. Randolph, MA: National Autism Center.

Q49
Which ASC Treatments May Cause Harm?

Patricia Howlin

Although there are many unproven claims for interventions for ASC, probably the most potentially harmful therapies are those based on the premise that autism is caused by toxins of various kinds (e.g., mercury from vaccines, lead, etc.). In fact, there is no evidence that these are a primary cause of ASC or that levels of toxins are elevated in the blood of children with autism. Nevertheless, "detoxification therapies" are becoming increasingly promoted. For example, chelation is a highly controversial, and potentially dangerous, intervention that involves using chemicals or other substances to "correct" the (presumed) chemical balance in the bodies of individuals with ASC. There is no reliable evidence that chelation is effective for this population, and the US National Institute for Mental Health has recently suspended a trial of chelation due to safety fears (Mitka, 2008). Some deaths have also been reported following the use of chelation therapy. Moreover, some commercially available chelating agents may already contain high levels of mercury. Other risks include: removal of essential minerals and vitamins from the body; increased risk of nausea, diarrhea, anorexia, fatigue, irritability, sleep disturbances and allergic reactions; worsening of autistic symptoms, and regression in language and behavior. Some chelating agents can also affect blood clotting, immune response to infections and other toxins, or cause lung, liver and kidney damage.

Other interventions that are potentially dangerous include the use of various drugs, mainly involving selective serotonin reuptake inhibitors (SSRIs) and tricycle medications, to modify the core symptoms of autism. Although such treatments may be effective for comorbid problems often associated with ASC (e.g., depression or agitation), there is little evidence that they have any positive effect on autism-specific behaviors. Information about the possible side effects of these drugs when used to treat children or adults with developmental disorders is very limited, although there is some indication that SSRIs may actually increase symptoms such as agitation.

Another potentially hazardous treatment involves immune globulin (given orally or by injection). This is an antibody used by the immune system to identify and neutralize bacteria and viruses. Its use is based on the belief that people with ASC are susceptible to immune deficiencies and that these deficiencies may produce some of the symptoms of autism. However there is no evidence that immune globulin is effective in the treatment of the majority of people with ASC: It is also expensive, inconvenient to use, and potentially harmful (Handen et al., 2009).

Secretin is a gastrointestinal hormone that helps promote digestion by stimulating the stomach to produce the enzyme pepsin, the liver to produce bile, and the pancreas to produce digestive juices that help neutralize acidity. It has been claimed that autism can be treated by taking secretin supplements, as this will prevent harmful chemicals from undigested food traveling to the brain. Again, there is no evidence that secretin treatment is effective (Sturmey, 2005). It can be very expensive and there are health risks arising from multiple injections, sometimes by unqualified practitioners.

Testosterone regulation involves using drugs, such as Leuprolide, to reduce the amounts of testosterone and estrogen in the body and has been suggested as a way of reducing sexually inappropriate behaviors in ASC. Those who believe that autism is caused by high levels of mercury also claim that reducing testosterone levels reduces the toxic effects of mercury. Leuprolide is a powerful drug designed to change the hormonal balance in adult men and women. Use on children or adolescents could cause irreversible damage to sexual functioning. It is also very expensive and there is no scientifically reliable research to show that Leuprolide is effective in reducing any of the problem behaviors associated with autism.

Other therapies may be hazardous for very different reasons. Facilitated communication (FC), for example, is a communication therapy in which a facilitator supports the individual client's hand, wrist, or arm while the client uses a keyboard or letter board to spell out words, phrases, or sentences. Not only is there no evidence that FC is effective (responses are almost invariably under the control of the facilitator, not the person with ASC (Mostert, 2001)), but there have been major concerns due to the many unsupported claims of sexual or physical abuse made by people with ASC while using this technique. The American Psychological Association (1994) concluded that FC is "a controversial and unproved procedure with no scientifically demonstrated support for its efficacy," and the American Academy of Pediatrics Committee on Children with Disabilities (1998) concluded that "there are good scientific data showing (FC) to be ineffective. Moreover, the potential for harm does exist, particularly if unsubstantiated accusations of abuse occur using FC." (p. 432)

Holding therapy, in which children are physically restrained in order to promote social contact with adults, or "packing," in which they are wrapped in cold wet blankets, have obvious physical and emotional risks. Strict exclusion diets may be potentially dangerous for children who already have very poor dietary intake. Another therapy that is to be discouraged, because of the potential physical risks, is Dolphin therapy, not only because of concerns about health dangers to humans, but equally because of the potential risks to the dolphins involved.

References

American Academy of Pediatrics Committee on Children with Disabilities (1998). Auditory integration training and facilitated communication for autism. *Pediatrics, 102*, 431–433.

American Psychological Association. (1994). Resolution on facilitated communication. Adopted in Council, August 14, 1994, p. 1–2. Los Angeles, CA.

Handen, B. L., Melmed, R. D., Hansen, R. L., Aman, M. G., Burnham, D. L., Bruss, J. B., & McDougle, C. J. (2009). A double-blind, placebo-controlled trial of oral human immunoglobulin for gastrointestinal dysfunction in children with autistic disorder. *Journal of Autism and Developmental Disorders, 39*, 796–805.

Mitka, M. (2008). Chelation therapy trials halted. *Journal of the American Medical Association, 300*, 2236.

Mostert, M. P. (2001). Facilitated communication since 1995: A review of published studies. *Journal of Autism and Developmental Disorders, 31*, 287–313.

Sturmey, P. (2005). Secretin is an ineffective treatment for pervasive developmental disabilities: A review of 15 double-blind randomized controlled trials. Research in Developmental Disabilities, 26, 87–97.

Further Reading

Santosh, P., & Baird, G. (2001). Pharmacotherapy of target symptoms in autistic spectrum disorders. *Indian Journal of Paediatrics, 68,* 427–431.

6

Q50
Why Is Early Intervention Important in ASC?

Zachary Warren & Wendy L. Stone

The unprecedented popular scientific, political, and media attention paid to ASC in recent years has created many controversies regarding the fundamental nature of autism and its optimal treatment. However, there is little controversy surrounding the importance of early intervention for young children with ASC. In recognition of the potential impact of early intervention, several professional groups, including the American Academy of Neurology, the American Academy of Child and Adolescent Psychiatry, the American Academy of Pediatrics, and the National Academy of Sciences have issued practice parameters endorsing early ASC screening and diagnosis in clinical settings. While there is at present no single accepted intervention, treatment, or known cure for ASC, there is growing consensus that early identification and appropriate intervention can significantly improve short- and long-term outcomes for individuals and their families. In short, early intervention is thought to be the best hope for the future for young children with ASC.

We are not far removed from an era when ASC was almost considered "untreatable." Individuals with ASC were once thought, as a rule, to display severe patterns of lifelong disability, including comorbid intellectual disabilities (i.e., mental retardation) and limitations in terms of achieving functional independence as adults. However, it is now clear that children who enter into autism-specialized intervention services at younger ages may show greater gains in cognitive and adaptive functioning and may be more likely to achieve fully integrated classroom placements at school age than children diagnosed at later ages (Cohen, Amerine-Dickens, & Smith, 2006; Harris & Handleman, 2000; Remington et al., 2007). Further, an increasing body of recent work suggests that the poor long-term outcomes traditionally associated with ASC (e.g., intellectual disability (ID), limited language) may not be as prevalent as once thought (Chakrabarti & Fombonne, 2005). Such changes in outcome are complex and are likely to be associated with many factors, including shifts in diagnostic practices. However, all available evidence suggests that early diagnosis and intervention can play a meaningful role in improving outcomes for children with ASC in the short and long term.

6

Fundamentally, early intervention provides children with instruction that builds on individual strengths to teach new skills, manage challenging behaviors, and remediate areas of vulnerability. As applied to young children with ASC, early intervention entails the use of specialized approaches and strategies to address deficits in social communication and minimize distress and impairment associated with atypical and rigid patterns of behavior. By addressing these specific areas of weakness at relatively early developmental time-points, early intervention programs may capitalize on the increased neurobehavioral plasticity presumed to be present at younger ages. Further, the remediation of deficits at young ages may serve to mitigate the cascading effects of early difficulties on later cognitive and skill development. In other words, the gaps between the social communication and behavioral development of children with ASC and typically developing children may be smaller at younger ages. Thus, early intervention may operate within an optimal window for making a significant long-term impact on development via relatively short-term treatment.

It is also important to recognize that the impact of early intervention extends beyond optimizing outcomes for children with ASC, and offers benefits for their families as well. There is mounting evidence that caregivers play a key role, not only by recognizing early signs of ASC, but also by fostering their child's social communicative and behavioral development. A critical aspect of early intervention is providing parents with specific information to better understand their child's behavior and needs, as well as specific techniques to address developmental vulnerabilities across a variety of settings. In addition, the presence of a child with ASC can have a substantial impact on a family, with parents frequently experiencing heightened stress and everyday challenges. By offering a family component, in terms of resources, support, and training, early intervention can help parents learn to work and play more effectively with their child with ASC. In this regard, early intervention can be important for minimizing distress and enhancing the quality of life for family members caring for children with ASC, in addition to providing support to those who can make a tremendous impact in terms of optimizing child-focused outcomes within the context of everyday routines (Stone & DiGeronimo, 2006).

Caring for a child with ASC places stressors not only on parents, but also on the larger community and its systems of care. Effective and appropriate treatment of ASC often comes with substantial financial costs for school, medical, behavioral, and other social systems (Järbrink & Knapp, 2001). The cost of this treatment presumably increases in direct relation to the cumulative impairments in the core and associated features of ASC. From a public health perspective, early intervention via remediation of deficits in the short-term may lessen the long-term functional impairments related to ASC. Thus, early intervention may ultimately reduce the considerable lifetime costs and service system demands associated with providing care and support to individuals with ASC and their families.

References

Chakrabati, S., & Fombonne, E. (2005). Pervasive developmental disorders in preschool children: Confirmation of high prevalance. *American Journal of Psychiatry, 162,* 1133–1141.

Cohen, H., Amerine-Dickens, M. S., & Smith, T. (2006). Early intensive behavioral treatment: Replication of the UCLA model in a community setting. *Journal of Developmental and Behavioral Pediatrics, 27,* 145–155.

Harris, S. L., & Handleman, J. S. (2000). Age and IQ at intake as predictors of placement for young children with autism: A four-to six-year follow-up. *Journal of Autism and Developmental Disorders, 30,* 137–142.

Järbrink, K., & Knapp, M. (2001). The economic impact of autism in Britain. *Autism, 5,* 7–22.

Remington, B., Hastings, R. P., Kovshoff, H., degli Espinosa, F., Jahr, E., Brown, T., ... Ward, N. (2007). Early intensive behavioral intervention: Outcomes for children with autism and their parents after two years. *American Journal of Mental Retardation, 112,* 418–438.

Stone, W. L. & DiGeronimo, T. (2006). *Does my child have autism? A parent's guide to early detection and intervention in autism spectrum disorders.* San Francisco, CA: Wiley.

Further Reading

Dawson, G. (2008). Early behavioral intervention, brain plasticity, and the prevention of autism spectrum disorder. *Development and Psychopathology, 20,* 775–803.

Rogers, S. J., & Vismara, L. A. (2008). Evidence-based comprehensive treatments for autism. *Journal of Clinical Child and Adolescent Psychology, 37,* 8–38.

6

Section 7

Specific Treatment Approaches in ASC

Q51

How Can the Behavior Challenges of Individuals with ASC Be Managed in Everyday Life?

Vera Bernard-Opitz

ASC tend to make everyday life difficult for the affected individual, as well as for those within their environment. For the individual with autism, over- or under-sensitivity to sensory stimuli and communicative and social deficits are major challenges. Sensory problems are seen in about 90% of individuals with ASC and are considered core features by many specialists (Geschwind, 2009). Educators and parents also struggle with noncompliance, oppositional or negativistic behavior, and sometimes even severe aggression or self-abusive behavior. In addition, eating and sleeping problems are common and can be quite disruptive to family life. Even in individuals with advanced cognitive skills or specialized skills, rituals or obsessive behaviors can have a significant impact on the social environment (Dominik, Davis, Lainhart, Tagar-Flushberg, & Folstein, 2007).

Making sense of their children's behavior has been an important agenda for parents faced with issues such as: Why does my child close his ears, throw frequent tantrums or refuse to eat anything new? Why does he/she constantly talk about one topic and ignore the interests of the listeners? Understanding underlying reasons of behavior problems has been the focus of behavior analysts as well. We now know that treatment methods are most successful if they are closely matched to the specific function of the problem. Over the last 15 years, the field of behavior analysis has developed practices that focus on the function(s) of problem behavior in order to prevent problems and to develop and teach positive alternatives (Horner, 2000). Through observations, interviews, or experimental manipulations, factors triggering and maintaining behavior challenges are explored, specifically, which events, settings, people, or times elicit a behavior and which consequences maintain the problem.

When dealing with behavior challenges, *prevention* is the first "line of defense." If a child acts up because of oversensitivity to sounds, preventing exposure to noisy environments or masking loud sounds through earplugs or headphones may be useful first steps. Catching first steps of behavior chains is another important strategy that can be used in everyday settings. Often se-

7

vere problems announce themselves in minor problems, such as irritability or negativism. Being hungry, tired, rushed, or frustrated often constitutes a breeding ground for bigger issues. If caught before behavior escalates, more difficult problems, such as meltdowns or aggression can often be prevented.

If medical issues, such as digestive problems, ear-infections, or other medical symptoms covary with the behavior challenges, taking care of these is obviously a first step. For some individuals, *pharmacological treatment* can be a crucial part of the solution. In the case of sleep problems, normalizing sleep-patterns can improve the child's overall behavior. Comorbid conditions such as ADHD often respond well to specifically tailored stimulant medication (Buitelaar & Willemsen-Swinkels, 2000).

Other individuals, most likely constituting the majority of children, will require behavioral and educational interventions to reduce challenging behaviors. In some cases, a *Functional Behavior Analysis (FBA)* may be recommended. Through experimental manipulation of variables potentially contributing to a problem behavior, the FBA identifies the biological, social, affective, and/or environmental factors leading to the behavior and the interventions that best address them (Cooper et al., 2007). Although a licensed behavior therapist is needed to explore these relations, parents and other family members remain a crucial part of the treatment team. The field of positive behavior support has grown rapidly over the last 10 years, as there is strong evidence that treatment methods are more successful if parents and other team members are involved in planning and implementing a program.

One of the useful strategies in a behavioral intervention is a focus on appropriate alternative behavior, instead of the challenging behavior. The general guideline "catch them being good" (before you end up struggling with a behavior challenge) is not only helpful for parents, but also for educators, siblings, and peers, who frequently benefit from training in *reinforcing positive alternative behaviors*. So, instead of telling the child, who climbs or runs away, "do not climb!" or "no running!," asking them to "come here," "sit down," or even,"throw this paper in the trash" has a higher chance of reducing the problem, especially if powerful reinforcers are used for following these instructions. In addition, positive instructions are less likely to be misunderstood by children, who focus only on the last part of an utterance (i.e., in this case: "...climb" or "...running"). For younger children, *compliance training* is often helpful for establishing responsiveness to simple commands, waiting behavior across different settings, or survival skills, such as traffic safety.

Many behavior problems are motivated by the wish to get attention, to avoid a demand, or to escape a difficult situation. Alternative positive ways to get attention or to communicate the need for an easier task, a break, or help can prevent problems motivated by these causes. Even nonverbal individuals have learned to indicate their needs more appropriately through hand signs or pictures, rather than through problem behaviors.

Children with ASC exhibit behavior challenges since they do not know what to expect and where, when, and how to do things. They may not know how long they have to do something and what will happen once the current situation has ended. Often a clearer presentation of the situation can prevent behavior problems. Through *visual support*, they understand more readily what is expected, where things happen, how to do things, and when things will be completed. Sequences of tasks and situations are visualized through pictures or words, replacing uncertainty and providing the preferred predictability (Bernard-Opitz & Häussler, 2010). Social stories, using words and pictures, help children anticipate what will happen in a social situation and prepare an appropriate response to it.

Consequential management is another positive response to challenging behavior. Individuals learn that their behavior leads to specific consequences, such as having to clean up after spilling something (restitution). Positive alternatives can be phrased, such as, "you can play the computer game quietly or you will have to leave the room." Choices can be visualized in contingency maps, so that children learn that positive behavior (e.g., asking to leave when it is too noisy) leads to positive consequences, while negative behavior (e.g., screaming) does not change the situation (Brown & Mirenda, 2006). *Token systems, behavior contracts, or video modeling* are other possible visual means to improve behavior in everyday settings (see Bernard-Opitz, 2007, for a summary).

For the last 15 years, the field of behavior analysis has been proven as a necessary basis for effective intervention. It tells us that, when dealing with behavior challenges, it is crucial to understand the individual function of the behavior problem and to match the respective intervention strategy to the individual with an ASC, as well as to their social environment. Another important general basis for behavior change is a social environment that encourages positive behavior, self-control and self-efficacy (Mesibov, 2004).

References

Bernard-Opitz, V. (2007). *Children with autism spectrum disorders: A structured teaching and experienced-based program.*Austin, TX: Pro Ed.

Bernard-Opitz, V., & Häussler, A. (2010). Praktische Hilfen für Kinder mit Autismus-Spektrum-Störungen (ASS): Fördermaterialien für visuell Lernende [Visual support for children with autism spectrum disorders]. Stuttgart, Germany: Kohlhammer.

Brown, K., & Mirenda, P. (2006). Contingency mapping: Use of a novel visual support strategy as an adjunct to functional equivalence training. *Journal of Positive Behavior Interventions, 8*, 155–164.

Buitelaar, J. & Willemsen-Swinkels, S. (2000). Medication treatment in subjects with autistic spectrum disorders. *European Child and Adolescent Psychiatry, 9*, 185–197.

Cooper, J. O., Heron, T. E., & Heward, W. L. (2007). *Applied Behavior Analysis (3rd ed.). Upper Saddle River, NJ: Pearson Education.*

Dominick, K. C., Davis, N. O., Lainhart, J., Tager-Flusberg, H., & Folstein, S. (2007). Atypical behaviors in children with autism and children with a history of language impairment. *Research in Developmental Disabilities, 28*, 145–162.

Geschwind, D. H. (2009). Advances in autism. *Annual Review of Medicine, 60*, 367–380.

Mesibov, G. (2004). Self-efficacy and students with autism. *Autism News of Orange County & the Rest of the World, 1*, 12–14.

7

Further Reading

Kern Koegel, L., Koegel, Ro. L., & Dunlap, G. (2001). *Positive Behavioral Support*. Baltimore, MD: Paul Brooks.

7

Q52

What is the Best Way to Treat Self-Injury, Aggression, and Stereotypy in ASC?

James K. Luiselli

Self-injury, aggression, and stereotypy are common behaviors demonstrated by people who have an ASC. Self-injury can produce tissue damage and health complications secondary to bodily harm (e.g., infections, contusions, etc.). Aggression poses a risk to parents, peers, and teachers. Stereotypy, sometimes referred to as ritualistic or perseverative behavior, interferes with learning and can be socially stigmatizing. Furthermore, people with ASC who have self-injury, aggression, and stereotypy often must receive educational and habilitation services within restrictive settings instead of their homes, schools, and the community-at-large.

The best way to treat self-injury, aggression, and stereotypy is to first identify the environmental "causes" of these behaviors. Professionals within the discipline of applied behavior analysis (ABA) have shown that a person's behavior is governed by the consequences it produces. Specifically, there are four behavior-consequence relationships:

Social positive reinforcement-attention: Behavior is described as being *attention maintained* when it produces pleasurable consequences, such as physical and verbal interaction with another person.

Social positive reinforcement-tangible: Behavior is described as being *tangible maintained* when it produces pleasurable consequences, such as access to food, toys, and activities.

Social negative reinforcement: Behavior is described as being *escape motivated* when it terminates (removes) an unpleasant condition or interaction, such as a compliance demand.

Automatic reinforcement: Behavior is described as being *automatically reinforced* when it produces pleasurable consequences, such as visual, auditory, and proprioceptive sensory stimulation.

In order to assess the environmental influences on self-injury, aggression, and stereotypy, a professional should conduct a functional behavioral assessment (FBA) or functional analysis (FA) (Hanley, Iwata, & McCord, 2003). An

7

FBA correlates problem behavior with environmental consequences through observation, direct measurement, and similar descriptive methods. With FA, environmental consequences are manipulated experimentally to isolate their controlling effects on problem behavior. The results of FBA and FA are used to formulate a treatment plan, as described below:

Social positive reinforcement: If self-injury, aggression, and stereotypy are reinforced by pleasurable social consequences, one component of treatment should be withholding these consequences immediately following the behaviors. For example, caregivers should not speak to or present a preferred object to a person who has an ASC when she/he demonstrates attention maintained and tangible maintained self-injury, aggression, and stereotypy. The next focus of treatment should be making the pleasurable social consequences contingent on behavior *other than* self-injury, aggression, and stereotypy. To illustrate, the parents of a child who has an ASC and self-injury could praise him/her enthusiastically when she performs any behavior that prevents her from harming herself. Similarly, an adult with an ASC who hits his peers could be treated by allowing him access to a favorite activity when he interacts cooperatively without aggression. In effect, positive reinforcement that maintains self-injury, aggression, and stereotypy is shifted so that it strengthens alternative behavior.

Negative social reinforcement: Recall that negative social reinforcement operates when problem behavior terminates an unpleasant condition or interaction. There are several treatment options when self-injury, aggression, and stereotypy have this function. One strategy is to reduce a person's motivation for escaping nonpreferred situations by increasing positive reinforcement for behavior, such as completing tasks, responding to instructions, and communicating properly. Another procedure is to decrease the "aversive" features of certain conditions and interactions, so that they no longer provoke escape-motivated behavior. In classrooms, for example, teachers can modify the duration, complexity, and effort requirements of instructional activities so that a child who has ASC does not learn to avoid them through self-injury, aggression, and stereotypy (Luiselli, 2008).

A procedure termed functional communication training (FCT) (Carr & Durand, 1985) also can be implemented to treat escape-motivated problem behavior. FCT entails teaching a person who has an ASC to request a "break" from difficult situations instead of engaging in self-injury, aggression, and stereotypy. These requesting responses can be verbalizations such as, "Can I stop now? " or nonverbal communication that conveys the same request via sign language or pointing to pictures.

Automatic reinforcement: When self-injury, aggression, and stereotypy are reinforced by behavior-contingent sensory consequences, treatment usually seeks to eliminate this source of reinforcement by substituting alternative stimulation. For example, the function of stereotypy in children and adults with an ASC, typically, is to access automatic reinforcement (Lerman & Rapp, 2006). In the case of a child, a stereotypy, such as repetitive hand clapping, might be reinforced by the consequent auditory stimulation. Treatment could be having the child play with music-producing toys, in effect, making a pleasurable sensory consequence contingent on a desirable leisure skill. As another example, an adult with an ASC may touch and stroke their hair frequently, a stereotypy that is maintained by tactile stimulation. Teaching the person to brush their hair appropriately could be an effective function-based treatment.

As outlined in these illustrations, successful treatment of self-injury, aggression, and stereotypy requires matching intervention procedures to behavior function. In situations where a child or adult with an ASC exhibits more than one of the behaviors, each treatment plan has to be matched accordingly, recognizing further that, most of the time, treatment plans include more than one procedure. Also, the focus of contemporary ABA treatment is teaching a person the skills necessary to support a meaningful lifestyle. Note, too, that pretreatment assessment should rule out acute and chronic medical conditions that might account for the problem behavior (Carr & Smith, 1995). Finally, treatment should be evaluated empirically by recording how frequently, and in what contexts, a person with an ASC exhibits self-injury, aggression, and stereotypy.

In some cases, medication may be prescribed in concert with a behavioral treatment plan for self-injury, aggression, and stereotypy. Different medications are used to alleviate conditions, such as depression and elevated anxiety, or to alter brain chemistry responsible for problem behavior. A combined behavioral-pharmacological intervention is typically considered for children and adults who have an ASC and have been nonresponsive to behavioral treatment alone or pose a severe risk to self, others, or the physical environment.

References

Carr, E. G., & Durand, V. M. (1985). Reducing behavior problems through functional communication training. *Journal of Applied Behavior Analysis, 18,* 111–126.

Carr, E. G., & Smith, C. E. (1995). Biological setting events for self-injury. *Mental Retardation and Developmental Disabilities Research Reviews, 1,* 94–98.

Hanley, G. P., Iwata, B. A., & McCord, B. E. (2003). Functional analysis of problem behavior: A review. *Journal of Applied Behavior Analysis, 36,* 147–185.

Lerman, D. C., & Rapp, J. T. (2006). Antecedent assessment and intervention for stereotypy. In J. K. Luiselli (Ed.), *Antecedent control: Innovative approaches to behavior support* (pp. 125–146). Baltimore, MD: Paul H. Brookes.

Luiselli, J. K. (2008). Antecedent (preventive) intervention. In J. K. Luiselli, S. Wilczynski, D. C. Russo, & W. P. Christian. *Effective practices for children with autism: Educational and behavior support interventions that work* (pp. 393–412). New York, NY: Oxford University Press.

Further Reading

Luiselli, J. K., Russo, D. C., Christian, W. P., & Wilczynski, S. (Eds.) (2008). *Effective Practices for Children with Autism: Educational and Behavior Support Interventions that Work.* New York, NY: Oxford University Press.

What Sleep Problems Are Common in Children with ASC, and How Can They Be Treated?

Ruth O'Hara & Carmen M. Schröder

Sleep problems are among the most common complaints reported by families of children with ASC. A limited number of studies have investigated sleep disturbances in children with ASC, and fewer still have considered the repercussion of these disturbances on the core symptoms and behavioral problems that hallmark this disorder. Indeed, sleep problems in this population are neither routinely nor systematically assessed in clinical practice, but their repercussions can extend beyond the patient themselves, negatively impacting the quality of life of the family. The literature to date indicates prevalence rates of sleep disturbances a high as 44–83% in children with ASC, compared to only 30% in typically developing children.

Sleep disturbance can result from very different sleep disorders, including insomnia, periodic limb movements (PLMs), restless leg syndrome (RLS), circadian rhythm disturbance (CRD), and obstructive sleep apnea (OSA). Several of these sleep disorders can be alleviated with a range of established and effective treatment approaches. However, we have very limited information on the prevalence of specific sleep disorders in children with ASC. Characterizing the type and severity of sleep disorder has been hampered by the difficulties with conducting full objective, overnight measures of sleep, such as polysomnography, in this patient population. Actigraphy, a small wrist or ankle band that records movement indicative of periods of activity and rest has been employed by several groups. It indicates that sleep disturbances exist in ASC but not which sleep disorder subserves the disturbance, and, thus, makes it difficult to determine the most effective treatment approach. Many studies rely on parental reports.

The most common sleep disturbance in ASC reported by parents is insomnia, with the child having difficulties initiating sleep and having frequent nocturnal awakenings, leading to decreased total sleep time, as well as irregular sleep-wake rhythms (Richdale, 1999; Gail Williams, Sears, & Allard, 2004). Although recent studies combining subjective and objective assessment of sleep in ASC suggest that parental reports do not always concur with more objective criteria, the few objective studies of sleep in ASC that have employed polysomnography confirm the symptoms of insomnia described by parents. These include increased sleep latency (SL) (i.e., a longer time to fall asleep) and increased wake-after-sleep-onset (WASO) (i.e., more or longer wake periods during the night), and decreased total sleep time (TST). Studies using actigraphy also indicate that children with autism have less TST in 24 hours than typically developing children or those with developmental disabilities.

Based on parental reports of irregular sleep-wake rhythms in their autistic children, along with difficulties falling asleep, investigators have examined CRD in children with autism. Emerging evidence from 4 independent groups suggests these disturbances may reflect abnormalities in melatonin secretion. Melatonin is an endogenous neurohormone secreted by the pineal gland that displays a distinct day/night profile with an increase in blood levels with the beginning of the dark period of the evening, a peak during the night, and a decrease towards dawn. Across studies, nocturnal melatonin seems to be deficient in the majority (63–65%) of children with ASC (Melke et al., 2008).

Although the prevalence of PLMs in ASC is unknown, studies have observed insufficient dietary iron intake, low ferritin levels, and subsequent improvement of sleep with iron supplementation in children with autism. Given that PLMS may cause hyperactivity in typically developing children and are frequently associated with iron deficits, PLMS may be a comorbidity that could be easily targeted in children with ASC.

Finally, OSA is a respiratory disturbance during sleep that is observed in about 3% of typically developing children. It is characterized by decreases or pauses in respiration during sleep, with frequent arousals from sleep and intermittent drops in blood oxygen levels. OSA is associated with cognitive deficits and behavioral disturbances in typically developing children that are reversible after appropriate treatment. A diagnosis of OSA requires polysomnography, and, so far, a minimal number of such investigations have been conducted in children with ASC. These studies do not suggest a higher prevalence of OSA in this population, but both studies conducted were conducted on very small samples.

Overall, sleep disturbances, in particular insomnia and CRD, appear to be common in autistic children, and they likely have a significant negative impact on daytime behavior. Though a full review of all treatment options is beyond the scope of this chapter, we will briefly outline the main therapeutic approaches to treating these sleep disorders. Coexisting medical, neurological, or psychiatric conditions should be ruled out first. For insomnia, a multimodal treatment approach, including behavioral intervention, pharmacotherapy and use of chronotherapeutics, is often successful. Behavioral intervention for autistic children and their parents includes education on sleep hygiene, establishment of a bedtime routine, establishment of regular bed- and wake-up times that are contingent upon the child's circadian cycle and sleep needs (sometimes with additional techniques, such as bedtime fading to decrease bedtime resistance), and programmed parent intervention during nighttime waking. Behavioral therapy specifically geared towards insomnia in autistic children has shown to be beneficial for children and their families (Reed et al., 2009). Pharmacotherapy should be given in association with behavioral intervention.

If the child's physician suspects presence of another primary sleep disorder besides insomnia, such as OSA or PLMS, a full night's recording with polysomnography in a sleep center is usually warranted. Enlarged tonsils are found in about 75% of children with a polysomnographically confirmed diagnosis of OSA. In those cases, adenotonsillectomy is indicated first. Continuous positive airway pressure (CPAP) is the second line treatment, but compliance with this device may be difficult for children with ASC. Polysomnography also confirms PLMS. Blood draw and analysis of ferritin levels, reflecting iron stores, are indicated, and in case of ferritin levels below 50 µg/l, iron supplementation is given first. If symptoms persist, dopaminergic agents, known to alleviate PLMs, may be the treatment of choice.

With respect to CRD, several studies have now investigated the effects of melatonin in a controlled manner. In the most recent, Wirojanan et al. (2009) found that, in patients with ASC, mean TST was longer on melatonin than placebo by 21 minutes, and mean SL was shorter by 28 minutes. Depending on the type of preparation (immediate versus controlled-release form) and on the dosage, melatonin has chronobiotic, chronohypnotic, or soporific effects, which clinicians should be aware of. Although its safety profile seems to be very favorable after wide use as a dietary supplement, melatonin is not FDA approved, and there are currently no long-term studies available. Light therapy is another chronotherapeutic that may be used for circadian rhythm abnormalities, but, to date, there are no studies in children with ASC. Light boxes that simulate dawn and dusk may be beneficial for children with irregular sleep-wake cycles, always in combination with behavioral therapy.

Overall, treating sleep disorders and CRD has the potential not only to improve sleep in children with ASC and, in turn, their families, but also to ameliorate daytime symptoms in these children. An increased emphasis on objective characterization of the type and severity of sleep problems in patients with ASC, and increased understanding of the relationships between these sleep problems and core symptoms of ASC, could point to effective targeting treatments for ameliorating or alleviating the specific sleep disorders, thus reducing clinical and cognitive symptomatology, alleviating caregiver burden, and improving long-term outcome and quality of life.

References

Gail Williams, P., Sears, L. L., & Allard, A. (2004). Sleep problems in children with autism. *Journal of Sleep Research, 13*, 265–268.

Melke, J., Goubran Botros, H., Chaste, P., Betancur, C., Nygren, G., Anckarsäter, H., ... Bourgeron, T. (2008). Abnormal melatonin synthesis in autism spectrum disorders. *Molecular Psychiatry, 13*, 90–98.

Reed, H. E., McGrew, S. G., Artibee, K., Surdkya, K., Goldman, S. E., Frank, K., ... Malow, B. A. (2009). Parent-based sleep education workshops in autism. *Journal of Child Neurology, 24*, 936–945.

Richdale, A. L. (1999). Sleep problems in autism: Prevalence, cause, and intervention. *Developmental Medicine and Child Neurology, 41*, 60–66.

Wirojanan, J., Jacquemont, S., Diaz, R., Bacalman, S., Anders, T. F., Hagerman, R. J., & Goodlin-Jones, B. L. (2009). The efficacy of melatonin for sleep problems in children with austism, fragile x syndrome, or austism and fragile x syndrome. *Journal of Clinical Sleep Medicine, 5*, 145–150.

7

Q54
How Can Feeding Problems in ASC Be Treated?

Richard M. Foxx & Keith E. Williams

Problems with eating have characterized ASC since Kanner's initial description of infantile autism, with the most commonly-reported problems involving some form of diet restriction. Children with ASC have been reported to be food selective by the type, texture, temperature, and color of food and to have more limited diets than children with typical development (Schreck, Williams, & Smith, 2004). While diet restriction is the most common feeding problem among children with ASC, additional feeding problems have included food refusal, liquid avoidance, packing, and rapid eating. Food refusal can be severe with children refusing to eat all or most foods and often suffering from insufficient calorie intake, swallowing deficits, oral motor problems, and even dependence upon supplemental tube feeds (Field, Garland, & Williams, 2003).

The etiology of selective eating is unclear. Although children with ASC are reported to have greater abnormalities in taste than other children with special needs, it is not known if they actually have greater taste acuity. It may be that the narrow diets found among children with ASD are an extension of their characteristic restriction in interests and activities. Children learn to eat a variety of foods by repeatedly tasting novel foods. This tasting is initiated by a range of social and environmental strategies, such as caregiver's prompts, modeling by peers, and exposures to novel foods in numerous settings including school. However, delays in language and poor social skills, the core deficits in ASC, may prevent these strategies from developing diet variety in children with ASC.

Prior to assessment or intervention development, it is necessary to determine if a child has a feeding problem. Guidelines for establishing that a feeding problem exists include: (1) The child is not gaining weight consistently and has been diagnosed as "failure to thrive," (2) the child is dependent on tube feedings but has the skills needed to eat by mouth, (3) the child has problems eating age-appropriate textures, (4) the child refuses to eat an age-appropriate variety of foods, and (5) mealtime behavior problems are disruptive to family functioning and may include crying, throwing food, excessive dawdling, spitting out food, or holding food in the mouth for excessive amounts of time.

Once it has been determined that a child has a feeding problem in need of intervention, several assessments may be required. Many children with feeding problems have comorbid medical issues, such as gastroesophageal reflux, constipation, or motility problems that may need to be addressed first. While some children with feeding problems have no delays in oral motor functioning, others have difficulty with chewing or swallowing, and evaluation by a speech pathologist or occupational therapist experienced in the assessment of oral motor status is necessary. There are documented reports of children with ASC, who have developed rickets and even blindness from extreme nutritional deficiencies. Although these cases are atypical, children who eat a limited volume or variety of foods are at risk for nutrition problems, and assessment by a dietician can provide information for diet planning.

It is important to distinguish between children who *won't* eat and those who *can't* eat. Children who can't eat have physiological conditions, such as problems with swallowing or certain metabolic abnormalities that result in unsafe oral feeding and usually require intensive, specialized interventions at a feeding clinic that is associated with or part of a medical facility. Children who won't eat have been identified as safe oral feeders by their primary physician or medical teams. These children, typically, are successfully treated with behavioral interventions (Williams & Foxx, 2007).

There is a growing literature documenting the successful use of behavioral interventions to treat the feeding problems of children with ASC (Williams & Foxx, 2007). These interventions often consist of a treatment package of two or more components, typically implemented by behaviorally trained personnel, who may later transfer programmatic control to the child's parents or caregivers.

One of the most important steps prior to developing and implementing a behavioral intervention is to identify antecedent conditions that can adversely affect feeding. Antecedents, which can include settings, events, or biological states, can have a profound impact on a child's feeding and the success of any intervention. Some antecedent conditions include the child's biological state, lack of sleep, medication side effects, including appetite suppression, tube feed schedules, and between meal snacks.

Preferred foods have been used to increase the consumption of novel foods. Both sequential presentation or the use of a preferred food as a reward for eating a novel food and simultaneous presentation or presenting the preferred and novel food together (e.g., a small piece of carrot on top of a corn chip) have been successfully used to increase diet variety. Another successful approach to introduce new foods, called "fading," involves gradually increasing the amount of the food the child is required to eat. In this intervention, a child is initially presented with a single bite of a small amount of a novel food. Across the course of treatment, the amount of novel food the child is required to eat is systematically increased. Another variant of fading has been used to teach children to drink novel beverages. In this intervention, a small amount of a preferred beverage is replaced with an equal amount of a novel beverage. Over time, increasing amounts of the preferred beverage are replaced with the novel beverage until the child is drinking only the novel beverage. Some children are selective by the texture of foods, and many of them eat only purees or other low textures. Fading has also been used to increase the texture eaten in presented foods by gradually increasing it over time.

It is well known that food preferences are acquired through repeated exposures to the *taste* of novel foods. Repeated taste exposure was recently utilized within a treatment package to increase diet variety in children with autism (Paul, Williams, Riegel, & Gibbons, 2007). The intervention involved offering novel foods in brief probe meals, during which the children were praised for eating but not required to do so. Foods not eaten in the probes were introduced in taste sessions. In a taste session, children were offered only a single pea-sized bite of one food, and the session was terminated when the bite was consumed. This repeated tasting of novel foods resulted in their increased consumption in subsequent probe meals, even when the children were not required to eat.

Feeding problems represent a major problem for children, families, and medical and educational services. Proper assessment, combined with empirically based behavioral interventions, can help insure that no-one with an ASC suffers because their nutritional concerns and feeding problems go unrecognized and untreated.

References

Field, D., Garland, M., & Williams, K. (2003). Correlates of specific childhood feeding problems. *Journal of Pediatrics and Child Health, 39*, 299–304.

Paul, C., Williams, K. E., Riegel, K., & Gibbons, B. (2007). Combining repeated taste exposure and escape prevention: A treatment for the treatment of extreme food selectivity. *Appetite, 49*, 708–711.

Schreck, K. A., Williams, K. E., & Smith, A. (2004). A comparison of eating behaviors between children with and without autism. *Journal of Autism and Developmental Disorders, 34*, 433–438.

Williams, K. E., & Foxx, R. M. (2007). *Interventions for treating the eating problems of children with autism spectrum disorders and developmental disabilities*. Austin, Texas: Pro-Ed.

Further Reading

Williams, K. E. & Seiverling, L. (2010). Eating problems in children with autism spectrum disorders. *Topics in Clinical Nutrition, 25*, 27–37.

Q55
What Is Applied Behavior Analysis (ABA)?

Richard M. Foxx

Applied behavior analysis (ABA), sometimes called behavior therapy, uses methods derived from scientifically established principles of behavior. ABA has been applied successfully to a wide range of populations and areas, including developmental disabilities, education, business, mental health, counseling, industrial safety, child abuse, and ASC. There is extensive evidence for the effectiveness of ABA with autism. Consider that (a) individuals of all ages have been successfully educated and treated for over 40 years; (b) over 1,000 peer reviewed, scientific articles describe ABA successes; (c) no other autism intervention has the support of The State of New York Health Department and US Surgeon General; (d) all individuals obtain some degree of benefit from ABA; (e) autism agencies using ABA have provided successful nonresidential and residential services for thousands of children; (f) no other autism intervention meets the standards of scientific proof met by ABA or produces similar outcome results; (g) investing in early ABA intervention for young children is financially worthwhile, whether the results lead to complete or partial effects; and (h) there has been growing evidence in the past 20 years that early intensive ABA intervention produces improved developmental progress and intellectual performance in young children with autism with the results for those under age 3 being particularly gratifying (Foxx, 2008).

ABA treatment of individuals with ASC seeks to construct socially and educationally appropriate repertoires and decrease or reduce inappropriate behaviors, through the use of specific, carefully programmed, environmental interventions. A variety of ABA methods are used to strengthen current skills and create new ones. Multiple, repeated opportunities are arranged each day for the individual to develop new skills and practice mastered ones. Positive reinforcement is used liberally to insure that the individual is maximally motivated.

Typically, a number of steps are chained together to form a behavioral repertoire. Some ABA methods used include (1) positive reinforcement, in which appropriate behavior is followed by a pleasurable event, such as praise, a token, or a favorite activity; (2) shaping, reinforcing the individual for behavior that approaches the target behavior or goal; (3) fading, reducing the individual's de-

7

pendence on the teacher or therapist for assistance; (4) prompting, providing cues to the individual to try to perform a behavior; and (5) maintenance and generalization strategies to insure that a recently learned behavior will last and be performed in other environments. Several strategies are employed to treat inappropriate behaviors, including analyzing and manipulating the antecedents that trigger the behavior, ignoring the behavior, or providing undesired or unpleasant consequences. The overall goal of ABA is to motivate the individual to want to achieve success.

Teaching or therapy trials are typically repeated a number of times until mastery is achieved. Accurate records are used to assess progress and indicate the need for programmatic changes. Each individual's program is unique to their needs and evolves with their progress. Several formats are used for teaching. The discrete trial format features one-to-one interaction with the trainer/educator, brief, clear instructions, careful use of prompting and fading, and immediate reinforcement for appropriate responding. Incidental teaching is a less structured format designed to facilitate learning in less structured situations. The overall programmatic goal is to systematically move the individual from one-to-one interaction with a trainer/educator to group instruction (Maurice, Green, & Luce, 1996).

ABA programming incorporates scientifically validated methods into a comprehensive but highly individualized package. A defining characteristic of ABA programs is that they are applied consistently (1) through the use of explicitly written programs for each skill to be taught or inappropriate behavior to be treated and (2) by having the behavior analyst who is responsible for the program train everyone who works with the individual to implement it. Critical to the achievement of the generalization of the treatment efforts is training therapists/parents to implement the programs across situations, settings, and people. Highly problematic behaviors, such as aggression and self-injury, are not reinforced, whereas specific, appropriate, alternative behaviors are either developed or maintained through positive reinforcement (Maurice, Green, & Foxx, 2001).

Before treatment, the individual's skill and developmental levels are assessed so that therapeutic goals can be selected. The determination of what skills to teach is made by examining all relevant skill domains, including academic, communication, leisure, play and self-care, and social skills. Each skill is then broken down into smaller and more easily taught component skills. The skills that are taught are increased in complexity as progress is achieved. The overall goal is to provide the kind of programming that will insure that each individual reaches their highest potential and level of independence (Green, www.behavior.org).

Critical to programmatic success is the direct and frequent measurement of the individual's progress. These data are graphed to display how each targeted skill and inappropriate behavior has responded to the intervention effort. The behavior analyst responsible for the program frequently checks the graphs and records to determine if progress is occurring and make any needed programmatic changes. Frequent review of the individual's responsiveness to the intervention permits any identified problems to be corrected quickly. To assure treatment consistency, the responsible behavior analyst frequently observes the intervention efforts in order to provide feedback to those implementing the program.

While universal ABA principles guide all programming efforts and activities, each individual is regarded as unique. The establishment and maintenance of a positive treatment environment is assured through the use of repeated and consistent presentations of material, individually selected and strategically used motivators, high levels of consistency, selective use of prompting and fading procedures, and systematic planning for generalization. The overall goal of ABA programs is to create intervention experiences that will lead to enduring positive changes over time and across all settings.

An appropriate ABA intervention is directed by a professional with advanced formal training in behavior analysis. Such professionals have met the educational, experiential, and examination performance standards of the Behavior Analyst Certification Board (BACB) and are Board Certified Behavior Analysts (BCBAs). ABA is sometimes confused with Positive Behavior Support. It is important to distinguish between them, because they are separate entities that differ in the depth and breadth of their scientific base and political correctness. ABA has played a vital role in revolutionizing treatment and education for individuals with autism by freeing them from the many behavioral, educational, and adaptive barriers that kept them dependent and devalued. To date, the only interventions that had been shown to produce comprehensive, lasting results in autism are those based on ABA principles.

References

Foxx, R. M. (2008). Applied Behavior Analysis (ABA), treatment of autism: The state of the art. *Child and Adolescent Psychiatric Clinics of North America, 17*, 821–834.
Green, G. Applied behavior analysis for autism. Retrieved from www.behavior.org.
Maurice, C., Green, G., & Luce, S. C. (1996). *Behavioral intervention for young children with autism: A manual for parents and professionals.* Austin, TX: Pro-Ed.
Maurice, C., Green, G., & Foxx, R. M. (2001). *Making a difference: Behavioral intervention for autism.* Austin, TX: Pro-Ed.

Further Reading

Lovass O. I. (1987) Behavioral treatment and normal educational and intellectual functioning in young autistic children. *Journal of Consulting and Clinical Psychology, 55*, 3–9.
Freeman, S. K. (2007). *The complete guide to autism tTreatments: A parent's handbook: Make sure your child gets what works!* Lynden, WA: SKF Books.
Metz, B., Mulick, J. A., & Butter, E. M. (2005). Autism: A late 20th century fad magnet. In: J. W. Jacobson, R. M. Foxx, & J. A. Mulick, (Eds.), *Controversial therapies for developmental disabilities: Fads, fashion and science in professional practice* (p. 237–264). London: Routledge.

Q56
What Is TEACCH?

Simonetta Panerai

Treatment and Education of Autistic and related Communication-handicapped CHildren (TEACCH; Mesibov, Shea, & Schopler, 2002) is an educational program developed in the 1960s at the University of North Carolina at Chapel Hill. It was founded by Eric Schopler and has spread all over the world because of its concepts, training activities, and scientific publications. It's one of the most visible and frequently cited autism programs, broadly requested and implemented in public schools of several countries and considered one of the most widely-known, comprehensive intervention models. Comprehensive approaches attempt to address a range of developmental abilities, emphasizing early and intensive intervention, actively involving families, and utilizing staff who are trained and specialized in ASC. TEACCH provides direct, long-life services for children with ASC and their families, as well as staff training and counseling for classrooms, group homes, and other services.

The philosophy of TEACCH is based on the "culture of autism." Autism is a disorder of neural development that affects the ways children think, feel, communicate, and behave, ways that need to be understood in order to make their life easier and more successful. What are the points of strength and weakness of autism? One of the points of strength is the visual information processing, which is preferred to auditory information processing, namely, verbal language. As for the points of weakness, the following have been found: Unusual sensory processing, difficulty in understanding meanings of personal experiences, focus on details, distractibility and attention deficits (focusing and shifting), difficulties in organizing ideas, materials, and activities and poor use and understanding of verbal and nonverbal language in social interactions, difficulties in generalization processes, strong routine and repetitive behaviors, limited social skills and low emotional empathy, as well as noncompliant behavior.

Given the cognitive and behavioral characteristics of ASC, the TEACCH philosophy suggests that children with ASC will benefit from a highly-structured teaching approach that provides routines and predictability in visually-based environments (Schopler, Mesibov, & Hearsey, 1995). Structured Teaching, which is the core of TEACCH approach, is based on several principles:

Individualized assessment: A formal and informal assessment is carried out by parents, teachers, and trainers to establish the Individualized Educational Program

(IED), particularly focusing on communication, self-care, vocational skills, and leisure time. To this purpose, Division-TEACCH has developed specific instruments namely: The CARS-Childhood Autism Rating Scale (Schopler, Reichler, & Renner, 1988), a diagnostic instrument for children that turned out to be suitable also for adolescents and adults; the PsychoEducational Profile-PEP (Schopler & Reichler, 1979) and its subsequent revisions, PEP-R (PEP-Revised) in 1990 and PEP-3 (PEP-third revision) in 2004, which are developmental-age instruments to assess a child's learning points of strength and weakness; and the Adolescent and Adult PsychoEducational Profile (AAPEP; Mesibov, Schopler, Schaffer, & Landrus, 1988) and its recent revision, the TEACCH Transition Assessment Profile – TTAP (2007), which are instruments assisting the transition from schools to vocational settings.

Using strengths and interests to facilitate the learning of adaptive skills: The teaching model addressed to ASC children is a competence-based, rather than deficit-based, model. TEACCH approach uses the autistic characteristics as a context to teach the skills required by surrounding environment. For example, since ASC persons are very attentive to visual stimuli, we can teach matching, sorting, and collating skills that are useful in daily life, or, since ASC persons show a strong adherence to routines and rituals, we might train them daily-living skills through "positive" routines.

Family involvement: Involvement is encouraged across all the phases of the program, since it facilitates the generalization of skills. Family lifestyles are "embedded" into the educational programs, and consequently, individuals with ASC are trained in those skills that are most appropriate for the family lifestyle.

Individualization: The educational program is designed on the basis of the peculiar features of each child, as resulting from careful assessment, objectives, methods, places, activities, materials and the communication system are all individualized. Children can communicate by using objects, pictures, drawings, and/or written words (augmentative communication system), according to their own developmental level.

Generalist training model: The holistic approach is evident in the attention focused on the child as a unique person, the "child-centeredness," rather than on professional specialties. All the professionals, besides their education and specialization, are trained on the "culture of autism" and the TEACCH practice – indeed, they must be able to face the autistic problem in a global manner and intervene to facilitate new learning within the developmental phase, as well as to reduce inappropriate and disruptive behaviors.

Structured Teaching has two complementary goals: (a) increasing individuals' skills and (b) making the environment more understandable and more consistent with the child's needs. It is appropriate for both children and adults and is used in multiple settings, such as schools, homes, job places, leisure-time settings, and so on.

Structured Teaching includes the following components:

Organization of the physical environment: This is based on the principle of place-activity correspondence (i.e., any designed space is adapted to a specific activity; spaces are structured by differently arranging the furniture). This makes the environment clearer and predictable to the children and facilitates their attention, calmness, independence, and effective work. Visual cues, such as colors or labels, can be used to support environmental structure. Younger students need areas for play, independent work, learning with teacher, self-help skills, and snack, while older children need areas for their leisure interests, vocational, domestic and self-help skills, group activities, independent work, and learning work.

Sequential Organization of activities: Children with ASC hardly remember activities' sequence, therefore, predictability is obtained with a visual schedule, showing the activities for the day. Consequently, time (which is an abstract concept) becomes "visible." Children can "see" the schedule of the day, and after the completion of a task, anxiety is reduced because they know what is going to happen later.

Visual schedules: These help to reduce problems deriving from verbal memory deficits and fleeting attention, as well as poor time orientation and spontaneous activities organization, in order to compensate verbal comprehension deficits, facilitate independence, and increase motivation. Indeed, this is a form of "memo" that makes visible the sequence of events, such as "work" and "reward". Visual schedules can be differently arranged, for example, written check-lists, photographs, pictures/drawings, and objects. Designing of schedules depends on the developmental level of each child. In the classrooms, 2 kinds of schedules can be used – the general classroom schedule and the individual student schedule.

Routines: Routines are encouraged since they represent an alternative way of predicting events and their sequence and correctly doing most of the activities during the day. Common examples of routines are the left-right work to facilitate independent activities, or those routines used during transition periods, when behavior problems can occur most prominently.

Work system: Work systems help children to understand which and how many tasks have to be done, how to progress with the tasks, when to finish the work, and what will happen at the end of activities. Just like a schedule, a work system is presented visually, based on the developmental level of the child: It can be presented, for example, as a written list or in a more concrete manner, such as using a certain number of boxes, each of them containing a task, placed on a shelf on the left side of the work-place. The child has to take a box, complete the task, and move the box in the "finished" area on the right side of the work-place.

Tasks and materials organization: Appropriate activity materials must be immediately available in the places where the activities are being carried out, in order to promote child independence during task performance, error reduction, and a fluently-progressing work, while also decreasing stereotypic behaviors, usually occurring when children manipulate the objects. Once more, visual instructions are being used (i.e., specifically-designed, highly-individualized, and perceptually clear materials are, therefore, arranged).

The TEACCH approach is a comprehensive educational program, based on a theoretical conceptualization of autism that provides ASC individuals, their families, teachers, and therapists with a model of good practice. TEACCH is addressed to individuals with ASC in all age ranges and at all developmental levels. From a social perspective, it is a highly valuable approach: That is the reason why it has been strongly appreciated and valued by parents, teachers, and therapists. It is being implemented in a variety of settings to help persons with ASC to organize themselves, to function more appropriately, independently, and successfully, and to enjoy social situations while improving social skills.

References

Mesibov, G. B., Schopler, E., Schaffer, B., & Landrus, R. (1988). *Adolescent and adult PsychoEducational Profile (AAPEP)*. Austin, TX: Pro-Ed.

Mesibov, G. B, Shea, V., & Schopler, E. (2002). *The TEACCH approach to autism spectrum disorders*. New York, NY: Springer.

Mesibov, G., Thomas, J. B., Chapman, S. M., & Schopler, E. (2007). *TTAP: TEACCH Transition Assessment Profile* (2nd Ed.). Austin, TX: Pro-Ed.

Schopler, E., Lansing, M. D., Reichler, R. J., Marcus, L. M. (2004). *Psychoeducational Profile: Third Edition (PEP-3)*. Austin, TX: Pro-Ed.

Schopler, E., Mesibov, G. B., & Hearsey, K. (1995). *Structured teaching in the TEACCH system.* In: E. Schopler & G. B. Mesibov (Eds.), *Learning and Cognition in Autism.* New York NY: Plenum Press.

Schopler, E., & Reichler, R. J. (1979). *Individualized assessment and treatment for autistic and developemtally disabled children: Vol. 1 – Psychoeducational Profile.* Baltimore: University Park.

Schopler, E., Reichler, R. J., & Renner, B. (1988). *The Childhood Autism Rating Scale (CARS).* Los Angeles, CA: Western Psychological Services.

Mesibov, G.B., Schopler, E., Schaffer, B., & Landrus, R. (1988). *Adolescent and Adult PsychoEducational Profile (AAPEP)*. Austin: Pro-Ed

Further Reading

Schopler, E. (Ed.) (2000). International priorities for developing autism services via the TEACCH model (special issue). *International Journal of Mental Health, 29 (1)*.

Panerai, S., Zingale, M., Trubia, G., Finocchiaro, M., Zuccarello, R., Ferri, R., & Elia, M. (2009). Special education versus inclusive education: The role of the TEACCH program. *Journal of Autism and Developmental Disabilities, 39*, 874–882.

Callahan, K., Shukla-Mehta, S., Magee, S., & Wie, M. (2010). ABA versus TEACCH: The case for defining and validating comprehensive treatment models in autism. *Journal of Autism and Developmental Disorders, 40*, 74–88.

7

Q57
What Is the Picture Exchange Communication System (PECS)?

Twyla Y. Perryman & Paul J. Yoder

The Picture Exchange Communication System (PECS) is a manualized alternative/augmentative communication approach that was developed for children with no or limited social communication skills. The PECS program has often been used to help children with ASD learn to communicate. PECS is based on behavioral principles that incorporate prompts and reinforcements as a means of teaching children to participate in communicative interactions with others using pictures. An important distinction to make is that PECS is a specific curriculum and set of teaching methods. It is not just the use of pictures or symbols (e.g., picture schedules, general use of pictures to label) to guide behavior. Additionally, PECS is not a general label for all methods used to teach children to communicate through pictures. The developers of PECS suggest that the overall goal of the program is to progressively fade prompts in a way that promotes attainment of spontaneous communication (Bondy & Frost, 2001).

Overview of the 6 Phases of PECS

The teaching structure is organized into 6 phases that begin with children learning to exchange a picture to make a request for an object and ends with them using combinations of pictures (i.e., sentences) to "comment" on things in the environment. After the first phase, children are provided with a communication binder (a binder of removable, plastic inserts with Velcro® attachments) that holds several pictures, allowing children to choose pictures and combine them into sentences in later phases. During the later phases, children will utilize sentence strips (removable oblong plastic pieces with attachments) that are given to the message recipient to convey a request, answer a question, or convey a "comment." (See Table 1 for a brief description of each phase.)

Table 1. Description of the 6 phases of the PECS approach

Phase	Goal	Procedures
I. Picture Exchange	Children are taught to exchange a picture for a desired item. Hand over hand prompts are used to teach this skill.	Two trainers, one acting as the physical prompter and the other as the communication partner (receiver of the symbol/picture), prompt the child to exchange the picture. Training often occurs at a table with a single picture and communication partner in close proximity to the child.
II. Distance	Children are taught to be persistent in their attempts to communicate with others by creating communication barriers (distance).	The distance between the child, picture, and communication partner is increased. Children are taught to walk to get the picture of the desired object and take it to their communication partner, who is no longer seated right in front of them.
III. Discrimination	Children are taught to discriminate between pictures to request a preferred object.	Children are prompted to choose between pictures representing a highly desired object and a nondesired item with visual cues, demonstration, and vocal praise from the trainer. After mastering this first step, the 2 selected pictures are adjusted to, gradually, become more equal in their level of desirability. Eventually, more pictures are added to increase discrimination between up to 6 pictures.
IV. Sentences	Children are taught to combine pictures in order to create short sentences to request items.	Children are initially taught to use sentence starters (i.e., combine 2 pictures) within a request. The 2 pictures are attached to a sentence strip and exchanged. The first picture represents the phrase, "I want" and the second picture will represent the desired object.
V. Questions	Children are taught to answer "What do you want?" questions, using short sentences.	Children are prompted to answer questions related to a request by exchanging the phrase "I want + (object)."
VI. Comments	Children are taught to use sentences to answer "What do you hear?" or "What do you see?" questions. The PECS curriculum calls this commenting.	Children are now prompted to answer questions about objects or events in their environment. During this phase, trainers are encouraged to provide only social reinforcements to the child's response to the question, instead of access to the object.

7

Training and Implementation

The creators of the PECS system offer training and workshops to become certi-fied implementers of the approach. Their basic training workshop is described as a 2-day intensive workshop at which participants learn the theory behind the PECS approach, how to teach the 6 phases, and how to transition to other communication modalities. At the time of writing (spring, 2010), the cost of the workshop was $295 for parents and $395 for professionals. When considering the human resources and time required for implementing the PECS program, it is important to bear in mind that 2 trainers are needed during the first phase and 1 trainer, the communication partner, throughout the remaining 5 phases. Train-ers also need to schedule time to continually update pictures, in order to stay current with the child's changing toy and object preferences. It is also helpful if the child can have access to these pictures across settings (i.e., available at school and at home). Materials needed for implementation often include a va-riety of desirable and nondesired foods/toys/objects, the communication binder and inserts, pictures (these may be purchased online at the developers' website or produced with the Board Marker Software), a laminating machine and pages, Velcro® loops, and the PECS manual.

Clinical Benefits and Limitations

Since its development, several studies have been conducted to look at the effec-tiveness of the PECS system for teaching communication skills. Many studies reported gains in a subset of children's communication skills (e.g., requesting desired objects), immediately following the intervention, within communication contexts very similar to those that were used to teach PECS. However, there is limited support showing that children are able to maintain and generalize (i.e., demonstrate the skills learned with new people or contexts long after the treat-ment phase ends) the skills gained from PECS training (Flippin, Reszka, & Wat-son, 2010). The lack of evidence regarding generalization and maintenance may be partially due to limited measures of such in the majority of studies. Addition-ally, it is likely that the PECS program will be more useful for some children than others. A few researchers have begun to look at which preexisting child characteristics make it more likely that children will benefit from the PECS pro-gram when compared with other treatments. One study found that children who start with low rates of joint attention initiations and a relatively strong interest in objects (Yoder & Stone, 2006a; 2006b) benefited more from the PECS interven-tion over a less-structured play-based approach. Another study found that PECS was more effective for teaching requests to a child with low motor imitation when compared to the same child being taught sign language (Tincani, 2004). It is also possible that PECS promotes gains in very specific skills (e.g., initiations, requests, etc.) rather than in more social pragmatic functions (e.g., commenting) or more general language use. In conclusion, PECS has been shown to promote at least short-term gains in mostly instrumental communication skills for some children. However, more research is needed to examine whether these gains are maintained and generalized.

References

Body, A. & Frost, L. (2001). The Picture Exchange Communication System. *Behavior Modification, 25*, 725–744.

Flippin, M., Reszka, S., & Watson, L. R. (2010). Effectiveness of the Picture Exchange Communication System (PECS) on communication & speech for children with autism spectrum disorders: A metanalysis. *American Journal of Speech-Language Pathology, 19*, 178–195.

Tincani, M. (2004). Comparing the Picture Exchange Communication System and sign language for children with autism. *Focus on Autism and Developmental Disabilities, 19*, 152–163.

Yoder P. J., & Stone, W. (2006a). Randomized comparison of two communication interventions for preschoolers with autism spectrum disorders. *Journal of Consulting and Clinical Psychology, 74*, 426–435.

Yoder, P. J., & Stone, W. (2006b). A randomized comparison of the effect of two prelinguistic communication interventions on the acquisition of spoken communication in preschoolers with ASD. *Journal of Speech Language and Hearing Research, 49*, 698–711.

7

Q58
What Is Social Skills Training?

Rhea Paul

Children with ASC, regardless of their level of function, have difficulty establishing and maintaining meaningful social relationships, especially with peers. Elliot, Racine, and Busse (1995) define social skills as those that "enable a person to interact with others in ways that elicit positive responses and assist the person in avoiding negative responses" (p. 1009). Bellini (2008) points out that in typically developing people (TD), skills such as engaging in conversation and initiating play with peers, while learned through experience, are clearly supported by a biological predisposition toward social interaction. For children with ASC, however, these biological tendencies are reduced or atypical. Thus, learning that comes easily through ordinary, informal experiences to children with TD is not acquired through the natural channels in children with ASC. For this reason, children with ASC require explicit, focused instruction, in order to learn the play and interactive skills that are second nature to typically developing children.

Social skill acquisition is crucial to the optimal development of children with ASC, because both emotional and cognitive development proceed through our interactions with others. Children learn to control their tempers and cope with their fears by observing others in similar situations, by experiencing others' reactions to them when they become aggressive or show excessive fearfulness, and by developing coping strategies through these observations and reactions. Cognitive and academic development is also closely tied to social interactive skills. Young children use dramatic play with peers to acquire and practice language and concepts; they learn to persist in difficult tasks because of a drive to please or be like others; they master the rules of school and playing field in response to motivation to be seen positively in others' eyes. Thus, the acquisition of social skills is important, not only as a way of getting along with others, but as a tool to enhance development across a range of domains.

Social skills training is an attempt to provide children with ASC with the tools they need to successfully engage in social interactions, in order to broaden their opportunities, not only to make friends and enjoy social contact, but to use these social situations to enhance their overall adaptive outcome. Generally, social skills training takes place in small group settings. Atwood (2003) argued that the curriculum for social skills groups needs to be determined by children's level of function. He argued that the quality of children's friendships changes from early childhood to adolescence, and the content of social skills groups needs to be carefully crafted to match the social expectations of each developmental level. Social skills training for young children, then, might focus on simple acts, such as greetings, joining a peer in play with a toy, or sharing a preferred object. Teaching methods might include practicing "scripts" for greeting or using video modeling to observe how typical peers greet each other, then practicing in role playing situations. English, Shafer, Goldstein, and Kaczmarek (2005) developed "buddy time" as a more generalized training program, in which pairs of young children (1 TD, 1 ASC) are given rewards for, at first, just "staying together" during a specified period of time. Later, requirements for the reward increase from merely staying together to "playing together, " and eventually to "talking together." Research suggests that all of these methods show some degree of efficacy for increasing social interaction and opportunities for young children with ASC.

For school-aged children, Bellini, Peters, Benner, and Hopf (2007) report that social skills group instruction that focuses on specific, discreet skills, such as turn-taking, giving compliments, etc., is more effective than programs that highlight more general "friendship" skills. Their analysis of published research further suggests that social skills training is more effective when delivered within a school setting, rather than at a separate location and when it is delivered with a high degree of intensity (i.e., more than once a week). Paul (2008) interpreted her summary of social skills training literature to suggest that the presence of typical peers within the social skills group significantly increases the efficacy, generalization, and maintenance of program goals.

Social skills training for adolescents typically focuses on the social issues faced by teenagers, such as peer group acceptance, dating, and understanding and expressing feelings. Strulovitch and Tagalakis (2003) advocate using social skills groups for adolescents with ASC that have a consistent session structure and employ techniques such as review of previously taught skills, modeling and role play of new skills, and guided practice in natural contexts.

In sum, social skills training is an important part of the intervention program for children with ASC. Social skills programs appear to be most effective when they focus on specific skills, include peer models, use research-based strategies, take place in school environments, and are relatively intensive.

References

Atwood, T. (2003). Social skill programs to teach friendship skills for children with Asperger syndrome. *Perspectives on Language, Learning, and Education, 10,* 16–20.

Bellini, S., Peters, J., Benner, L., & Hopf, A. (2007). A meta-analysis of school-based social skills interventions for children with autism spectrum disorders. *Remedial and Special Education, 28,* 153–162.

Bellini, S. (2008). *Building social relationships.* Shawnee Mission, KS: AAPC.

Elliott, S., Racine, C. & Busse. R. (1995). Best practices in preschool social skills training. In A. Thomas & J. Grimes (Eds.), *Best practices in school psychology* (3rd ed.) (pp. 1009–1020). Washington, DC: NASP.

English, K., Shafer, L., Goldstein, H., & Kaczmarek, L. (2005). Teaching buddy skills to preschoolers. In M. Wehneyer & M. Agran (Eds.), *Mental retardation and intellectual disabilities: Teaching students using innovative and research-based strategies* (pp. 177–195). Annapolis Junction, MD: American Association on Mental Retardation.

Paul, R. (2008). Interventions to improve communication in autism. *Child and Adolescent Psychiatric Clinics of North America, 17,* 835–856.

Strulovitch, J., & Tagalakis, V. (2003). Social skills groups for adolescents with Asperger syndrome. *Perspectives on Language, Learning, and Education. 10,* 20–22.

Further Reading

McAfee, J. (2002). *Navigating the Social World.* Arlington, TX: Future Horizons.

Weiss, M. & Harris, S. (2001). *Reaching out, joining in: Teaching social skills to young children with autism.* Bethesda, MD: Woodbine House.

7

Section 8

Pharmacological Treatments of ASC

Q59

What Is the Value of Medication in ASC?

L. Eugene Arnold, Michael Aman, & Benjamin Handen

At this point, the main value of medication for ASC is for the associated symptoms of hyperactivity, irritability, aggression, self-injury, and anxiety. Despite one encouraging report of improved joint attention with methylphenidate (Jahromi et al., 2009), there is currently no medication proven effective for the core symptoms of social and communication impairment, and the pharmacology of repetitive, stereotyped behavior and restricted interests is a mixed picture. Psychopharmacology of ASC is further complicated by the high rate of co-occurring intellectual disability (ID), which can make pharmacotherapeutics more complex (Aman, Buican, & Arnold, 2003).

Stereotypy, repetitive behavior, obsessive-compulsive symptoms

Attempts to treat this cluster of core ASC symptoms have constituted one of the more perplexing efforts in psychopharmacology. Theoretically, serotonergic antidepressants (selective serotonin reuptake inhibitors (SSRIs) and clomipramine) should be useful because of their efficacy in typically developing children for obsessive-compulsive disorder (OCD) and anxiety and because serotonin abnormalities have been documented in autism. For a while, this theory dominated the field (e.g., Aman, Arnold, & Armstrong, 1999). Indeed, Gordon (1993) reported positive results for clomipramine, while also noting increased irritability, temper outbursts, and uncharacteristic aggression in 75% of probands. However, 2 recent multi-site SSRI trials failed to show any effect of citalopram (King et al., 2009) or low-dose fluoxetine (neuropharm.co.uk/aboutus/portfolio_pipeline/autism_programme/) on repetitive behaviors in young people with autism. This deserves more research, including attempts to determine if age is an important moderator of outcome.

On the other hand, antipsychotic drugs do have documented evidence of efficacy for stereotypy in ASC. For example, the Research Units on Pediatric Psychopharmacology (RUPP) Autism Network found a highly significant in-

8

cidental effect on the Stereotypy subscale of the Aberrant Behavior Checklist (ABC) in a 5-site randomized clinical trial comparing risperidone to placebo for irritability, aggression, tantrums, and self-injury in youth with autistic disorder (RUPP Autism Network, 2002). Similar results have been found with other antipsychotics (e.g., Aman & Madrid, 1999). Consequently, in contrast to the typically developing population, in ASC the pharmacology of stereotyped, repetitive behavior, and obsessive-compulsive symptoms relies more on antipsychotics than on antidepressants.

Irritability, Tantrums, and Aggression

This cluster of associated symptoms actually has an approved indication by the US Food and Drug Administration (FDA). Risperidone and aripiprazole are approved for irritability in autism on the basis of a multi-site randomized clinical trials showing a large effect on the irritability subscale of the ABC (RUPP Autism Network, 2002; Owen et al., 2009; Marcus et al., 2009) and, in the case of risperidone, on parent-selected target symptoms (Arnold et al, 2003). Those with the greatest baseline severity benefited the most. It is likely that other antipsychotics would show similar results. However, the significant benefit is bought at the expense of a concerning side effect, at least with risperidone, and probably with other atypical antipsychotics. The increased appetite that most patients experience can result in excessive weight gain, risk of type II diabetes, and possibly cardiovascular sequelae.

Self-Injury

Self-injury could in some ways be considered a core symptom under the rubric of stereotyped behavior. However, it is not specifically listed in DSM-IV-TR, and most cases of autism do not show it, at least not to a significant degree. When it occurs, it can be devastating, with such complications as blindness due to retinal detachment from self-hitting the head or open wounds from picking. Naltrexone is helpful in a few cases, possibly when release of endorphins is a sustaining reinforcer. Cases in which anxiety, frustration, or irritability is the main cause might be helped by antipsychotic or antianxiety agents. In children with autistic disorder selected for irritability, the antipsychotic risperidone decreased self-injury substantially compared to placebo (Arnold et al., 2003).

Hyperactivity

Hyperkinetic symptoms are so common in ASC that one is not supposed to diagnose attention-deficit/hyperactivity disorder (ADHD) in the presence of ASC.

Although not a core symptom, it is one of the most troubling symptoms for young children with ASC and can be dangerous due to such actions as darting into the street. It sometimes responds to the same medication as in typically developing children, such as stimulants and atomoxetine (RUPP Autism Network, 2005; Arnold et al., 2006). Unfortunately, the stimulant response rate is lower and intolerable side effects rate higher than for typically developing children.

Anxiety

Anxiety, although not considered a core symptom of ASC, is often the driving force behind other symptoms. Unfortunately, it does not respond as well to the usual antianxiety agents, such as SSRIs, as in typically developing children. Again, this symptom may respond to an antipsychotic agent.

References

Aman, M. G., Arnold, L. E., & Armstrong, S. (1999). Review of serotonergic agents and perseverative behavior in patients with developmental disabilities. *Mental Retardation and Developmental Disabilities Research Reviews, 5*, 279–289.

Aman, M. G., Buican, B., & Arnold, L. E. (2003). Methylphenidate treatment in children with low IQ and ADHD: Analysis of three aggregated studies. *Journal of Child and Adolescent Psychopharmacology, 13*, 27–38.

Aman, M. G.,& Madrid, A. (1999). Atypical antipsychotics in persons with developmental disabilities. *Mental Retardation and Developmental Disabilities Research Reviews, 5*, 253–263.

Arnold, L. E., Vitiello, B., McDougle, C. J., Scahill, L., Shah, B., Gonzalez, N. M., ... Tierney, E. (2003). Parent-defined target symptoms respond to risperidone in RUPP Autism Study: Customer approach to clinical trials. *Journal of the American Academy of Child and Adolescent Psychiatry, 42*, 1443–1450.

Arnold, L. E., Aman, M. G., Cook, A. M., Witwer, A. N., Hall, K. L., Thompson, S., & Ramadan, Y. (2006). Atomoxetine for hyperactivity in autism spectrum disorders: Placebo-controlled crossover pilot trial. *Journal of the. American Academy of Child and Adolescent Psychiatry, 45*, 1196–1205.

Gordon, C., State, R. C., Nelson, J. E., Hamburger, S. D., & Rapoport, J. L. (1993). A double-blind comparison of clomipramine, desipramine, and placebo in the treatment of autistic disorder. *Archives of General Psychiatry, 50*, 441–447.

Jahromi, L. B., Kasari, C. L., McCracken, J. T., Lee, L. S., Aman, M. G., McDougle, C. J., ... Posey, D. J. (2009). Positive effects of methylphenidate on social communication and self-regulation in children with pervasive developmental disorders and hyperactivity. *Journal of Autism and Developmental Disorders, 39*, 395–404.

King, B. H., Hollander, E., Sikich, L.,McCracken, J. T., Scahill, L., Bregman, J. D., ... Ritz, L., for the STAART Psychopharmacology Network (2009). Lack of efficacy of citalopram in children with autism spectrum disorders and high levels of repetitive behavior. *Archives of General Psychiatry, 66*, 583–590.

Marcus, R. N., Owen, R., Kamen, L., Manos, G., McQuade, R. D., Carson, W. H., & Aman, M. G. (2009). A double-blind, randomized, placebo-controlled study of fixed-dose aripiprazole in children and adolescents with autistic disorder. *Journal of the American Academy of Child and Adolescent Psychiatry*, *48*, 1110–1119.

Owen, R., Sikich, L., Marcus, R. N., Corey-Lisle, P., Manos, G., McQuade, R. D., ... Findling, R. L. (2009). Aripiprazole in the treatment of irritability in children and adolescents with autistic disorder. *Pediatrics, 124, 1533–1540.*

Research Units on Pediatric Psychopharmacology (RUPP) Autism Network (McCracken, J. T., McGough, J., Shah, B., Cronin, P., Hong, D., Aman, M. G., ... McMahon, D.) (2002). Randomized clinical trial of risperidone for irritability in autism. *New England Journal of Medicine, 347,* 314–321.

Research Units on Pediatric Psychopharmacology (RUPP) (2005). Autism Network: A randomized controlled crossover trial of methylphenidate in pervasive developmental disorders with hyperactivity. *Archives of General Psychiatry, 62*, 1266–1274.

Further Reading

Aman, M. G., Hollway, J. A., McDougle, C. J., Scahill, J., Tierney, E., McCracken, J., ... Posey, D. J. (2008). Cognitive effects of risperidone in children with autism and irritable behavior. *Journal of Child and Adolescent Psychopharmacology, 18*, 227–236.

Research Units on Pediatric Psychopharmacology (RUPP) Autism Network (2005). Risperidone treatment of autistic disorder: Longer-term benefits and blinded discontinuation after 6 months. *American Journal of Psychiatry, 162*, 1361–1369.

8

Q60
When Are Psychiatric Medications Used in the Treatment of ASC?

Wendy Froehlich, Linda Lotspeich, & Antonio Y. Hardan

At this time, there are no medications to address the social and communication deficits in autism. However, medication may help reduce specific symptoms associated with autism that interfere with a child's daily functioning. For example, children with ASC may have significant symptoms of hyperactivity and impulsivity that overlap with a diagnosis of attention-deficit/hyperactivity disorder (ADHD); overwhelming fears similar to children with anxiety; interfering rituals or repetitive behaviors like children with obsessive-compulsive disorder (OCD); or symptoms of mood disorders like children with depression or bipolar disorder. Determining whether these symptoms are due to the same cause as the autism or two separate and coexisting disorders can be very difficult and, at times, near-impossible to determine. However, current practice supports using similar approaches in choosing medications regardless of whether the symptoms are felt to be due to autism or a coexisting, but separate disorder. Thus, support for the use of various medications comes from studies in both children and adults, both with and without autism, who suffer from the specific targeted symptom(s) for the given medication(s). For example, in the US, patients with ASC who experience a depressive episode are treated with an antidepressant approved by the US Food and Drug Administration (FDA) for this condition in typically developing individuals. Similarly, although this question focuses on psychiatric symptoms and psychiatric medication, it should be noted that children with autism may also have associated nonpsychiatric symptoms, such as gastrointestinal symptoms (including diarrhea or constipation) or neurologic symptoms (such as seizures). In these cases, medication to help control these symptoms may be prescribed by pediatricians, gastroenterologists, or neurologists.

In general, there are currently not as many extensive reviews for biologic therapies specifically for individuals with autism as there are published recent reviews for educational and behavioral treatments.

It should be noted that all medications, whether prescribed or over-the-counter, have potential risks and side effects. Whenever possible, nonmedication therapies should be implemented either before beginning medication or, in severe cases, in addition to medication when symptoms are considerably dis-

8

abling. Thus, a few behavioral treatments for specific symptoms that can be used prior to and alongside medication will also be discussed briefly in this section. There is evidence that children with ASC are more sensitive to medications, both in terms of having potential side effects, as well as requiring slower titration schedules. A general rule of thumb in psychiatry for treating children with ASC with psychiatric medication is "start low and go slow." In other words, children with ASC may be started at very low doses of medications. It should be noted that many of the medications used for children (with and without autism) have not been approved by the FDA for specific uses in children. This is a result of many research trials typically being performed on adults, and not including children. Due to the lack of research on psychiatric medications in children, physicians often use medications with FDA approval in adults to treat the same or similar symptoms in children. As with the general treatments for autism, it is important to consider the individual values and preferences of parents, service providers, and the person with autism.

Children with ASC and extreme hyperactivity and impulsivity that interferes with their ability to learn may benefit from school-based behavioral interventions and/or medications for ADHD-like symptoms. The school may address these strategies, such as having the child sit near the teacher, receive extra help with organizational skills, be allowed extra time on exams, etc. Medication may also prove to be useful. The most commonly used classes of medications for ADHD-like symptoms are stimulants (i.e., methylphenidate, amphetamine/dextroamphetamine, and dexmethylphenidate), alpha-agonists (i.e., clonidine and guanfacine), and the recently approved atomoxetine. As with all other medications, these carry risks. Stimulants may cause side effects, such as appetite suppression, jitteriness, sleep disturbance, and increase in heart rate, among others. Alpha-agonists may cause the child to feel tired. At higher doses, they may also cause decreases in blood pressure. Atomoxetine can lead to decreased appetite, upset stomach, and sedation. Thus, children taking medication for ADHD-like symptoms should have their height, weight, and vital signs monitored closely by the prescribing physician.

Children with ASC and prominent symptoms of anxiety or OCD may benefit from therapies and/or medications aimed at addressing obsessions and compulsions. Similarly, children with ASC and symptoms consistent with mood disorders (i.e., depression or bipolar disorder) may benefit from therapies and/or medications for depression or bipolar disorder. The most widely-accepted non-medication therapy for anxiety, OCD, and depression is cognitive-behavioral therapy (CBT). Despite the long name, the basic principles of CBT can be made quite simple and CBT may therefore be beneficial for any child (including a child with an ASC) who is capable of verbalizing their thoughts and labeling their feelings. However, since many children with ASC have difficulties labeling and verbalizing emotions, this does limit the number of individuals who can potentially benefit from this intervention. Just as CBT is the most widely accepted nonmedication therapy for symptoms of anxiety, OCD, and depression, the class of medication generally used first-line for all of these disorders are the SSRIs. These include medications such as fluoxetine, sertraline, citalopram, and others. While this class of medication is often the first type tried, there may be other factors (i.e., family history, medication interactions, allergies, and side effect profiles) leading the prescribing physician toward other medications. The main advantages of SSRIs are that they are relatively safe and can often lead to a significant decrease in targeted symptoms. The down sides of SSRIs are that it takes several weeks to know if they are going to be of benefit. It is difficult to know which individual will benefit from which SSRI, and, as with all medications, SSRIs carry side effects and risks. Potential side effects for SSRIs are vast and include changes in sleep, stomach discomfort, headache, dizziness, irritability, agitation, and others. Most side effects are mild and tend to go away as the body adjusts to the medication. Rarely, more serious side effects occur. All antidepressants carry a "Black Box" warning mandated by the FDA, because some studies have suggested antidepressants, including SSRIs, may worsen depression and lead to an increase in suicidal thoughts in a very small percentage of individuals (Hammad, Laughren, & Racoosin, 2006).

Bipolar disorder can be an extremely difficult diagnosis to make in children without ASC, let alone those with ASC. As with all of the discussed diagnoses, it should be diagnosed with caution by a professional trained in both ASC and other psychiatric disorders. When bipolar disorder is present in conjunction with ASC, it should be treated with medications appropriate for bipolar disorder, typically mood stabilizers and antipsychotics. Again, these medications may be quite beneficial, but they also carry the risk of several potential and serious side effects. They usually require close monitoring and regular bloodwork.

Finally, although aggression is not a true psychiatric diagnosis, antipsychotics are frequently used to target this behavior. It should be mentioned that risperidone and aripiprazole are currently the only two medications with FDA approval for treating children with autism and irritability. They are frequently prescribed, in addition to other medications from this class, to treat aggression. Risperidone and aripiprazole are in a class of medication known as atypical antipsychotics. They do not treat the core symptoms of autism. However, they may be helpful for decreasing aggressive behaviors in children with autism and severe aggression. Aggression may be the result of a variety causes. It can be especially difficult to determine the trigger in children with poor communication abilities. Therefore, it can be very difficult to know if a child with an ASC is becoming aggressive because they are anxious, depressed, in pain, hungry, thirsty, frustrated, etc. A functional behavior analysis, or an assessment to determine why a child engages in a given behavior, may help determine the cause of aggression and should be performed by a behaviorist trained in functional behavior analysis. In cases where aggression is felt to be due to another cause, such as depression or anxiety, it is appropriate to treat the underlying presumed cause. Although risperidone and aripiprazole are the only medications with FDA indications specifically for children with autism, other techniques and medications may be tried instead, especially if targeted at a potential underlying cause. For example, if aggression is thought to be due to anxiety or depression, an SSRI may be more appropriate than an antipsychotic, such as risperidone. In cases where the trigger is unclear and/or other interventions have failed, risperidone or aripiprazole may be appropriate and beneficial for reducing aggression. However, parents should be aware that potential side effects include, among others, weight gain, somnolence, high cholesterol, type II diabetes, movement disorders, and abnormal heart rhythms.

In summary, medications do not treat the social or communication deficits seen in ASC. However, psychiatric medication may be useful for some individuals with ASC who have severe impairing symptoms, such as hyperactivity, anxiety, obsessions/compulsions, depression, mood instability, or aggression. Medications may help reduce some of these symptoms. It is difficult to know which individual will respond best to which specific medication. Furthermore, it may take some time, weeks to even months, to reach an appropriate dose at which symptom reduction is notable. Finally, all medications have potential side effects and risks that must be weighed carefully prior to initiating any medication.

References

Hammad, T. A., Laughren, T., & Racoosin, J. (2006). Suicidality in pediatric patients treated with antidepressant drugs. *Archives of General Psychiatry, 63*, 332–339.

8

Q61
Are Antipsychotic Medications Useful in ASC?

Lovina Chahal & Antonio Y. Hardan

In individuals with ASC, antipsychotic medication is usually a last resort after behavior therapy, educational interventions, and other medications have been tried. Individuals who are exhibiting aggressive behaviors or severe symptoms of inattention and hyperactivity are examples of some of the severe conditions that may be helped by these medications. In adults without ASC, these medications are used to treat thought disorders with delusions, hallucinations, and paranoia. Antipsychotics were first used to help individuals with schizophrenia and, over time, have become useful in treating other disabling mental conditions like bipolar disorder, obsessive compulsive disorder (OCD), and psychotic depression. The success in treating adults led doctors to explore the possibility of helping children with these medications, especially for symptoms that are not successfully treated with any other modality. In individuals with autism, antipsychotics are frequently used to target aggressive behaviors, irritability, and impulsivity, mainly after other commonly used medications have failed to controls these symptoms.

There are two general groups of antipsychotic medications, *typical* and *atypical*. The name for these categories may seem confusing, and that is because these titles are a historical reference. The older generation of antipsychotics discovered in the 1950s was marked by a noticeable side effect of movement disorders, such as involuntary rhythmic movements of the body, muscle spasms, and tremors at higher doses. When the new generation of antipsychotics, also called second-generation antipsychotics, was developed in the 1980s, there was a marked absence of these movement changes, and the new medications were termed "atypical." Both categories of medications help treat symptoms through their effect primarily on the dopamine system in the brain. Each medication in both classes is unique in how much it blocks the dopamine system. Some of the atypical antipsychotics also affect other neurotransmitters, like serotonin and norepinephrine, which also makes each of the medications unique in how it treats symptoms. Each typical and atypical medication has a unique pattern of effects on these important neurotransmitter systems and may lead a doctor to pick one medication over another, depending on what the child needs help with.

8

A doctor will pick a specific antipsychotic medication on the basis of 2 main criteria. Initially, the doctor will determine the pattern of symptoms an individual has (e.g., aggressivity, impulsivity, tic symptoms, or repetitive behaviors). Once the pattern has been determined, there are probably some antipsychotic medications that research shows to be more helpful than others. Thus, the doctor first makes a decision on narrowing down the choice of medications that may likely be helpful. Second, each antipsychotic medication has a different pattern of possible side effects. Depending on the individual's medical health, some antipsychotic medications may be more suitable than others. After weighing the risks and benefits, the most appropriate medication is chosen. It is important to note that the US Food and Drug Administration (FDA) has recently approved 2 atypical antipsychotics, risperidone and aripiprazole, to treat behavior-related problems associated with autism in children. Despite that these medications are approved only in children and adolescents, most physicians also use these medications in adults with autism. The philosophy in using medications in individuals with autism is "to start low and go slow." So, usually the lowest possible starting dose is chosen, and the child is monitored over a period of weeks and months to see if they are improving from the medication and tolerating it. It can take time for the medication to be effective, so the improvements and side effects have to be observed for over a period of weeks to months rather than days. The doses can be broken up over the day, because children are sometimes fast metabolizers. As a child gets older and their metabolism and body size change, the dose may need to be adjusted.

Although these medications are helpful in improving the quality of life, they are to be used cautiously. As mentioned before, the typical antipsychotic medications, like haloperidol or thioridazine, have the significant side effect of tardive dyskinesia, a neuromuscular abnormality, resulting in involuntary rhythmic movement. The major concern with tardive dyskinesia is that it can be irreversible, and individuals experiencing this side effect might experience permanent consequences with considerable suffering and functional limitations. Conversely, atypical antipsychotic medications have a much lower risk of tardive dyskinesia but have other problematic side effects. Sometimes people taking atypical antipsychotics can develop an intense desire to eat, leading to significant weight gain (i.e., 10–15 pounds or more). Sometimes, the weight gain can result in metabolic disorders, such as diabetes and hyperlipidemia (high cholesterol). Thus, deciding between medications can be a difficult choice, weighing the advantages of improvement in the quality of life and the disadvantages of the medical risks of side effects.

Certain antipsychotics are more commonly prescribed, and those are risperidone, quetiapine, and aripiprazole. Each medication's usual dose range, side effects, and monitoring are described in the following. Risperidone (Risperdal®) is approved by the FDA for treatment of irritability and associated dysfunctional behaviors in children with autism. It acts on key receptors in the brain, such serotonin and dopamine. It comes in several different forms, including a regular tablet, a dissolving tablet, a liquid, and a longer acting injection. Typical doses in children are in the range of 0.25–3.0 mg daily, either given all at once or broken up into 2 doses over the day. The average dose in the clinical studies that have been conducted in children and adolescents was around 1.5–2.0 mg per day. Aripiprazole (Abilify®) is a relative newcomer to the treatment of behaviors associated with autism, especially aggression, self-injury, and impulsivity. It was approved by the FDA for the treatment of irritability in children and adolescents with autism in 2009. It also works on the dopamine and serotonin systems. It comes in several different forms, including a regular tablet, an oral solution, and a short acting injection. The usual doses can range from 10–15 mg daily that can be given all at once or broken up into 2–4 doses spread over the day. Quetiapine (Seroquel®) is a medication that is useful for aggression and hyperactivity. It acts on several brain receptors including dopamine, serotonin, and histaminic receptors. It is available as a short-acting tablet or longer-acting tablet. The typical dose range is 25–800 mg that may be given all at once or broken up into partial doses given throughout the day.

Regarding side effects, things to keep track of are sleepiness, weight changes, and sexual side effects. Weight gain is especially important to monitor when taking these medications. An individual taking any of the antipsychotics, especially atypical ones, will need to have blood tests done every few months to monitor glucose, triglycerides and cholesterol levels. It is also important to monitor for involuntary motor movements that can be observed with this class of medications, because they can be irreversible.

In summary, antipsychotic medications are very effective agents to target disruptive behaviors in individuals with autism, including aggression and irritability. Choosing to use an antipsychotic medication should be made carefully. This class of medications gives powerful relief of severe symptoms that might not respond to other agents and/or behavioral treatment. However, an individual's health would need close observation for common side effects like sedation and weight change. Other monitoring may involve regular doctor's visits, occasional blood tests, and electrocardiograms (ECGs). Although it is tough and sometimes overwhelming to consider having someone take antipsychotic treatments, these medications are necessary at times, and assessing the risks and benefits of these agents is crucial before making a decision.

8

Q62
Are Antidepressants Useful in ASC?

Lovina Chahal & Antonio Y. Hardan

Antidepressants are a frequently used class of medications because they help with anxious and depressive symptoms in children and adults with autism. They are safe and effective medications with limited side effects. Although they are called antidepressants because of their powerful effect on mood in adults, they have also been helpful with anxiety syndromes such as obsessive compulsive disorder (OCD). For example, when children with autism appear to be nervous about being in unfamiliar places or feeling down and depressed, antidepressants may be used. Benefits from this class of medications are thought to happen through their modulation of 2 neurotransmitters systems involving norepinephrine and serotonin. There are several different categories of antidepressants that vary by their effect on neurotransmitters, and thus help guide physicians to choose which ones may be particularly helpful for each individual.

Antidepressants vary from each other based on their particular blend of effects on the serotonin, norepinephrine, and other neurotransmitter systems. They also differ from each other with regard to side effects. Therefore, the choice of medication will depend on the most prominent symptoms experienced by the individual. For low mood and low interest, low to moderate doses of antidepressants may be used. For anxiety, higher doses of antidepressants may be chosen as anxiety responds better to higher doses. For repetitive behaviors, which are thought to be related to OCD, the average dose is higher than that usually used for the treatment of depressive and anxiety symptoms. Additionally, if an individual with autism is having trouble sleeping, some of the antidepressants with a sedating effect, like mirtazapine and trazadone, are sometimes prescribed.

Selective Serotonin Reuptake Inhibitors (SSRIs)

The SSRI type of antidepressant is commonly recommended because of its safety profile, limited side effects, and ease of use. As its name suggests, SSRIs primarily work through the serotonin system, which makes them particularly useful for anxiety conditions like panic and obsessive-compulsive behavior (OCBs). Fluoxetine (Prozac) is used for depression, repetitive behaviors, and OCB at

8

20–80 mg a day with the occasional side effects of increased hyperactivity and insomnia. Sertraline (Zoloft) is also used for OCB and reduces anxiety, aggression, and repetitive behaviors at doses ranging from 25 mg to 200 mg daily with side effects similar to fluoxetine. Citalopram (Celexa) is used for anxiety, depression, OCB, repetitive behaviors and irritability at doses of 10 mg to 60 mg, usually well tolerated, with side effects of headaches, agitation, and sedation. Escitalopram (Lexapro) is a molecularly purified version of citalopram that maybe used for similar reasons. Fluvoxamine (Luvox) is also used in individuals with autism at 75–300 mg daily with the main side effect of sedation and nausea. Fluvoxamine has been found to be beneficial in targeting OCB in adults but not children with autism. Paroxetine (Paxil), another SSRI, may also be used in autism at doses ranging from 10 mg to 50 mg per day. Some common side effects of all SSRIs are short-term increases in agitation, stomach discomfort, and physical restlessness, which commonly dissipate over time. Sometimes there is an increase in suicidal thoughts that should be monitored for carefully.

While SSRIs are commonly used in children and adolescents with ASC, studies have not been successful in showing the benefits of these medications in this population. The US National Institutes of Health (NIH) sponsored a randomized controlled trial (the most rigorous type of clinical trial) with 149 participants with ASC. In this trial, citalopram was compared to placebo for treatment of repetitive behaviors and no difference was found between the 2 groups. Thus, this trial does not support the use of citalopram for repetitive behaviors. Another study that casts doubt on the effectiveness of SSRIs in patients with autism is the Study of Fluoxetine in Autism (SOFIA), an industry-sponsored trial conducted through the Autism Clinical Trials Network (ACTN). ACTN is an organized attempt to verify the safety and efficacy of medications in autism. The study evaluated the efficacy and safety of a new low-dose form, melt-in-the-mouth formula of fluoxetine. Although the study showed a decrease in repetitive behaviors with both fluoxetine and placebo, no differences between the 2 groups were found. Thus, the study does not support the use of fluoxetine for repetitive behaviors in ASC.

Other Antidepressants

Tricyclic antidepressants (TCAs) are among the oldest groups of antidepressants and named after their 3-ring chemical structure. Clomipramine is one that might be used for irritability or repetitive behavior in doses of 75–200 mg a day. Some side effects are dry mouth, constipation, sedation, and tremor. They can be lethal in overdose by causing an abnormal rhythm in the heart and, therefore, need to be monitored by occasional ECGs and regular blood levels.

There are other antidepressants that are commonly used to treat symptoms in ASC but haven't been extensively studied in children and adolescents. Trazodone is an antidepressant that is more commonly used for insomnia. Mirtazapine (Remeron) is also helpful for children to reduce self-injury, irritability, anxiety, insomnia, depression, and hyperactivity at doses ranging from 7.5 mg to 45

8

mg daily. It works on both the serotonin and norepinephrine neurotransmitter systems. Mirtazapine has side effects similar to those of the SSRIs and is usually well tolerated. Venlafaxine and duloxetine also work on the serotonin and norepinephrine neurotransmitter systems and are used for similar symptoms. At lower doses, venlafaxine is used to treat hyperactivity and irritability. Some patients can see an improvement in repetitive behaviors, socialization, communication, and inattention.

What to Worry About with Antidepressants

Relative to other medication classes, e.g., antipsychotics, there are fewer major side effects to be concerned about. Gastrointestinal distress, sedation, and headache are common to most of them but usually abate after some time. Some may experience dry mouth and insomnia with some of the medications. Some individuals with autism may have in increase in energy, activity, and aggression, which can be concerning as that is usually the opposite of the desired outcome. A most concerning adverse event is the increase of suicidal ideation in people less than the age of 24. Please note that, although there is an increase in suicidal ideation, this has not been linked to an increase in suicide attempts and has not been clearly reported in individuals with autism. Nevertheless, this is important to monitor in children who are verbal and adults and may prompt a prescriber to switch medications.

In summary, antidepressants are useful medications due to their safety and tolerability in the treatment of repetitive behaviors, anxiety, and depression in individuals with autism. However, recent studies have cast doubt on the efficacy, of SSRIs in particular, for repetitive behaviors in children with autism. This makes treating symptoms even more challenging and confusing for both parents and physicians.

Q63
Are Stimulants Useful in ASC?

L. Eugene Arnold, Michael Aman, & Benjamin Handen

This question naturally arises because hyperactivity, impulsivity, and inattention are common complaints in ASC (Aman, Farmer, Hollway, & Arnold, 2008). Stimulants are not as useful in ASC as in other children but are worth trying in individual patients, because (1) some patients with ASC have an excellent response and (2) the result can be ascertained quickly due to the immediate effect of stimulants, whether beneficial or adverse.

It has been known for some time that the response rate in autism and intellectual disability (ID) is lower than in other children (Handen, Breaux, Gosling, Ploof, & Feldman, 1990; Handen et al., 1992). Indeed, at one point, it was thought that stimulants were contraindicated in autism (Aman, 1982). Children with IQs below 45 or mental age below 4½ years seem particularly unresponsive (Aman, Buican, & Arnold, 2003). Nevertheless, there were some children in the lower functional levels who benefited from stimulants.

The Research Units on Pediatric Psychopharmacology (RUPP) Autism Network undertook a multi-site, double-blind study to determine methylphenidate response and side effects in ASC (RUPP Autism Network, 2005; Posey et al., 2006). Children age 5 to 14 years entered a 4-week balanced crossover with random assignment to order of placebo and three doses of immediate-release methylphenidate, all given 3 times a day, with the third dose sculpted to approximately half of each of the first 2 doses. The total daily dose ranged from 7.5 mg (low dose) to 25 mg (high dose) for the lightest children and 12.5 mg (low dose) to 50 mg (high dose) for the largest children. The target daily total averaged about 0.315 mg/kg for the low dose, 0.625 mg/kg/day for the medium dose, and 1.25 mg/kg for the high dose. Prior to the double-blind, random-order month, all subjects had a single-blind safety "test dose" week, in which placebo and all three doses appropriate for their size were given in ascending order. Those who could not tolerate at least the medium dose exited the study. Those who could tolerate the medium, but not the high dose, had the high dose deleted from their double-blind crossover, with an extra medium dose week substituted. The double-blind possible orders were censored to prevent the high dose from ever immediately following the placebo. Responders to one of the active doses during the double-blind phase entered an 8-week open continuation.

8

The results showed a 49% response rate, in contrast to the response rate of 70% or more consistently reported for typically developing children (e.g., The MTA Cooperative Group, 1999, which used approximately the same doses in a placebo-controlled titration in combined-type ADHD). The average effect size on teacher rating, for the optimal dose, was also lower than usually reported for typically developing children, although parent rating showed a similar effect as in typically developing children, possibly even nominally better. The small effect seen by teachers may, at least partly, be explained by highly structured school programs, which takes away some of the variance for showing an effect. Importantly, the intolerable adverse event rate was extremely high: 13 of 72 had to drop out because of intolerable side effects, especially increased irritability. This 18% rate of intolerable side effects contrasts with less than 4% reported in typically developing children with ADHD with similar doses (The MTA Cooperative Group, 1999).

Thus, the likelihood of good response (about half) is lower and the likelihood of intolerable adverse events (almost 1 in 5), is higher in ASC than in typically developing children with ADHD. However, for the half who do have a good response, the benefit may be remarkable. The adverse events are generally short-lived, wearing off as the drug washes out, usually by the next day. Therefore, a stimulant trial may be indicated in individual children with ASC and hyperactivity, despite the discouraging group statistics. Although little harm usually comes from brief cautious trials, it is important that practitioners not keep raising doses of stimulants in hopes of improving the clinical response when early indications are that a child is deteriorating behaviorally.

Nevertheless, it would be desirable to have alternatives to stimulants. Two possibilities have emerged with potential special value in ASC. The first is atomoxetine, a nonstimulant approved for ADHD by the US Food and Drug Administration (FDA). Arnold et al. (2006) reported a double-blind, balanced crossover with random assignment to 6 weeks each of placebo and clinically titrated atomoxetine, with 1-week washout between and random assignment to order. On the primary outcome, the Hyperactivity subscale of the Aberrant Behavior Checklist (ABC), atomoxetine was superior to placebo. It was also superior on a 0-to-3 rating of the nine DSM-IV-TR ADHD hyperactive/impulsive symptoms, but missed significance on the nine inattentive symptoms. Nine of the 16 probands responded to atomoxetine, of whom 2 also responded to placebo (43% placebo-controlled response rate). Most encouraging, only 1 of the 16 had to drop out because of intolerable side effect. Two larger placebo-controlled studies of atomoxetine are currently being carried out.

The other emerging possibility for treating ADHD symptoms in ASC is guanfacine. The RUPP Autism Network conducted a 25-child open trial for the 13 dropouts from the methylphenidate trial described above, plus some additional children who had failed screen because of previous adequate trial of methylphenidate (Scahill et al., 2006). Doses of guanfacine were 1 to 3 mg/day in 2 or 3 divided doses. Pre-post effect size on the primary outcome (Hyperactivity scale of the ABC) were large for parent and teacher ratings. Twelve of the 25 (48%) were considered responders. Although a placebo-controlled study is needed to draw definite conclusions, it is noteworthy that these were children for whom methylphenidate had been unsatisfactory. Handen, Sahl, and Hardan (2008) recently conducted a double-blind, placebo-controlled crossover trial of guanfacine in 11 children with ID ($n = 4$) or ASC ($n = 7$). Four of the seven individuals with ASC were found to be responders, based upon > 50% improvement on the Hyperactivity scale of the ABC.

References

Aman, M. G. (1982). Stimulant drug effects in developmental disorders and hyperactivity: Toward a resolution of disparate findings. *Journal of Autism and Developmental Disorders, 12*, 385–398.

Aman, M. G., Buican, B., & Arnold, L. E. (2003). Methylphenidate treatment in children with low IQ and ADHD: Analysis of three aggregated studies. *Journal of Child and Adolescent Psychopharmacology, 13*, 27–38.

Aman, M. G., Farmer, C. A., Hollway, J. A., & Arnold, L. E. (2008). Treatment of inattention, overactivity, and impulsiveness in autism spectrum disorders. *Child and Adolescent Psychiatric Clinics of North America, 17*, 713–738.

Arnold, L. E., Aman, M. G., Cook, A. M., Witwer, A. N., Hall, K. L., Thompson, S., & Ramadan, Y. (2006). Atomoxetine for hyperactivity in autism spectrum disorders: Placebo-controlled crossover pilot trial. *Journal of the. American Academy of Child and Adolescent Psychiatry, 45*, 1196–1205.

Handen, B. L., Breaux, A. M.,.Gosling, A., Ploof, D. L., & Feldman, H. (1990). Efficacy of Ritalin among mentally retarded children with ADHD. *Pediatrics, 86*, 922–930.

Handen, B. L., Breaux, A. M., Janosky, J., McAuliffe, S., Feldman, H., & Gosling, A. (1992). Effects and noneffects of methylphenidate in children with mental retardation and ADHD. *Journal of the American Academy of Child and Adolescent Psychiatry, 31*, 455–461.

Handen, B. L., Sahl, R., & Hardan, A. (2008). Guanfacine in children with developmental disabilities. *Journal of Developmental and Behavioral Pediatrics, 29*, 303–308.

The MTA (Multimodal Treatment Study of Children with ADHD) Cooperative Group. (1999). A 14-month randomized clinical trial of treatment strategies for attention-deficit/hyperactivity disorder. *Archives of General Psychiatry, 56*, 1073–1086.

Posey, D. J., Aman, M. G., McCracken, J. T., Scahill, L., Tierney, E., Arnold, L. E., ... McDougle, C. J. (2006). Positive effects of methylphenidate on inattention and hyperactivity in pervasive developmental disorders: An analysis of secondary measures. *Biological Psychiatry, 61*, 538–544.

Research Units on Pediatric Psychopharmacology (RUPP) Autism Network (2005). A randomized controlled crossover trial of methylphenidate in pervasive developmental disorders with hyperactivity. *Archives of General Psychiatry, 62*, 1266–1274.

Scahill, L., Aman, M. G., McDougle, C. J., McCracken, J. T., Tierney, E., Dziura, J... Vitiello, B. (2006). A prospective open trial of guanfacine in children with pervasive developmental disorders. *Journal of Child and Adolescent Psychopharmacology, 16*, 589–598.

Q64
Are Nutritional Supplements or Special Diets Useful in ASC?

Sven Bölte

There are claims that people with ASC have nutritional problems (for instance, abnormal levels of amino acids, vitamins, or minerals) caused by either damaged metabolism, food refusal, or eating rituals, and that those are key factors in causing or managing some autistic behaviors. This view is not widely accepted by the scientific community, owing to weak, inconsistent, nonexistent or negative empirical evidence (e.g., Millward, Ferriter, Calver, & Connell-Jones, 2008; Nye & Brice, 2005). Moreover, such claims are often rather unspecific to ASC, also demanding validity in other disorders, such as ADHD (Weber & Newmark, 2007). Nevertheless, a variety of nutritional supplements and diets are offered for treating people with ASC, and a substantial minority of parents try to help their children with these approaches (Green et al., 2006).

Dietary supplements are vitamins, minerals, herbs, and other substances meant to improve nourishment. A wide range of supplements are available. They come in many shapes and forms, as pills, capsules, powders, liquids, and injections. Among the food supplements often recommended for ASC are vitamins A, B6 combined with magnesium, B12, C, E, dimethylglycine, thiamine, carnosine folic acid, cad liver oil, fatty acids (omega 3 and 6), zinc, glyconutrients, phytonutrients, and probiotics.

The special diets most widely recommended for ASC are those avoiding gluten and casein. It has been hypothesized that ASC may be aggravated by opioid peptides that are metabolic products of gluten and casein. Gluten is a composite of the proteins gliadin and glutenin, which exist in oat, wheat, rye, and barley. Casein is a protein that occurs in milk, yogurt, and cheese, but is often also admixed in energy bars, drinks, and processed foods. It has a molecular structure similar to that of gluten. Therefore, some gluten-free diets are combined with casein-free diets. Other diets sometimes recommended are yeast free (combined with antifungal medication), high fat, adequate protein, low carbohydrate, so-called ketogenic (used for the treatment of intractable seizures), excluding complex carbohydrates (such as those found in rice and potatoes) and replacing them with simple carbohydrates (such as those found in bananas and squashes), as well as avoidance of salicylates, food dyes, and simple sugars.

As mentioned above, there is no reliable general evidence that special diets or food supplements help people with ASC. Apart from being potentially expensive and inconvenient, these alternative interventions are also not without risk. They are not harmless just because they are "alternative" or "natural." For instance, some high-dosage vitamins and minerals accumulate in the organism and can reach toxic levels. Some special diets may cause deficiency symptoms. Also, there are no long-term safety data for most of these treatments.

There are recommendations to combine diets with chelation therapy, a method to remove heavy metals (e.g., lead, arsenic, and mercury) from the body using dimercaptosuccinic acid or other chemical agents. Its application in ASC is controversial and has led to fatalities (Brown, Willis, Omalu, & Leiker, 2006).

Specific diets or supplements may help some persons with ASC, if nutritional problems are medically validated in individual cases, using accurate blood testing. The use of special diets and nutritional supplements should always be supervised by a physician or nutritionist.

References

Brown, M. J., Willis, T., Omalu, B., & Leiker, R. (2006). Deaths resulting from hypocalcemia after administration of edetate disodium: 2003–2005. *Pediatrics, 118,* e534–536.

Green, V. A., Pituch, K. A., Itchon, J., Choi, A., O'Reilly, M., & Sigafoos, J. (2006). Internet survey of treatments used by parents of children with autism. *Research in Developmental Disabilities, 27,* 70–84.

Millward, C., Ferriter, M., Calver, S., & Connell-Jones, G. (2008). Gluten- and casein-free diets for autistic spectrum disorder. *Cochrane Database Systematic Reviews, Apr 16,* (2) CD003498.

Nye, C., & Brice, A. (2005). Combined vitamin B6-magnesium treatment in autism spectrum disorder. *Cochrane Database Systematic Reviews, Oct 19,* (4) CD003497.

Weber, W., & Newmark, S. (2007). Complementary and alternative medical therapies for attention-deficit/hyperactivity disorder and autism. *Pediatric Clinics of North America, 54,* 983–1006.

Further Reading

Levy, S. E., & Hyman, S. L. (2008). Complementary and alternative medicine treatments for children with autism spectrum disorders. *Child and Adolescent Psychiatric Clinics of North America, 17,* 803–820.

Volkmar, F. R., & Wiesner, L. A. (2004). *Healthcare for children on the autism spectrum: A guide to medical, nutritional, and behavioral issues.* Bethesda, MD: Woodbine House.

8

Section 9

School, Education, Employment, and Independent Living

Q65
What Kinds of Problems Do Individuals with ASC Encounter in School?

Lara Delmolino

Cognitive Skills

Individuals with ASC exist along a spectrum spanning average or above average cognitive ability to all levels of intellectual disability (ID). In addition, students with autism typically display uneven patterns of cognitive skill at all levels of the IQ continuum (Tsatsanis, 2005). This uneven development underscores the need for thorough and ongoing assessment to ensure that a student is receiving appropriate instruction.

Learning Style

The optimal learning format for an individual with ASC requires consideration. Some students with ASC may have strong skills in areas such as visual processing but struggle with language and abstract reasoning, which may be relatively weak in comparison. Alternately, some students may be easily distracted by visual input and find verbal scripts or rehearsal to be successful learning strategies.

Adaptive Behavior and Independence

Even in the absence of cognitive delay, individuals with ASC often show delays or deviance in the development of independent and adaptive behavior to a degree that is discrepant from their cognitive functioning. A student who is advanced academically may have significant difficulty mastering the nonacademic aspects of a school environment and daily activities, such as navigating the school building, organizing school materials, and interacting with teachers

9

and classmates. Social peer contact and interaction is a strong source of motivation for many typically developing students to attend school and participate in activities. The diminished capacity for an individual with ASC to be motivated by or successful with typical social contact is a potential problem. The performance of students with ASC may need to be addressed via contrived and individualized systems of motivation (Delmolino & Harris, 2004). In addition, being socially ostracized, bullied, or uncomfortable in social settings may affect school attendance and participation for a student with ASC.

Behavioral Characteristics

The restricted interests, preoccupations, or repetitive behavior of individuals with ASC may pose difficulty in school. These behaviors are both socially stigmatizing and potentially distracting to peers and may interfere with a student's learning. Potent interventions to address these behaviors may be impractical or challenging to provide in some school settings. In addition, disruptive, aggressive, and self-injurious behaviors are common in the repertoire of learners with ASC and pose a challenge to educators (Simpson & Otten, 2005). Because communication difficulties or nonpreferred activities are fairly common in the school experience of learners with autism, they may express their distress through challenging behaviors. The use of antecedent strategies and functional assessment is a fundamental part of addressing these issues.

Social Integration

In an inclusive educational setting, the impact of the students with ASC on classmates should also be considered. Awareness of difference, tolerance, and diversity are important components of typical social development and could take various forms, depending on the age and peer group. Settings that have the opportunity of including peer training and support may benefit classmates, as well as students with ASC.

Resources

The behavioral and learning characteristics of individuals with ASC often require richness of resources and significant adaptation of materials and curriculum. These adaptations and resources are costly, in terms of time and financial considerations, and pose a dilemma for educational settings.

References

Delmolino, L., & Harris, S (2004*). Incentives for change: Motivating people with autism spectrum disorders to learn and gain independence.* Bethesda, MD: Woodbine House.

Tsatsanis, K. D. (2005). Neuropsychological characteristics in autism and related conditions. In F. Volkmar, R. Paul, A. Klin, & D. Cohen (Eds.), *Handbook of autism and pervasive developmental disorders* (3rd ed.) (pp. 365–381). Hoboken, NJ: Wiley.

Simpson, R., & Otten, K. (2005). Structuring Behavior Management Strategies and building social competence. In D. Zager, D. (Ed.), *Autism spectrum disorders, identification, education and treatment* (pp. 367–394*)*. Mahwah, NJ: Erlbaum.

Further Reading

Wilczynski, S., Menousek, K., Hunter, M., & Mudgal, D. (2007). Individualized education programs for youth with autism spectrum disorders. *Psychology in the Schools, 44*, 653–666.

Klin, A., Saulnier, C., Sparrow, S., Cicchetti, D., Lord, C., & Volkmar, F. (2007*).* Social and communication abilities and disabilities in higher functioning individuals with autism spectrum disorders: The Vineland and the ADOS. *Journal of Autism and Developmental Disorders, 37*, 748–759.

Klin, A., Saulnier, C., Tsatsani, K., & Volkmar, F. (2005). Clinical evaluation in autism spectrum disorders: Psychological assessment within a transdisciplinary framework. In F. Volkmar, R. Paul, A. Klin, & D. Cohen (Eds.), *Handbook of autism and pervasive developmental disorders* (3rd ed.) (pp. 365–381). Hoboken, NJ: Wiley.

9

Which Form of Education Is Best for Individuals with ASC?

Sandra L. Harris

The optimal setting and teaching methods for children and adolescents with an ASC vary with the individual's degree of autistic involvement, age, and cognitive ability. An older learner with very substantial symptoms of an ASC and serious intellectual disabilities requires a different educational experience than a person with Asperger syndrome, who has strong cognitive skills and milder symptoms. Similarly, a very young child often benefits most from a one-to-one teaching ratio, while an older learner should ideally be functioning in a group setting.

The Very Young Learner with ASC

Researchers have recently identified several behaviors of infants and toddlers that predict a diagnosis of an ASC in children by the age of 3 years (Chawarska, Klin, & Volkmar, 2008). Although we are just starting to develop the most effective interventions for children this young, there is good reason to expect that very early intervention will be beneficial for many youngsters. For infants and toddlers, treatment is probably best effected in the home with considerable parental involvement.

The Preschool Child with ASC

Since Lovaas (1987) published his landmark study, we have known that intensive intervention for preschool aged children can significantly alter the developmental trajectory of approximately half of these youngsters. This finding has been replicated a number of times. We also know that for preschool-aged children, the intensive use of Applied Behavior Analysis (ABA) has the best empirical support. These methods can be applied in public or private schools or in home based settings. The crucial variables appear to be the intensity of intervention and the application of empirically based treatments. A respect for the developmental needs of the child is also important. Generic treatments, even if used intensively, do not achieve the outcome that may be accomplished with ABA (e.g., Howard, Sparkman, Cohen, Green, & Stanislaw, 2005).

The Older Learner with ASC and Impaired Cognitive Skills

After the preschool years, those children who do not make major educational gains in a high quality, ABA-based program require ongoing intensity to support their learning. As is the case with preschool children, this can be done in a public or private school, as long as an appropriate student to staff ratio is maintained and the learning goals are consistent with the potential of the learner. The use of home-based instruction as the primary teaching context is no longer fitting for most learners beyond kindergarten, but supplementing a school-based program with additional home-based work is often helpful. The use of photographic or written activity schedules may be important in allowing these students to gain greater independence throughout the day (e.g., McClannahan & Krantz, 1999).

The Older Learner with Strong Cognitive Skills

Some children and adolescents on the autism spectrum are capable of taking good advantage of being fully included in a regular education classroom. They may, however, need supplemental support. For example, in the elementary school years, they may still require a one-to-one aide to learn to attend to the teacher, follow group directions, initiate social interaction, and so forth. Over time, that support is often faded, although many adolescents with high-functioning ASC continue to need help in organizing their work, engaging in appropriate social behavior, and learning to control their emotional expression. This learning may be done individually or in small groups, depending on the educational setting, and may be continued even at the college level or during the entry level stages of employment. The use of ABA teaching methods that emphasize self-management strategies, including self-reinforcement, can be quite helpful for these learners. Similarly, the older, higher-functioning person with an ASC can make the transition from a photographic or written activity schedule to using a hand-held electronic organizer to stay on schedule and remind themselves of upcoming events.

9

References

Chawarska, K., Klin, A., & Volkmar, F. (Eds.) (2008). *Autism spectrum disorders in infants and toddlers. Diagnosis, assessment, and treatment.* New York, NY: Guilford.

Howard, J. S., Sparkman, C. R., Cohen, H. G., Green, G., & Stanislaw, H. (2005). A comparison of intensive behavior analytic and eclectic treatments for young children with autism. *Research in Developmental Disabilities, 26*, 359–383.

Lovaas, O. I. (1987). Behavioral treatment and normal educational and intellectual functioning in young autistic children. *Journal of Consulting and Clinical Psychology, 55*, 3–9.

McClannahan, L. E., & Krantz, P. J. (1999). *Activity schedules for children with autism: Teaching independent behavior*. Bethesda, MD: Woodbine House.

Further Reading

Harris, S. L., Handleman, J. S., & Jennett, H. K. (2005). Models of educational intervention for students with autism: Home, center and school based programming. In F. Volkmar, R. Paul, A. Klin, & D. Cohen (Eds.), *Handbook of Autism and Pervasive Developmental Disorders* (3rd ed., pp. 1043–1054). Hoboken, NJ: Wiley.

9

Q67
Are There Special Schools for People with ASC?

Sandra L. Harris

There are a variety of ways to approach the education of people with ASC. These range from full inclusion in a regular education class, to home-based treatment, to a residential placement. One model for educating people with ASC is in special schools with a staff that is deeply and broadly trained in educating individuals on the spectrum of autism (Harris, Handleman, & Jennett, 2005). The depth of technical talent in such a setting allows appropriate teaching to oc- cur even if a teacher is out sick or a speech therapist is on maternity leave. In a regular education setting, the success or failure of a special education classroom for children with ASC often hinges on the presence or absence of a specific teacher, and if this person leaves, the integrity of the entire program may be threatened.

Special schools are appropriate for very young children with an ASC be- cause the learners can receive the intensity of empirically supported treatment they require in a setting where staff members are well trained and well super- vised in the use of Applied Behavior Analysis (ABA). By the time they reach kindergarten age, many children with ASC are ready to move into a regular education class and do not need the intensity of one-to-one services they once required. In all likelihood, however, many of them will continue to benefit from specialized supports for a period of time. That interval can vary from needing a dedicated classroom aide in the early school years, to having such assistance through the high school years. Access to resource room teachers for some sub- jects and to social skills groups for improving interpersonal connections are fairly common on-going needs.

Not every young child who receives intensive ABA instruction in a spe- cialized school is ready to make the transition to a regular education setting or to a special education class in a regular school. There is a group of learners who continue to have very substantial needs as they grow up, and for some of these students a specialized school maybe the most effective and efficient set- ting throughout their school life. This group includes some students who pose serious aggression or life-threatening behavior problems. In addition, there are children who were transitioned to regular education settings at an early point

9

but were unable to adapt to a regular education class and who learned maladaptive behaviors that require, at least temporarily, a specialized school program. Similarly, there is a small group of individuals with ASC who may have been in regular education classes since they started school but later develop behavior management issues of a serious nature and need to be removed from a classroom to protect them as well as those around them. In that case, a specialized school may be a better alternative than placing the student in home instruction.

References

Harris, S. L., Handleman, J. S., & Jennett, H. K. (2005). Models of educational intervention for students with autism: Home, center and school-based programming. In F. Volkmar, R. Paul, A. Klin, & D. Cohen (Eds.), *Handbook of autism and pervasive developmental disorders* (3rd ed., pp. 1043–1054). New York, NY: Wiley.

Further Reading

Handleman, J. S., & Harris, S. L. (Eds) (2006). *School aged educational programs for children with autism.* Austin, TX: Pro-Ed.
Handleman, J. S., & Harris, S. L. (Eds.) (2008). *Preschool programs for children with autism.* Austin, TX: Pro-Ed.

9

Q68
When Should People with ASC Move Out of the Family Home?

Sandra L. Harris

For most families, making a decision about when their child with an ASC should move out of their home is one of the most emotionally complex decisions they will ever make. In many countries around the globe, parents have few options about whether or when such a move should be made. Even in places relatively rich in resources for adults for ASC, parents may find the decision difficult, and many families are inclined to keep their adult child at home. However, that choice may not, ultimately, prove to be the best course of action, in terms of the quality of life for parents or children.

Ruth Christ Sullivan (2005) points out that childhood is brief and adulthood is long for most people with ASC. This is a source of serious concern for parents who want to ensure the best for their child, even after he/she enters adulthood. Parental concern is heighted by the knowledge that they are aging, and, even if they live a long and healthy life, they will, in all probability, die before their child. Sullivan (2005) also highlights the relative lack of community-integrated residential services for adults and notes a "staggering disconnect" between the number of adults requiring out-of-home living arrangements and the spaces available (p. 1256). She also remarks that the needs of adults with ASC are often very different from those of people with intellectual disabilities (Sullivan, 2005).

Given limited resources, it is not simply a question of when a person with an ASC should leave home but what living resources can be found that are trust-worthy and respectful in their treatment. To whom can parents entrust the future well being of their child? Some families will answer that by saying they will keep their child at home as long as they are physically able and then charge their other adult children with providing care. Sometimes siblings are willing to assume that responsibility (Heller & Kramer, 2009), but often they are not. If siblings are willing to take a brother or sister with an ASC into their home, then the problem is solved, at least until the sibling becomes unable to provide care. If the sibling is unwilling, but unable to share that reluctance with the parents, then the person with an ASC may be moved to a residential setting, often with-out any preparation for the change, after the parents die.

9

Perhaps the best arrangement is one in which the person with an ASC moves into a community-integrated residential living arrangement as a young adult. That allows the parents to ease the transition and to have home visits for many years before they die or become incapacitated. It also allows the parents to have a less physically demanding and more peaceful life as they age. Finally, it creates a situation in which a sibling is more likely to be willing to assume the guardianship role and visit and support their adult brother or sister with an ASC.

For a person whose ASC is not accompanied by an intellectual disability (ID), it is, in most cases, possible and desirable to live on their own or in a supervised apartment where they can have support when they need it, as well as a great deal of independence. Such individuals are often their own guardians.

Reference

Heller, T., & Kramer, J. (2009). Involvement of adult siblings of persons with developmental disabilities in future planning. *Intellectual and Developmental Disabilities, 47,* 208–219.

Sullivan R. C. (2005). Community-integrated residential services for adults with autism: A working model (based on a mother's odyssey). In F. Volkmar, R. Paul, A. Klin, & D. Cohen (Eds.), *Handbook of autism and pervasive developmental disorders* (3rd ed., pp. 1255–1264). Hoboken, NJ: Wiley.

Further Reading

Saunders, R. R. (2007). Residential and day services. In J. W. Jacobson, J. A. Mulick, & J. Rojahn (Eds.), *Handbook of intellectual and developmental disabilities* (pp. 209–226). New York, NY: Springer.

9

Q69
What Kinds of Jobs and Professions Are Conceivable for People with ASC?

Matthias Dalferth

Participating in work and, thus, in social life is of far-reaching consequence for the personal development and future perspective of people with ASC. Having a job means getting self-affirmation, having a structured day, maintaining social contacts, achieving financial independence, and participating in economic life. The kind and extent of participation, however, depend on the severity of the disability and the work and training opportunities a society offers. Jobs in sheltered workshops or in integration companies/departments as well as competitive jobs (in supported employment) on the regular labor market can be possibilities here. Internationally, only 25% of individuals with an ASC have a job (Howlin, 2003), the majority of whom work in sheltered or partly sheltered employment. Only 5–6% are in full-time employment (Dalferth, 2007). An estimated 25–75% of adults concerned (rates vary between countries) do not participate in any productive work whatsoever.

However, far more people with ASC do have the capacity to acquire a profession or work in the regular labor market, provided that they are suitably supported while gaining the necessary job qualifications and that their fields of activity meet their interests and inclinations. A special interest (e.g., mechanics, computing, music, etc.) or a talent (e.g., photographic memory, analytical thinking, perceptual sensitivity, etc.) is always a good basis for a suitable job, and this applies particularly to individuals with an ASC. The following courses of action are open to them, depending on their individual circumstances:

The participation of adults with multiple disabilities in *occupational therapy measures and prevocational training programs.*

For the majority of adults with an ASC, a *job in sheltered employment* may be a possibility. This can help them acquire a qualification in a specific field and thus improve their chances in the regular labor market. People with considerable impairments also have a good chance of vocational development if the workshops adapt their requirements and learning strategies to the special needs of people with autism (e.g., TEACCH).

9

The last decade has shown that high-functioning young people with an ASC can successfully complete vocational training and find *employment in the regular labor market* (Dalferth, 2009). A growing number of trainees who successfully finish their vocational training prove that the potential of people with autism is not exhausted by far and can be further developed under the right conditions. However, a systematic vocational assessment and profiling are absolutely necessary to ensure the best possible vocational orientation for each individual.

Many people with Asperger syndrome or other high-functioning forms of ASC are able to acquire a university degree and work as engineers, natural scientists, computer scientists, translators, etc.

ASC are heterogeneous, and a large variety of jobs are conceivable for people with ASC, depending on the nature of their condition and, of course, the choices any individual society offers.

Depending on the kind and severity of a person's ASC, as well as their particular interests that may be confined to sub-areas of a job (i.e., smell, form, color of a material; arranging, collecting, listing, etc.), various kinds of specific *qualified jobs* can be carried out by people with an ASC – they may train as ornamental or landscape gardeners, metal workers, librarians, drivers, mechanics, cooks, tailors, lab technicians, painters, textile cleaners, or draftspersons, as well as in the catering and hotel industry, building industry, or domestic services. Especially talented autistic adults may become IT/electronics technicians, programmers, computer scientists, or mechanics. Special abilities and interests may equally lead a person to aim for a job as a piano tuner, in a registrar's office, a library, or in administration or financial controlling.

Unqualified jobs available include factory work, kitchen work, assemblage, packaging and car washing, as well as basic office, retail or farm work that does not require specific training.

Generally speaking, activities that are clearly structured and require neither team work, communication, and cooperation skills nor leadership qualities or didactic skills, and only very little creativity or flexibility are particularly suitable for people with ASC (i.e., jobs with limited complexity that allow specialization in sub-areas, are attached to a certain place, and do not require changing the workplace; tasks that can be based on detailed specifications, executed independently and in one's own time, and require accuracy, precision, and logical thinking.) Jobs characterized by a certain repetitiveness (monotony) may also be particularly suitable for people with ASC.

By contrast, activities that are accompanied by a high noise level, require multitasking or involve strongly varying demands (e.g., higher levels of efficiency at certain peak times) are rather less appropriate for individuals with ASC, as are jobs that involve large amounts of social interaction (e.g., dealing with customers), do not have any clear objectives or structures or require flexible time management. Tasks that revolve around the weighing up of alternatives and setting of priorities are likely to be found highly demanding, and jobs that involve instructing others or otherwise require strong communication skills (e.g., teaching, human resource management) are often too socially demanding for individuals with ASC.

In general, people with ASC possess many talents and may be able to do very demanding jobs, particularly those of a highly specialized nature (i.e., programming, compiling statistics, web and software design, computer animation, etc.). However, they always need help to get used to how the company works and to understand subliminal social signals and conventions. For a person with an ASC to succeed in the workplace, working conditions should be created in which their sensibilities are respected and their behavioral characteristics tolerated.

References

Dalferth, M. (2007). *How to get a job with Asperger syndrome. The Abensberg Vocational Training Programme (ATP) and job placement of people with ASD*. Paper presented at the 8th International Congress Autism-Europe, Oslo [author: please provide page range, publisher location and name; if unpublished poster or paper presented at the conference, please provide type of contribution and month of conference].

Dalferth, M. (2009). Die Bedeutung der beruflichen Rehabilitation für die Lebensqualität von Menschen aus dem autistischen Spektrum. Ergebnisse des 2. BMAS Projekts zur beruflichen Teilhabe [The importance of employment rehabilitation for the quality of life of individuals with autism spectrum conditions. Results of the 2nd Federal Ministry of Employment and Social Affairs project on integration in employment]. 12. Bundestagung Autismus Deutschland, Hamburg 2009 (pp. 165–178). Hamburg: Deutschland e.V.

Howlin, P. (2003). *Longer-term educational and employment outcomes: Learning and behavior problems in Asperger syndrome* (pp. 269–293). New York, NY: Guilford.

Further Reading

Dalferth, M., Baumgartner, F. & Vogel, H. (2009). Berufliche Teilhabe für Menschen aus dem autistischen Spektrum [Employment integration options for individuals with autism spectrum conditions]. Heidelberg, Germany: Winter.

Hawkins, G. (2006). *How to find work that works for people with Asperger syndrome*. London, Philadelphia: JKP.

Smith, M. D., Blecher, R. G., & Juhrs, P. D. (1994). *A guide to successful employment for individuals with autism*. Baltimore, MD: Paul Brookes.

9

Q70

What Problems are Encountered by People with ASC When Looking for a Job?

Luitgard Stumpf

When leaving school, many people with ASC have no idea what kind of job might be suitable for them, although almost all are highly motivated to find their way into the job market. They have spiky ability profiles, often intense or special interests, but little or no work experience and deficits in communication skills compared to non-ASC individuals of the same age and education. Appropriate assessment of the vocational abilities of people with ASC is still lacking. Besides intellectual capabilities, vocational and social skills are important to make the right career choice. For example, most jobs necessitate the ability to work independently, manage time schedules and stress, master conflicts, cooperate in teams, and cope with changing job expectations. If such demands are small, workplace tasks are concrete and transparent, and people are available that autistic individuals can talk to, this will greatly help them to get jobs and keep them.

Although the general situation for individuals with ASC has improved in recent years, they are still likely to encounter obstacles when trying to find a job or maintain one (Bölte, Wörner, & Poustka, 2005). Furthermore, if employment is achieved, the position is often below their level of educational attainment. People with ASC can also have unrealistic career expectations, as they find it hard to realize the importance of social and communication skills for different positions and professions. Moreover, they don't always take into consideration that, the higher the vocational qualification is, the more important a capacity for communication, teamwork, and leading other people will be. Because individuals with an ASC cannot easily cope with social skills demands, their jobs are often less qualified (Stumpf, 2009). This can lead to lower confidence levels and self-esteem, as they feel overqualified for a given position.

As there is often not enough information on ASC, employers can find it difficult to integrate autistic employees. They are often unable to convey instructions and expectations in a way that is helpful and supportive for people with ASC. In some instances, it would, for example, be better to give instructions in a visual format, rather than a verbal one, as language processing in social situations is highly demanding for autistic people and a verbal message may not be received correctly. People with ASC also benefit from a complex task being broken down into smaller individual tasks to make it more comprehensible. Job requirements should be made as explicit and clear as possible (Stumpf, 2009). Spontaneous new demands and unexpected changes should be avoided. It also has to be remembered that autistic people are often not used to asking for help and may just wait until someone realizes that work is not being continued.

Autistic people often aim for perfection and cannot accept mistakes, including their own. They may also find it very hard to accept advice, because it appears to them that the only possible reason for advice being given is that they have made a mistake. In such situations, it is very important for them to learn how to cope with the emotions that rise, such as frustration, anxiety, and anger. Another difficulty is time management. Because of the primacy of perfection, many autistic people are not aware that it might be as important that things are done within a certain time and that they themselves are responsible for time keeping. Finally, some individuals with an ASC have problems with grooming and personal hygiene. This is a very sensitive issue in the workplace and difficulties in this area can quickly lead to removal from a job (Attwood, 2007).

When first applying for a job, people with ASC are rarely able to handle a job interview on their own. Many will also need assistance in writing cover letters and CVs, making telephone inquiries, and getting prepared for a job interview itself. Without guidance, they often do not understand the explicit and implicit rules that apply in communications with a potential employer. For instance, they may not know what information might be important for the employer, and what irrelevant. During the job interview, it may be difficult for people with ASC to know when it is time to talk and when to listen, respectively, and when they do talk, how to convince the employer of their qualities that recommend them for the particular position in question. An interview situation requires a significant amount of flexibility and perspective taking. A crucial issue in a job interview for people with an ASC is, of course, when and how to disclose information about their diagnosis and explain what kind of support might be helpful for them (Stumpf, 2009).

Once on the job, individuals with an ASC who do not have any prior work experience (gathered, for instance, through voluntary work) often struggle with executive functioning demands because they are not used to planning various stages of their work independently, to problem solving, and to controlling the results of their work. They are likely to have difficulty with appropriate verbal and nonverbal reciprocal communication (e.g., keeping eye contact during conversations and showing recognizable facial expressions and gestures as well as interpreting those of their opposites). Equally, individuals with ASC may talk too much, not listen to their counterparts, or not show any interest in the concerns, thoughts, and opinions of others. This makes it hard for them to conduct a conversation because they have difficulty in anticipating what the other person is going to say or do or their reactions to what other people do or say may appear odd. Imagine, for example, a young man with an ASC working in an office, who is good at calculating, does not talk much, and has to learn how to handle stress and unexpected changes. Having worked for the company for a year, he starts making jokes his colleagues do not like. They have to tell the young man that they cannot tolerate this kind of behavior. This is often very hard for colleagues, because they do not want to hurt their co-worker's feelings. Furthermore, it is not always easy to explain what was wrong, why it was wrong, and how to behave more appropriately.

For an individual with an ASC to successfully sustain employment over a longer period, they need to acquire insight into unwritten social rules of communication and behavior, and efforts in terms of supporting structures have to be made by both the employer and other employees (Stumpf, 2009). As a result, successful employment will be possible for an individual with an ASC, which can lead to better job performance and improved social behavior as well as higher self-confidence (Howlin, Alcock, & Burkin, 2005).

References

Attwood, T. (2007). *The complete guide to Asperger syndrome*. London, UK: Jessica Kingsley.

Bölte, S., Wörner, S., & Poustka, F. (2005). Kindergarten, Schule, Beruf: Die Situation in einer Stichprobe von Menschen mit autistischen Störungen [Kindergarten, school, employment: Observations in a sample of individuals with autism spectrum conditions]. *Heilpädagogik online, 01*, 70–83.

Howlin, P., Alcock, J., & Burkin, C. (2005). An 8-year follow-up of a specialist supported employment service for high-ability adults with autism or Asperger syndrome. *Autism, 9*, 533–549.

Stumpf, L. (2009). Berufliche und soziale Integration. In: S. Bölte (Ed.), *Autismus. Spektrum, Ursachen, Diagnostik, Intervention, Perspektiven* [Autism. Spectrum, causes, diagnosis, intervention] (pp. 321–332). Huber: Bern.

Further Reading

Gerhardt, P. F., Holmes, D. L. (2005). Employment: Options and issues for adolescents and adults with autism spectrum disorders. In F. Volkmar, R. Paul, A. Klin, & D. Cohen. (Eds.), *Handbook of autism and pervasive developmental disorders* (pp. 1087–1101). Hoboken, NJ: Wiley.

Hawkins, G. (2004). *How to find work that works for people with Asperger syndrome*. London, UK: Jessica Kingsley.

9

Q71
What Can Help People with ASC Find and Keep Employment?

Ernst VanBergeijk, Ami Klin, & Fred Volkmar

This is an extremely relevant question, given the recent worldwide economic downturn that led to unemployment rate approaching 10% in industrialized countries (US Bureau of Labor Statistics, 2009). The parents we work with often lament that their adult children who are on the spectrum are "the last hired and the first fired." This adage is never truer than during tough economic times. According to the Organization for Autism Research, the unemployment rate for all individuals with ASC approaches 90% (Gerhardt, 2009).

The first step in finding and keeping employment is obtaining an accurate assessment of an individual's strengths, aptitudes, and interests, as well as their areas of deficits. This critical first step should act as a blueprint for the subsequent steps an individual needs to take in searching for and maintaining employment. The Vineland Adaptive Behavior Scales will provide a global picture of the individual's functioning in 5 different domains, including communication, self-care, fine and gross motor skills, and communal living. The assessment of vocational skills should attempt to match career interests with aptitudes. Often, higher-functioning individuals on the spectrum do not accurately assess their own abilities and need an objective third-party assessment. Part of the comprehensive assessment should include an analysis of the individual's travel skills. The lack of reliable transportation is a major impediment to obtaining and sustaining employment. Many individuals on the spectrum will not learn to drive. Therefore, an assessment of their travel training skills and access to public transportation is crucial. Likewise, an assessment of sensory integration issues and impairments in executive functioning is also essential. Addressing these issues prior to employment can increase the likelihood that an individual will retain employment for a longer period of time.

The second step is to decide whether or not more education or training is necessary once the individual leaves the secondary school environment. Many individuals with Asperger syndrome or PDD-NOS have strong academic skills and may be capable of taking college-level academic courses. However, it is imperative that sufficient scaffolding be put in place to help the individual navigate the social demands of the college environment and compensate for their impairments

9

in executive functioning (VanBergeijk, Klin, & Volkmar, 2008). The problem for individuals pursuing a college degree is that the connection between the course work and skills for the world of work is abstract. Individuals with an ASC need training in job skills directly related to the field they are pursuing. Some individuals on the spectrum do not see the value of a liberal arts education. They see no connection between taking a required course, such as English, and their interest in a field, such as computers. These individuals should be encouraged to pursue vocational training in computer languages, networking, and repair. Vocational programs offer a wide range of career choices from small animal care to more traditional vocational training in areas such as plumbing, carpentry, automotive, and electrical repair. Transitional programs combine aspects of a college degree program and a vocational training program. These programs offer training, not only in vocational fields and in academics, but also in areas of social skills and independent living. Transitional programs offer internships in the student's chosen occupation. Job coaches are available to help the individual with an ASC navigate the social aspects of the work site. Training is directly related to the job at hand. Often, if an intern is successful, then they are hired as an employee. Transitional programs also train individuals on the spectrum in resume writing, job searches, proper dress for the particular work environment, and interviewing.

The third step in securing employment is the job search. Use personal or familial connections. It is estimated that 80% of jobs are found through personal connections (GovCentral, 2009). Individuals on the spectrum are, therefore, at a disadvantage because they have limited social circles. The family of the individual can be instrumental in providing this vital link. Through family contacts, an individual on the spectrum is more likely to secure employment. Traditional job searches are now done through the internet, but only 15–20% of available positions are advertised in any media (Hansen, 2010).

The fourth step in obtaining employment is the job interview. The social nature of a job interview puts individuals with an ASC at a distinct disadvantage. Repeated rehearsals or role plays of a job interview are paramount. Videotaping mock interviews and providing the individual with specific feedback will help reduce anxiety and increase the probability that they will successfully complete the interview. Give them rules about how much eye contact they should make. Practice the art of small talk. Review the importance of proper grooming and dress. The small talk aspects of the job interview are perhaps the most stressful portions of the process for individuals with ASC. Teach the job candidate how to focus upon skills and past accomplishments. Often a portfolio can be used to draw attention away from the candidate and allow them to demonstrate their skills (Grandin & Duffy, 2004).

The fifth step in obtaining and sustaining employment is learning the employment and antidiscrimination laws that are in effect. Identify reasonable accommodations that would enhance success. In particular, an individual will need help knowing what triggers their anxiety and effective coping strategies that can be enacted. Having the individual practice stress reduction techniques can keep them prepare for such situations. Some of these techniques might need to be shared with the employer to avoid misunderstandings. Identifying natural mentors in an organization will help an individual with an ASC in interpreting ambiguous social situations (Edmonds & Beardon, 2009). Knowing employees in the human resources department before there is a problem can also be a tremendous help to an individual on the spectrum. They can help implement reasonable accommodations and mediate in situations where the person's disability is interfering with his or her effectiveness at work.

A person on the autism spectrum and their family should consider utilizing state or federal vocational rehabilitation agencies when their own efforts have failed in securing employment. These agencies can conduct job-related functional assessments. Eligibility for these services is not only based upon the IQ of the individual, but also their adaptive functioning. The assessment of the latter set of skills is imperative for higher-functioning individuals whose IQ may fall into the average to superior range but whose adaptive functioning skills are clearly delayed. After making a careful assessment, vocational rehabilitative agencies can place an individual in an appropriate work setting. For lower-functioning individuals on the spectrum, this will most likely be a sheltered work setting. Sheltered work settings are created specifically to train individuals with a variety of disabilities to work. The most familiar example of sheltered workshop programs is Goodwill Industries. They are a private, nonprofit, social services agency. In the US, it is most widely recognized for its thrift stores that sell second-hand goods to fund the social services it provides across the country. It is also one of the largest private agencies that provide vocational training and sheltered workshop experiences to clients with a variety of disadvantages. For a complete description of the services Goodwill Industries offers, please visit www.goodwill.org/page/guest/about.

A second type of work setting in which a rehabilitative agency may place an individual is a supportive work site, where the employer works with the agency to provide the person on the spectrum with employment. Often the agency provides the individual and their employer with a job coach, who helps the individual decode the social requirements of the job and helps them break down tasks into manageable pieces. The job coach also helps to identify stressful situations that interfere with the individual's job performance as well as helping the person develop coping strategies at the work site. A customized employment site is one where a job is restructured or "carved" to suit the needs, interests, and abilities of the disabled individual and, simultaneously, meet the needs of the employer (Gerhardt, 2009). Finally, a vocational rehabilitative agency may also place an individual on the spectrum in a competitive work site. Competitive work sites are simply job sites where the individual earns a competitive wage. The salary is earned through their contribution to the company. No subsidies are provided to the employer for the individual's wages, and little, if any, support is provided to the individual at the work site. Competitive work sites provide an individual on the spectrum the highest level of community integration. Volunteering at a nonprofit organization while looking for paid employment is a strategy used by many people, both on and off the spectrum (Edmonds & Beardon, 2009). References from these sources can be invaluable in later job searches. Sometimes, a volunteer can be so invaluable that it can lead to the creation of a paid position. Volunteering at an organization or a position that one is passionate about allows the skills and strengths of an individual on the spectrum to shine.

References

Edmonds, G., & Beardon, L. (Ed.) (2009). *Asperger syndrome & employment: Adults speak out about Asperger syndrome.* London, UK: Jessica Kingsley.

Gerhardt, P. (2009). *The current state of services for adults with autism.* Draft Report. Advancing Futures for Adults with Autism Think Tank. New York, NY: Center for Autism.

GovCentral. (2009). *Network to get a government job guide.* Retrieved from http://gov-central.monster.com/benefits/articles/8498-network-to-get-a-government-job-guide.

Grandin, T., & Duffy, K. (2004). *Developing talents: Careers for individuals with Asperger syndrome and high-functioning autism.* Shawnee Mission: Autism Asperger Publishing Company.

Hansen, R. (2010). 15 myths and misconceptions about job-hunting. Retrieved October 18, 2010 from http://www.quintcareers.com/job-hunting-myths.html.

US Bureau of Labor Statistics (2009). *CPS database: Labor force statistics including the national unemployment rate.* (LNS14000000). Washington, D.C.: U.S. Government Printing Office. Retrieved from http://data.bls.gov/PDQ/servlet/SurveyOutputServle t;jsessionid=a2302ab78b717254c553

VanBergeijk. E. O., Klin, A., & Volkmar, F. (2008). Supporting more able students on the autism spectrum: College and beyond. *Journal of Autism and Developmental Disorders, 38,* 1359–1370.

Further Reading

Bolles, R. N., & Brown, D. S. (2004). *Job-hunting for the so-called handicapped or people who have disabilities.* New York, NY: Ten Speed Press.

Smith, M. D. (1995). *A guide to successful employment for individuals with autism.* Baltimore, MD: Brookes.

Wehman, P. (2006). *Life beyond the classroom: Transition strategies for young people with disabilities (4th ed.).* Baltimore, MD: Brookes.

9

Q72
What Forms of Living Are Useful and Available for Adults with ASC?

Sigan L. Hartley & Marsha Mailick Seltzer

The typical "launching stage," in which sons and daughters leave the family home as young adults to live independently, is often altered in families with children with an ASC, as individuals with an ASC often continue to need assistance in daily living into their adulthood. Determining where a person with an ASC will live as an adult is a difficult decision for families. This decision has consequences, not only for the adult with an ASC, but also their parents, siblings, and often other family members. Consideration of the goodness-of-fit for both the adult with an ASC and this broader family system must be taken into account.

Individuals with an ASC often experience "postponed launching" or delayed departure from the family home until well into their adulthood or after parents are deceased. Data from state agencies in New York and Massachusetts in 1998 suggest that about one-quarter to one-third of adults with an ASC in their 30s continue to live with their parents (Seltzer, Krauss, Orsmond, & Vestal, 2000). Thus, long-term family-based living occurs for a marked portion of adults with an ASC, although this rate is lower than the rate of coresidence reported for adults with intellectual disability (ID), due to other types of etiologies (see Seltzer et al., 2000 for discussion of findings).

There are many reasons for continued coresidence of adults with an ASC with their families, including parental preference and worries about the quality of and/or limited availability of appropriate community-based residential services. Parents who continue to have their adult son or daughter with an ASC live with them often highlight the enjoyment that the family derives from the presence of their offspring with an ASC at home and peace of mind that they have in ensuring the well-being of their adult child (Krauss, Seltzer, & Jacobson, 2005). Commonly expressed negative aspects of continued coresidence of adults with an ASC include added strain from caregiving activities and restrictions on the family (e.g., difficulty in spending time away from home and lack of "private couple time"). In addition, families often incur significant out-of-pocket expenses as there is limited financial reimbursement for family-based residential care of adults with ASC.

9

Adults with an ASC who do not coreside with family generally live in the community, either independently, in supported living settings, in group homes, or with host families. In terms of deciding which community residential setting is most appropriate, there is wide agreement within the field of ID that adults be placed in the most independent and integrated community setting appropriate for their support needs and that the adult is an active participant in determining where they live, who their service providers are, and the type of services received. In line with these goals, there has been a trend away from large institutional settings (16 or more residents) to smaller and more independent residential settings (Prouty, Smith, & Lakin, 2006).

High-functioning adults with an ASC often live independently in their own rented or owned home, either by themselves or with friends, spouses, and/or children. In supported community living settings, adults own or rent their own homes but receive some assistance services, either regularly or intermittently. Supported living services may include helping the adult find or move into a home, supervision of personal finances/budget, support for certain activities of daily living, and assistance in becoming an active member of the community. Group homes, which usually involve 6 of fewer persons with ID living together, are the most common out-of-the-family placement for adults with ID (Prouty et al., 2006). Group homes generally have on-site care staff, who provide supervision and support for activities of daily living, employment, and social and leisure activities. The number of adults with ID residing in a host family arrangement, in which the adult with ID lives with a support person or family, has increased in the last decade (Prouty et al., 2006). A smaller number of adults with ID continue to live in larger private or public institutional settings, nursing homes, or mental health facilities. Residential services are typically operated on a combination of federal and state government funding (e.g., Medicaid in the US), local monies, private pay, and charitable income. Waiting lists for community residential services can be quite long.

The decision for an adult with an ASC to move out of the family home is complex and related to several factors. Out-of-family placement occurs more often when adults have more severe autism symptoms and more severe ID, poorer functional skills, and cooccurring maladaptive behaviors. Circumstances related to the family situation also contribute to placement decisions, including caregiver stressors and burden, parental well-being and health, poor social support networks, and dissolution of the marital relationship. A greater use of formal disability services is also related to out-of-family placement, likely because the use of services decreases family misgivings and worries about the community residential service system.

Common advantages of having an adult with an ASC live away from the family home, as voiced by parents, include having the son or daughter receive better services, get increased opportunities to learn new skills, gain greater independence, and family members having an increased peace of mind and reduced negative feelings of guilt or burden (Baker & Blacher, 2002; Krauss et al., 2005). Mothers whose adult son or daughter with an ASC lives outside of the family home also report having more free time and being less fatigued than mothers of coresiding sons and daughters with an ASC (Krauss et al.,

2005). Recent analyses from the author's longitudinal study of 406 mothers of adolescents and adults with an ASC also indicate that mothers experience a decrease in overall level of anxiety subsequent to their son or daughter moving out of the family home. However, having the adolescent or adult son or daughter move out of the family home was not related to a change in depressive symptoms (Barker et al, in press). Thus, it may be that although the mother's anxiety about her son or daughter's day-to-day activities subsides when the child leaves the family home, there may be an enduring effect of stressful parenting on negative affect. Frequent disadvantages of having an adult with an ASC live away from the family home, as voiced by parents, include feeling unease or guilt about not fulfilling the parent role of providing direct care (Baker & Blacher, 2002) and missing daily contact with the son or daughter and increased worries about their child's future (Krauss et al., 2005).

The transition out of the family home and into community residential settings is often gradual. Parents generally play a central role in this transition. Research indicates that mothers are actively involved in the selection of their son's or daughter's residential placement and are often in regular contact with the residential program in the first few years after the transition into these programs. Thus, even when adults with an ASC are in out-of-family placements, family members continue to remain close with the son or daughter with an ASC.

References

Baker, B. L., & Blancher, J. (2002). For better or worse? Impact of residential placement on families. *Mental Retardation, 40*, 1–13.

Barker, E. T., Hartley, S. L., Seltzer, M. M., Floyd, F., Greenberg, J. S., & Orsmond, G. I. (in press). Trajectories of emotional well-being in mothers of adolescents and adults with autism. *Developmental Psychology*.

Krauss, M. W., Seltzer, M. M., & Jacobson, H. T. (2005). Adults with autism living at home or in non-family settings: Positive and negative aspects of residential status. *Journal of Intellectual and Developmental Disability Research, 49*, 111–124.

Prouty, R., Smith, G. & Lakin, K. (Eds.). (2006). *Residential services for persons with developmental disabilities: Status and trends through 2005.* Minneapolis, MN: University of Minnesota, Research & Training Center on Community Living. Available at: www. rtc.umn.edu/RISP

Seltzer, M. M., Krauss, M. W., Orsmond, G. I., & Vestal, C. (2000). Families of adolescents and adults with autism: Uncharted territory. In L. M. Glidden (Ed.), *International Review of Research on Mental Retardation* (Vol. 23) (pp. 267–294). San Diego, CA: Academic Press.

9

Further Reading

Esbensen, A. J., Seltzer, J. M., & Krauss, M. W. (in press). Life course perspectives in autism and mental retardation research: The case of family caregiving. In J. A. Burack,

R. M. Hodapp, & E. Zigler (Eds.), *Handbook of mental retardation and development* (2nd ed.). Oxford, UK: Oxford University Press.

Kozma, A., Mansell, J., & Beadle-Brown, J. (2009). Outcomes in different residential settings for people with intellectual disability: A systematic review. *American Journal on Intellectual and Developmental Disabilities, 114*, 193–212.

Section 10

Legal Issues, Organizations, and Resources

Q73
What Rights Do People with ASC and Their Families Have?

Autism Europe

People with Autism are Rights Holders

The *Convention on the Rights of Persons with Disabilities* came into force on May 3, 2008. It is a landmark treaty meant to guarantee the rights of people with disabilities worldwide. Because of the complexity of their needs, people with autism represent a *particularly excluded population*, even among disabled populations themselves. Some people with autism may have high or complex dependency needs, such as assistance in the activities of daily living, a high level of support, intensive education, and continuing assistance for safety purpose. As a general rule, aside from the fact that people with autism must benefit from the same human rights, they may need *a right to compensation* of their disability.

Mainstreaming and Positive Measures

For people with high or complex dependency needs, the mainstreaming approach may be either an inadequate response or only a partial response to cover their needs. The fundamental rights of these people are rarely effective if positive measures are not adopted and if compensation is not effectively granted and put in place

Effectiveness of Rights

The *individual* project of life must be adapted, flexible, *evaluated* all life long, taking into account the *needs* and *desires* of the person. This project must be defined under the so called rights-based approach (i.e., compensation must be based on each of the fundamental rights). The *quality of life* must be ensured and

10

effective all life long under a global approach for the person. Needs cannot be generally defined, such as standards. Each situation must be taken into account because they are complex and diverse.

Right to Early Diagnosis

Early and systematic identification permits not only an early and accurate diagnosis but also the introduction of early intervention to reduce the degree of disability and prevent the aggravation of the disability. Diagnosis must be based on international classifications (ICD-10, DSM-IV-TR).

Right to Receive Adapted Care All Life Long

People with autism must have access to appropriate care and treatment, not only for their mental health, but also for their physical health. Ordinary and common treatment must be performed, and people with autism must benefit from disease control and prevention programs. Appropriate right to receive adapted care means that treatment must be limited to the individual's needs (i.e., people with autism must not receive any inappropriate and/or excessive medication). They must not receive permanent treatment or medical care, unless such treatment is really indispensable. And, of course, recourse to irreversible means of contraception must be neither abusive nor inappropriate.

Right to Life-Long Education

States must guarantee an effective exercise of individuals with ASC's right to education in mainstream schools, and/or in special schools, *only if* inclusion in mainstream schools is not possible *and* if this decision is agreed with the parents. Special schools must be linked with mainstream schools and transition between mainstream and special schools must be encouraged because the child's situation may require both. Education must be adapted. This also means that apart from teaching academic skills, education of individuals with autism must include preparation for an independent life, adaptive behaviors, and social skills. Adaptive skills are critical factors in determining the supports the person requires for success in school, work, community, and home environments. Adult education should provide the maximum range of opportunities and include not only special education or participation in mainstream adult educational programs, but also training in basic skills, self-management, and living skills, at all ages (no retirement).

10

Right to Work

Working conditions must always be adjusted to the needs of the person with autism in the ordinary working environment. Where this is not possible by reason of the disability, sheltered employment according to the level of disability must be created. In certain cases, such measures may require recourse to specialized support services. The principle to be kept in mind is that a true career with flexible transitions to and from the ordinary environment must be possible for people with autism.

Access to Private Housing and to Private Life

Full integration and participation in the social life of those who are the most dependent and disabled require closing large institutions, living at home as independently as possible with home services, or living in small, quality structures as an alternative to living in an institution. A broad range of community-based services with all safety measures, including transport, must, therefore, be provided with qualified personnel. Appropriate, adequate, and non-abusive guardianship systems must also be provided.

Qualified Personnel

Achieving these goals requires competent general practitioners and specialists, qualified personnel in charge of education, of training, of job-coaching, and interdisciplinary teams.

Duty of Society as a Whole

Effective rights for all oblige society to positive measures. Positive measures have a cost, but for the majority of countries the answer is possible. The person and their needs must be at the heart of the project, not the supposed financial constraints. It is a national responsibility of States to ensure and guarantee same rights for all, on the whole national territory. Finally, the financing of the individual project must not influence the choice of the disabled person. Reaffirming the dignity and worth of every person with autism is also the duty of society as a whole.

10

Further Reading

Office of the United Nations High Commissioner for Human Rights. (2006). Convention on the rights of persons with disabilities. Retrieved from: http://www2.ohchr.org/english/law/disabilities-convention.htm.

10

Which Organizations Help People with ASC and Their Families?

Autism Europe

World Autism Organisation (WAO)

The WAO has as its main objective to improve the quality of life for people with autism and their families in all parts of the world. This covers various aspects, for instance: Sharing information and creating awareness by national public institutions in addition to international organizations, such as the United Nations Educational, Scientific, and Cultural Organization (UNESCO), the World Health Organization (WHO), and the United Nations; encouraging parents and autistic individuals to participate in associations representing their countries or to form such organizations, if none exist as yet where they live; raising awareness among professionals in the fields of health and education in relation to the specific needs of individuals with autism; promoting interest in working with people with autism; sharing initial and continuing vocational education and training in countries that need it urgently; facilitating worldwide information exchange to enrich knowledge everywhere through general participation in specific experience. For further information on WAO, see *www.worldautismorganization.org.*

Autism Europe (AE) and Its National Members

AE is an international association whose main objective is to advance the rights of persons with autism and their families and to help them improve their quality of life. AE ensures effective liaison among more than 80 member associations uniting parents of persons with autism in 30 European countries, including 20 Member States of the European Union, as well as government, European, and international institutions. AE plays a key role in raising public awareness and in influencing European decision-makers on all issues relating to autism, including the promotion of the rights of people with autism and other disabilities involving complex dependency needs. At the national level, people with ASC and their families may be helped and assisted by the national and local organizations that

10

are members of AE. More information regarding AE is available on their web-site: www.autismeurope.org.

Autism Society of America (ASA)

ASA exists to improve the lives of all affected by autism by means of increasing public awareness about the day-to-day issues faced by people on the spectrum, advocating for appropriate services for individuals across the lifespan, and providing the latest information regarding treatment, education, research, and advocacy. Founded in 1965 by Bernard Rimland, Ruth Sullivan, and many other parents of children with ASC, ASA is the leading source of trusted and reliable information about autism in North America. Through its strong chapter network, ASA has spearheaded numerous pieces of state and local legislation, including the 2006 Combating Autism Act, the first federal autism-specific law. ASA's website is one of the most visited websites on autism in the world, and its quarterly journal, *Autism Advocate*, has a broad national readership. For further information on ASA, see www.autism-society.org.

Q75
Are There Self-Help Organizations for Autistic People Run by Autistic People?

Sebastian Dern

There is a growing number of diverse self-help and self-advocacy initiatives for autistic people, ranging from groups for autistic people within established autism organizations run by nonautistic parents of autistic children to registered charities run entirely by autistic adults for autistic adults. The form of these self-help and self-advocacy initiatives ranges from individual blogs and publications through autistic communities to internet discussion boards to entire social network sites and groups for autistic people using networks such as Flickr, Facebook, Second Life, and Twitter. Autistic people use internet networks to directly share advice, writing, artwork, science, programming, products, job offers, experiences with relationships, practical help, emotional support, discussion of special interests, as well as discussion of life in the nonautistic world. Some autistic adults with limited speech use type-to-voice computers to talk from their homes via YouTube videos and explain to the world what they think. Sometimes verbal autistic adults may rely on alternative communication, too. Internet communication enhances participation in society and collaboration with others, which is especially true for autistic people. Internet communication facilitates contact between autistic people online as well as in person and includes autistic adults who have been living in social isolation prior to joining an autistic community. Events hosted by established autism parent self-help organizations, autism research conferences, electronic mailing lists, and internet discussion boards have traditionally been starting points for the emergence of peer-to-peer communication and the creation of groups of autistic people.

Parent self-help autism organizations differ in their approach as to representing the views of autistic people themselves, with some autism organizations completely integrating autistic adults into their organization and agenda and others having no representation of autistic adults. Joint initiatives between parents of autistic children and autistic adults exist, some of these include autism professionals. Other initiatives are comprised of autistic adults and autism professionals. There are groups for autistic parents, groups for autistic adults

10

and their partners, groups for university students on the spectrum, and groups for autistic people working freelance. Initiatives differ, due to respective regional, social, and cultural circumstances, regional expertise, and support services for autistic people and range from practical self-help groups to research collaborations to civil, disability, autistic, diversity, and neurodiversity rights movements. Issue-based groups include initiatives against neuroleptic abuse of autistic people, groups in support of computer and information technology as alternative and augmentative means of communication, and groups demanding that written and long-distance psychotherapy be available for autistic people. Several new partnerships between autistic adults and autism researchers aid autistic self-advocacy.

Autism Network International

Autism Network International (ANI; www.autreat.com) is a nonprofit initiative based in the US and run by autistic people for autistic people. It publishes a newsletter entitled *Our Voices* and runs an electronic mailing list called *ANI-L*. ANI has been a pioneer in accessibility of autism conferences for autistic people as well as creating offline and online autism communities. Beginning in 1996, ANI has hosted an annual retreat, "Autreat," a conference for autistic people where presenters address autistic people directly about positive ways of living with autism. Autreat inspired an annual autism conference, "Autscape," for autistic people in the UK, which has been running since 2005. Other camps for autistic adults have taken place in Germany and Sweden.

Autistic Self-Advocacy Network

The Autistic Self-Advocacy Network (ASAN; www.autisticadvocacy.org) is a volunteer-run nonprofit organization founded in the US in 2007. The network's membership comprises autistic adults and youth, crossdisability advocates, family members, professionals, educators, and friends. ASAN works to improve societal acceptance, services and support resources, and community understanding of all people on the autism spectrum, regardless of diagnosis and age, and seeks to empower autistic adults and improve the participation of autistic people in all aspects of society, specifically including autistic individuals in decisions concerning the autistic community. The network is active in public policy advocacy, advocacy and social support for people on the autistic spectrum and their families, public speaking, and collaboration with the crossdisability community. ASAN campaigns against autism organizations that focus on funding cures against autism and portray autistic individuals as burdens on families and society as a means to raise funds. The organizaion promotes quality of life approaches in autism research and supports community-oriented research, whilst warning against eugenic applications of autism research in the future. ASAN has state and regional chapters in the US and one in Australia and partners with *The Autism Acceptance Project* (www.taaproject.com) in Canada, run by autistic people and friends and family of autistic individuals who promote acceptance and accommodation of autistic people in society.

ASAN is a community partner of the *Academic Autism Spectrum Partnership in Research and Education* (AASPIRE) project (http://aaspire.org) and adheres to research that is inclusive to autistic adults, in equal partnership with autistic adults, answers research questions considered relevant by autistic people, and uses research findings to facilitate positive change for individuals on the autistic spectrum. One research priority of AASPIRE is access to general healthcare and reducing barriers to healthcare experienced by autistic adults.

Aspies e.V.

Aspies e.V. (www.aspies.de) is a registered charity in Germany, established in 2004. It is a self-help organization for autistic people run by autistic people with about 160 members in Germany and neighboring countries and an office at Berlin's House for Democracy and Human Rights. The majority of members have been diagnosed with Asperger syndrome and a few with autistic disorder. Aspies e.V. publishes a newsletter, *Aspies!*, runs an annual summer camp, provides a library, and operates the only public internet directory of self-help groups, autism professionals, and other resources in Germany, Austria, and the German-speaking part of Switzerland. Most publications and activities are free of charge and accessible online with about 40,000 visits per month. The organization runs a public self-help discussion board, an internet chat, a calendar, and a wiki to share and produce information relevant to autistic people and the autism community. Aspies e.V. facilitates contact between autistic adults and actively supports the creation of local self-help groups for autistic people. Membership conferences allow online participation to enhance accessibility. The association presents at events, autism research conferences, and governmental hearings.

Members of the charity are involved in media coverage on autism, organize regular meetings between autistic adults and autism professionals, and are developing an organization to create appropriate jobs for people on the autistic spectrum. Members contribute to a research project at Berlin's Max Planck Institute for Human Development and the Free University Berlin in equal partnership with autistic adults in Berlin to study topics that autistic adults consider relevant. Members present on autism independently, as well as jointly with autism professionals. The charity sends a delegate to the board of the Germany-based Society for Research in Autism Spectrum Conditions (www.wgas-autismus.org) to represent the perspective of autistic adults. Among the goals of Aspies e.V. are that autism research focuses on autistic abilities and how autistic people can live well as an individual with autism. Central to the goals of Aspies e.V. are the pursuit of autistic individuals' right to participate in all areas of society, including access to and reduction of barriers to appropriate employment, education, and health care.

10

Further Reading

For a listing of autistic-run organizations worldwide see http://aspies.de/english.php
The Global Registry of Autistic-Run Organizations can be found at http://www.wrong
   planet.net/postt58920.html.
A copy of The Global Registry of Autistic-Run Organizations can be found here http://
   www.aspiesforfreedom.com/showthread.php?tid=12262&pid=3553428.

Q76
Which Organizations Seek to Enhance ASC Research?

Sven Bölte

Research interest in ASC has increased significantly in recent years. There are also growing efforts to raise money for studies of ASC, as well as to enhance cooperation, networking, and synergy effects between scientists and disciplines. The International Society for Autism Research (INSAR; www.autism-insar.org) was established in 2001 and is devoted to advancing knowledge about ASC in all areas. Its main organs are the annual International Meeting for Autism Research (IMFAR) and the society's journal entitled *Autism Research*.

Autism Speaks (www.autismspeaks.org) was founded in 2005. It is an advocacy organization that supports ASC research and tries to generate autism awareness. Autism Speaks is originally US-based, but its mission is to act as globally as possible and it is expanding its organizational structures into Europe, starting with the UK (www.autismspeaks.org.uk). Aside from supporting four main research areas (i.e., etiology, biology, diagnosis/epidemiology, therapies), Autism Speaks funds several research initiatives: The Autism Genetic Resource Exchange (AGRE), a DNA repository and family registry of genotypic and phenotypic information that is available to autism researchers worldwide; the Autism Tissue Program, a network of researchers that manages and distributes brain tissues donated for autism research; and the Clinical Trials Network, which focuses on new pharmacological treatments. Autism Speaks also supports the Toddler Treatment Network, which develops new interventions for infants and toddlers.

The Simons Foundation Autism Research Initiative (SFARI; http://sfari.org/web/sfari/home) seeks to improve ASC research by establishing and supporting certain core projects. Its primary goal is to collect a permanent repository of genetic samples from 2,000 families with extensive behavioral characterization. The SFARI Simplex Collection is operated in collaboration with 13 university-affiliated research clinics.

The Organization of Autism Research (OAR; researchautism.org) was created in 2001 and set out to use applied science to answer questions that parents, families, individuals with autism, teachers, and caregivers confront daily. OAR funds pilot studies and targeted research within specific modalities and issues affecting the autism community, primarily studies whose outcomes offer new insights into the behavioral and social development of individuals with ASC with an emphasis on communications, education, and vocational challenges.

The National Institutes of Health (NIH; www.nih.gov) and the National Institutes of Mental Health (www. nimh.nih.gov) in the US systematically support autism research activities even beyond American borders, for instance the Autism Research Network (www.autismresearchnetwork.org), dedicated to understanding and treating ASC, and the National Database for Autism Research (http://ndar.nih.gov/ndarpublicweb), a program to simplify the process of data sharing and collaboration.

There are many additional regional and national organizations trying to support or organize autism research. An example is the Germany-, Austria-, and Switzerland-based Society for Research in Autism Spectrum Conditions (www. wgas-autismus.org), which, among other things, arranges annual conferences, awards scientific excellence, funds research projects, and advocates for cooperation between researchers as well as good scientific practice.

10

Q77
Where Do I Find the Latest Information on Progress in ASC Research?

Sven Bölte

There are many sources for information on ASC. However, often and increasingly, the fastest and cheapest resource is, of course, the internet. There are countless sites offering information and newsletters on causes, symptomatology, diagnostic procedures, and, particularly, intervention options. Unfortunately, the internet is rather a black-box when it comes to the quality of information provided. A lot of the online material on ASC is unproven, nonsense, biased, or simply voices the opinions and attitudes of a few, rather than hard evidence or common sense of experts. Exercizing caution and critical judgment are therefore always necessary when browsing for ASC information on the internet. Nevertheless, there are also a good number of highly reliable pages run by recognized organizations and centers. A selection is listed in the following.

PubMed (www.ncbi.nlm.nih.gov/pubmed) is a scientific literature search and documentation service by the US National Library of Medicine (NLM) and the National Institutes of Health (NIH). Users can search for relevant ASC research results in 5,200 biomedical and psychological journals. All abstracts are free to read, and there is a growing number of free full-text articles. As PubMed is an open resource for professionals, rather than laypersons, the level of complexity is often high. Several specialized ASC journals are included in PubMed, for instance *Autism: The International Journal of Research and Practice*, the *Journal of Autism and Developmental Disorders*, and *Autism Research*. Also included are the Cochrane Reviews, a database of systematic reviews and meta-analyses that summarize and interpret the results of high-quality medical research.

The UK-based Research Autism (www.researchautism.net) is a charity exclusively dedicated to research into interventions in ASC. It provides independent research into new and existing health, education, social, and other interventions and is supported by leading ASC experts. Research Autism is closely connected with the Autism Research Centre (www.autismresearchcentre.com), another valuable source of autism information, at the University of Cambridge.

10

In the US, the Yale Child Study Center (http://medicine.yale.edu/childstudy/) at Yale University School of Medicine in Newhaven, CT, has an Autism Program that provides comprehensive clinical services to children with autism spectrum disorders and their families (http://childstudycenter.yale.edu/autism/). The center has been recognized by the NIH as an autism center of excellence.

The Medical Investigation of Neurodevelopmental Disorders Institute (M.I.N.D. Institute; www.ucdmc.ucdavis.edu/MINDInstitute) is a research center that supports critical research designed to understand the causes and to develop effective diagnoses, treatments, preventions, and, ultimately, cures for autism, fragile X, and other neurodevelopmental disorders.

The University of Michigan Autism & Communication Disorders Centers (www.umaccweb.com) focus on research, education, and clinical services in ASC. A core research project is the further development and validation of the standard diagnostic ASC instruments.

Lastly, a newly established competence center for research, education, and development in neurodevelopmental disorders, including ASC, in Sweden is the Karolinska Institutet Center of Neurodevelopmental Disorders (KIND; www.ki.se/KIND).

Where Do I Find Helpful Links on the Web?

Autism Europe

World
World Autism Organisation
www.worldautismorganization.org

North America
Autism Society of America
www.autism-society.org

Europe
Autism Europe
www.autismeurope.org

Individual Countries
Austria
ÖAH Österreichische Autistenhilfe
www.autistenhilfe.at

Belgium
APPA
www2.ulg.ac.be/apepa/
Inforautisme
www.inforautisme.be
Vlaamse Vereniging Autisme
www.autismevlaanderen.be

Croatia
A.C.A.P.
www.autizam-ri.hr
gzr
www.gzr.hr

10

Czeck Republic
Autistik Club
www.volny.cz/autistik
APLA
www.praha.apla.cz

Denmark
Landsforeningen autisme
www.autismeforening.dk

Finland
F.A.A.A.S.
www.autismiliitto.fi

France
Association Française de Gestion de Services et d'Etabillsements pour Personnes Autistes
www.afg-web.fr
Sésame Autisme
www.sesame-autisme.com
Autisme France
http://autisme.france.free.fr/
ProAid Autisme
www.proaidautisme.org/

Germany
Autismus Deutschland
www.autismus.de

Greece
Greek Society for the Protection of Autistic People
www.autismgreece.gr

Hungary
Hungarian Autistic Society (HAS)
www.esoember.hu

Iceland
Umsjonarfelag einhverfra
www.einhverfa.is

Ireland
Irish Society for Autism
www.autism.ie

10

Italy
Autismo Italia
www.autismoitalia.org
ANGSA
www.angsaonlus.org

Luxemburg
Autisme Luxembourg
www.autisme.lu
Fondation Autisme Luxembourg
www.fal.lu/
APPAAL
www.appaal.lu/fr/index.php

Macedonia
Macedonian Scientific Society for Autism
http://mssa.org.mk/en/index.php

The Netherlands
N.V.A.
www.autisme-nva.nl

Norway
Autismeforeningen i Norge
www.autismeforeningen.no

Poland
Synapsis Foundation
www.synapsis.waw.pl/

Portugal
A.P.P.D.A. Lisboa
www.appda-lisboa.org.pt/
Federacao Portuguesa de Autismo
www.appda-lisboa.org.pt/federacao/

Romania
Autism Romania
www.autismromania.ro

Serbia
Serbian Society of Autism
www.autizam.org.yu

10

Slovakia
SPOSA
www.sposa.sk
Slovenia
Center za Avtizem
www.avtizem.org/

Spain
APAFAC, CERAC and Fundacio Congost
www.autisme.com
APNA-Espana
www.apna.es
Autismo-Espana
www.autismo.org.es/AE/default.htm
Autismo Burgos
www.autismoburgos.org
Autismo Galicia
www.autismogalicia.org
Gautena
www.gautena.org/intro/intro.html
Fundacion Menela
www.menela.org
Nuevo Horizonte
www.autismo.com

Sweden
Riksföreningen Autism
www.autism.se

Switzerland
Autisme Suisse Romande
www.autisme.ch
Autismus Schweiz
www.autismus.ch

Turkey
TODEV
www.todev.org

UK
National Autistic Society
www.nas.org.uk
Scottish Society for Autism
www.autism-in-scotland.org.uk
Autism Initiatives
www.autisminitiatives.org

10

Autism Anglia
www.autism-anglia.org.uk
Northern Ireland Autism Society
www.autismni.org
Hampshire Autistic Society
www.has.org.uk
Autism West Midlands
www.autismwestmidlands.org.uk/

10

Appendix

Contributors

Brett Abrahams
Departments of Genetics & Neuroscience
Price Center for Genetic & Translational Medicine
Albert Einstein College of Medicine
Bronx, NY, USA
brett.abrahams@einstein.yu.edu

Michael Aman
Department of Psychology
Ohio State University
Columbus, OH, USA
aman.1@osu.edu

L. Eugene Arnold
Nisonger Center
Ohio State University
Columbus, OH, USA
arnold.6@osu.edu

Autism Europe
Brussels, Belgium
secretariat@autismeurope.org

Simon Baron-Cohen
Department of Psychiatry
Autism Research Centre
Cambridge University
Cambridge, UK
sb205@cam.ac.uk

Vera Bernard-Opitz
Editor Autism News of Orange County & the Rest of the World
verabernard@cox.net

Jonathan A. Bernstein
Department of Pediatrics
Stanford University School of Medicine
Stanford, CA, USA
jon.bernstein@stanford.edu

Sven Bölte
Department of Women's and Children's Health
Karolinska Institutet Center of Neurodevelopmental Disorders (KIND)
Karolinska Institutet
Stockholm, Sweden
sven.bolte@ki.se

Lovina Chahal
Department of Psychiatry and Behavioral Sciences
Stanford University School of Medicine
Stanford, CA, USA

Tony Charman
Centre for Research in Autism and Education
Department of Psychology and Human Development
Institute of Education
London, UK
t.charman@ioe.ac.uk

John N. Constantino
Department of Psychiatry / Division of Child Psychiatry
Washington University School of Medicine
St. Louis, MO, USA
constantino@wustl.edu

Matthias Dalferth
University of Applied Sciences
Regensburg, Germany
matthias.dalferth@hs-regensburg.de

Michelle Dawson
Pervasive Developmental Disorders Specialized Clinic
Hôpital Rivière-des-Prairies
Montréal, QC, Canada
naamichelle@yahoo.ca

Lara Delmolino
Douglass Developmental Disabilities Center
Rutgers, the State University of New Jersey
New Brunswick, NJ, USA
delmolin@rci.rutgers.edu

Sebastian Dern
Aspies e.V.
Berlin, Germany
sebastian.dern@gmx.de

Isabel Dziobek
Cluster of Excellence "Languages of Emotion"
Free University Berlin
Berlin, Germany
isabel.dziobek@fu-berlin.de

Viviana Enseñat
Faculty of Medicine & Dentistry
University of Alberta
Edmonton, AB, Canada
vivanaensenat@gmail.com

Megan A. Farley
Department of Psychiatry
University of Utah School of Medicine
Salt Lake City, UT, USA
megan.farley@hsc.utah.edu

Carl Feinstein
Division of Child and Adolescent Psychiatry
Lucile Packard Children's Hospital
Stanford University School of Medicine
Stanford, CA, USA
carlf@stanford.edu

Susan E. Folstein
Department of Psychiatry and Behavioral Sciences
University of Miami Miller School of Medicine
Miami, FL, USA
sfolstein@med.miami.edu

Eric Fombonne
Department of Psychiatry
McGill University
The Montreal Children's Hospital
Montreal, QC, Canada
eric.fombonne@mcgill.ca

Richard M. Foxx
ABA Program
Penn State Harrisburg
Middletown, PA, USA
rmf4@psu.edu

Wendy Froehlich
Division of Child and Adolescent Psychiatry
Department of Psychiatry and Behavioral Sciences
Stanford University
Stanford, CA, USA
wendyf@stanford.edu

Mina Hah
School of Medicine
Stanford University
Stanford, CA, USA
mhah@stanford.edu

Joachim Hallmayer
Division of Child and Adolescent Psychiatry
Department of Psychiatry and Behavioral Sciences
Stanford University
Stanford, CA, USA
joachimh@stanford.edu

Francesca Happé
MRC Social, Genetic and Developmental Psychiatry Centre
Institute of Psychiatry
King's College London
London, UK
francesca.happe@kcl.ac.uk

Benjamin Handen
School of Medicine
University of Pittsburgh
Pittsburgh, PA, USA
handenbl@upmc.edu

Antonio Y. Hardan
Stanford University Medical Center
Psychiatry and Behavioral Sciences
Child and Adolescent Psychiatry and Child Development
Stanford, CA, USA
hardanay@stanford.edu

Sandra L. Harris
Rutgers, The State University of New Jersey
New Brunswick, NJ, USA
sharris@rci.rutgers.edu.

Sigan Hartley
Human Development and Family Studies
Waisman Center
University of Wisconsin-Madison
Madison, WI, USA
hartley@waisman.wisc.edu

James D. Herbert
Department of Psychology
Drexel University
Philadelphia, PA, USA
james.herbert@drexel.edu

Irva Hertz-Picciotto
Division of Environmental and Occupational Health
Department of Public Health Sciences
M.I.N.D. Institute
University of California Davis
Davis, CA, USA
ihp@phs.ucdavis.edu

Patricia Howlin
Department of Psychology
Institute of Psychiatry
King's College
London, UK
patricia.howlin@iop.kcl.ac.uk

Rita Jordan
Autism Centre for Education & Research
College of Social Sciences
University of Birmingham
Birmingham, UK
r.r.jordan@bham.ac.uk

Ami Klin
Child Study Center
Yale University
New Haven, CT, USA
ami.klin@yale.edu

Ann Le Couteur
Institute of Health & Society
Newcastle University
Newcastle, UK
a.s.le-couteur@newcastle.ac.uk

Li-Ching Lee
Department of Epidemiology
John Hopkins Bloomberg School of Public Health
Baltimore, MD, USA
llee2@jhsph.edu

Scott O. Lilienfeld
Department of Psychology
Emory University
Atlanta, GA, USA
slilien@emory.edu

Linda Lotspeich
Autism and Developmental Disabilities Clinic
Lucile Packard Children's Hospital, Child and Adolescent Psychiatry
Stanford University Medical Center
Stanford, CA, USA
ljl@stanford.edu

James K. Luiselli
May Institute
Randolph, MA, USA
jluiselli@mayinstitute.org

William M. McMahon
Department of Psychiatry
University of Utah School of Medicine
Salt Lake City, UT, USA
william.mcmahon@hsc.utah.edu

Nancy J. Minshew
NIH Autism Center of Excellence (ACE)
University of Pittsburgh School of Medicine
Pittsburgh, PA, USA
minshewnj@upmc.edu

Laurent Mottron
Department of Psychiatry
Rivière-des-prairies Hospital
University of Montréal
Montréal, Canada
mottronl@istar.ca

Svend Erik Mouridsen
Department of Child and Adolescent Psychiatry
Bispebjerg University Hospital
Copenhagen, Denmark
svend.erik.mouridsen@regionh.dk

Michele Noterdaeme
Department of Child and Adolescent Psychiatry and Psychotherapy
Josefinum
Augsburg, Germany
noterdaeme.michele@josefinum.de

Susanne Nußbeck
Department of Special Education and Rehabilitation
Faculty of Human Sciences
University of Cologne
Cologne, Germany
susanne.nussbeck@uni-koeln.de

Ruth O'Hara
Department of Psychiatry and Behavioral Sciences,
Stanford University School of Medicine,
Stanford, CA, USA
roh@stanford.edu

Simonetta Panerai
Oasi Maria SS
Institute for Research on Mental Retardation and Brain Ageing
Troina, Italy
spanerai@oasi.en.it

Jeremy Parr
Institute of Neuroscience
Newcastle University
Newcastle Upon Tyne, UK
jeremy.parr@newcastle.ac.uk

Rhea Paul
Child Study Center
Yale School of Medicine
New Haven, CT, USA
rhea.paul@yale.edu

Twyla Y. Perryman
Department of Special Education
Kennedy Center
Vanderbilt University
Nashville, TN, USA
twyla.perryman@vanderbilt.edu

Carmen M. Schröder
Department of Psychiatry and Mental Health, Division of Child Psychiatry
Department of Neurology, University Sleep Clinic
University Clinics Strasbourg
Strasbourg, France
carmen.schroder@chru-strasbourg.fr

Marsha Mailick Seltzer
Waisman Center
University of Wisconsin-Madison
Madison, WI, USA
mseltzer@waisman.wisc

Marjorie Solomon
Department of Psychiatry and Behavioral Science
M.I.N.D. Institute
University of California, Davis
Sacramento, CA, USA
marjorie.solomon@ucdmc.ucdavis.edu.

Wendy L. Stone
Department of Psychology
UW Autism Center
University of Washington
Seattle, WA, USA
stonew@uw.edu

Luitgard Stumpf
Integration Center for Individuals with Autism – MAut
Munich, Germany
stumpf.luitgard@m.gfi-ggmbh.de

Peter Szatmari
Department of Psychiatry and Behavioural Neurosciences
McMaster University
Hamilton, OT, Canada
szatmar@mcmaster.ca

Digby Tantam
Centre for the Study of Conflict and Reconciliation
School of Health and Related Research
University of Sheffield
Sheffield, UK.
D.Tantam@sheffield.ac.uk

Wesley K. Thompson
Department of Psychiatry
Stein Institute for Research on Aging
University of California, San Diego
La Jolla, CA, USA
wkthompson@ucsd.edu

Rabindra Tirouvanziam
Center for Excellence in Pulmonary Biology
Department of Pediatrics
Stanford University School of Medicine
Stanford, CA, USA
tirouvan@stanford.edu

Roberto Tuchman
Autism and Neurodevelopment Program
Miami Children's Hospital Dan Marino Center
Center for Autism and Related Disorders
University of Miami Miller School of Medicine
University of Miami-Nova Southeastern University
Miami, FL, USA
rtuchman@me.com

Ernst VanBergeijk
Vocational Independence Program
New York Institute of Technology
evanberg@nyit.edu

Fred R. Volkmar
Child Study Center
Yale University
New Haven, CT, USA
fred.volkmar@yale.edu

Zachary Warren
Departments of Pediatrics and Psychiatry
Vanderbilt University Medical Center
Nashville, TN, USA
zachary.warren@vanderbilt.edu

Keith E. Williams
Feeding Program
Penn State Hershey Medical Center
Hershey, PA, USA
feedingprogram@hmc.psu.edu

Paul J. Yoder
Department of Special Education
Kennedy Center,
Vanderbilt University
Nashville, TN, USA
paul.yoder@vanderbilt.edu

Lonnie Zwaigenbaum
Autism Research Centre
Glenrose Rehabilitation Hospital
Edmonton, AB, Canada
lonnie.zwaigenbaum@albertahealthservices.ca

Abbreviations & Acronyms

AAP	American Academy of Pediatrics
AAPEP	Adolescent and Adult Psycho Educational Profile
AASPIRE	Academic Autism Spectrum Partnership in Research and Education
ABA	Applied Behavior Analysis
ABC	Aberrant Behavior Checklist
ACTN	Autism Clinical Trials Network
AD	autistic disorder
ADHD	attention deficit hyperactivity disorder
ADI, ADI-R	Autism Diagnostic Interview (R = revised version)
ADOS	Autism Diagnostic Observation Schedule
AGRE	Autism Genetic Resource Exchange
ANI	Autism Network International
APGAR	Appearance (skin color), Pulse (heart rate), Grimace (reflex irritability), Activity (muscle tone), and Respiration
AS	Asperger syndrome
ASA	Autism Society of America
ASAN	Autistic Self Advocacy Network
ASC	autism spectrum condition
ASD	autism spectrum disorder
ATSDR	US Agency for Toxic Substances and Disease Registry
AUT	childhood autism
BACB	Behavior Analyst Certification Board
BAP	broader autism phenotype
BCBAs	board-certified behavior analysts
CAMs	complimentary and alternative medicines
CBT	cognitive-behavioral therapy
CD	conduct disorder
CDC	Centers for Disease Control and Prevention
CDD	childhood disintegrative disorder
CDI	MacArthur Communicative Development index
CELF-4	Clinical Evaluation of Language Fundamentals
CGH	comparative genomic hybridization
CHARGE	Childhood Autism Risk from Genetics and the Environment
CNS	central nervous system
CNS	Child Neurology Society
CNTNAP2	contactin-associated protein-like 2
CNVs	copy number variants
CPAP	continuous positive airway pressure
CRD	circadian rhythm disturbance/disorder
DLPFC	dorsolateral prefrontal cortex

DSM-IV-TR	Diagnostic and Statistical Manual of Mental Disorders, 4th ed., Text Revision
DTI	diffusion tensor imaging
DZ	dizygotic
EEG	electroencephalogram
EKGs	electrocardiograms
EPA	Environmental Protection Agency
FA	functional analysis
FBA	functional behavior analysis
FC	facilitated communication
FCT	functional communication training
FDA	US Food and Drug Administration
FG	fusiform gyrus
FISH	fluorescent *in situ* hybridization
fMRI	functional magnetic resonance imaging
GAS	Goal Attainment Scaling
GDD	global development delay
HC	head circumference
HIV	human immunodeficiency virus
ICD-10	International Classification of Diseases and Related Health Problems, 10th Revision
ID	intellectual disability
IED	individualized educational program
IL	interleukin
IMFAR	International Meeting for Autism Research
INF	interferon
INSAR	International Society for Autism Research
JA	joint attention
KIND	Karolinska Institutet Center of Neurodevelopmental Disorders
LDS	Church of Jesus Christ of Latter-Day Saints
M.I.N.D.	Medical Investigation of Neurodevelopment Disorders
MECP2	methyl CpG binding protein 2
MMR	measles, mumps, rubella
MRI	magnetic resonance imaging
mRNA	messenger (ribonucleic acid)
MZ	monozygotic
NIH	National Institutes of Health
NTs	neurotypicals
OAR	Organization of Autism Research
OCB	obsessive-compulsive behavior
OCD	obsessive-compulsive disorder
OSA	obstructive sleep apnea
PDD	pervasive developmental disorders

PDD-NOS	pervasive developmental disorders – not otherwise specified
PECS	picture exchange communication system
PEP, PEP-R, PEP-3	Psycho Educational Profile (and its revisions)
PET	positron emission tomography
PFC	prefrontal cortex
PLMs	periodic limb movements
PVC	polyvinyl chloride
RCT	randomized control trials
RLS	restless legs syndrome
RPMT	Responsive Education and Prelinguistic Milieu Training
RUPP	Research Units on Pediatric Psychopharmacology
SFARI	Simons Foundation Autism Research Initiative
SL	sleep latency
SMR	standardized mortality ratio
SOFIA	Study of Fluoxetine in Autism
SP	symbolic play
SRS	Social Responsiveness Scale
SSRIs	serotonin reuptake inhibitors
TCE	trichloroethylene
TD	typically developing individuals
TEACCH	Treatment and Education of Autistic and related Communication-Handicapped Children
TGF	transforming growth factor
TNF	tumor necrosis factors
ToM	theory of mind
TST	total sleep time
TTAP	TEACCH Transition Assessment Profile
UNESCO	United Nations Educational, Scientific, and Cultural Organization
VABS	Vineland Adaptive Behavior Scales
WAO	World Autism Organization
WASO	wake-after-sleep-onset
WHO	World Health Organization

Kalyna Z. Bezchlibnyk-Butler & Adil S. Virani (Editors)

Clinical Handbook of Psychotropic Drugs for Children and Adolescents

2nd, revised and expanded ed. 2007, ii + 346 pages, spiral-bound
ISBN: 978-0-88937-309-9, US $62.00 / £ 37.00 / € 49.95

This book is designed to fill a need for a comprehensive but compact and easy-to-use reference for all mental health professionals dealing with children and adolescents. The new edition of the widely praised handbook summarizes the latest information from the

published literature (scientific data, controlled clinical trials, case reports) and clinical experience in compact and easy-to-use charts and bulleted lists for each class of psychotropic drugs used in children and adolescents.

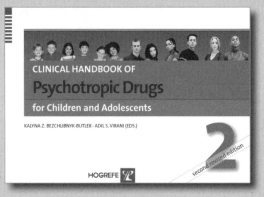

The spiral-bound handbook includes for each class of drugs both monograph statements on use in children and adolescents and approved indications, as well as the available data concerning off-label indications, findings from open and double-blind studies concerning doses, adverse affects, and other considerations in these age groups.

From the Foreword:

"...the editors have succeeded in improving on their first edition, already a "must-have" for those prescribing psychotropic medications in children and adolescents. It remains by far the most user-friendly and comprehensive handbook available for prescribers, teachers, students, and others working or interested in the field of child and adolescent psychopharmacology"

Pieter Joost van Wattum, MD, MA, in *The Journal of Clinical Psychiatry* 2009, Volume 70

"As a first time user of this handbook, I have already found it invaluable in clinical practice as well as psychiatric research. [...] It is a pleasure to have such a comprehensive resource on medications used in child and adolescent psychiatry. [...] The handout sheets at the end are very helpful to patients. This second edition is necessary because of the constant evolving nature of the field."

Corey Goldstein, MD(Rush University Medical Center) in *Doody's Book Review*

Hogrefe Publishing
30 Amberwood Parkway · Ashland, OH 44805 · USA
Tel: (800) 228-3749 · Fax: (419) 281-6883
E-Mail: customerservice@hogrefe.com

Hogrefe Publishing
Rohnsweg 25 · 37085 Göttingen · Germany
Tel: +49 551 999 500 · Fax: +49 551 999 50 425
E-Mail: customerservice@hogrefe.de

Hogrefe Publishing c/o Marston Book Services Ltd
PO Box 269 · Abingdon, OX14 4YN · UK
Tel: +44 1235 465577 · Fax +44 1235 465556
E-mail: direct.orders@marston.co.uk

HOGREFE   www.hogrefe.com

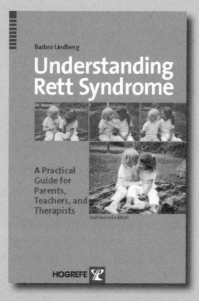